Abuse of the Elderly

Abuse of the Elderly

**A Guide to Resources
and Services**

Joseph J. Costa

LexingtonBooks
D.C. Heath and Company
Lexington, Massachusetts
Toronto

Library of Congress Cataloging in Publication Data

Main entry under title:

Abuse of the elderly.

   Bibliography: p.
   Includes index.
   1. Aged—United States—Abuse of. 2. Aged—United States—Crimes
against. 3. Aged—Services for—United States. I. Costa, Joseph J.
HV1461.A28   1984   362.8'8'0880565   82–48472
ISBN 0–669–06142–5 (alk. paper)

Second printing, June 1985

Published simultaneously in Canada

Printed in the United States of America on acid-free paper

International Standard Book Number: 0–669–06142–5

Library of Congress Catalog Card Number: 82–48472

Again,
This effort, this work,
this life,
for the greater honor and glory of God

Contents

List of Figures

List of Tables

Preface

Senior-citizen abuse, elder abuse, granny-bashing: Call it what one wants, abuse of the elderly is a modern social problem that demands increased attention and public awareness. Sources and resources in this subject area are limited. This compilation organizes the sources and resources that are available to senior citizens, advocacy groups, and prevention organizations and informs those in need that someone does care.

One difficulty encountered in assembling such information is knowing that new and different research is being conducted at every moment. Because of this aspect of research and assembling, readers must realize that this book cannot claim to be exhaustive.

In works of this nature, acknowledgments are of primary importance. The author wishes to acknowledge the following for their support and efforts: Nancy R. King, deputy director of the Center for Women Policy Studies, Washington, D.C., for permission to reprint her article; the Pennsylvania Commission on Crime and Delinquency, James Thomas, executive director; Dr. Frank Clemente of Pennsylvania State University, Dr. Jaber F. Gubrium of Marquette University, and Dr. Sheldon S. Tobin of the Institute of Gerontology, State University of New York at Albany, for permission to reprint their articles; Mrs. Fran Cable, reference librarian, Pennsylvania State University, and Mrs. Lorraine Stanton, library assistant, Schuylkill campus, Pennsylvania State University, for reference services; and Shenandoah Valley Junior-Senior High School students Donna Hancher, Janet Norbert, Angie Yarnitsky, Helene Ruth, Ann Marie Sendlock, Andrea Young, Chris James, Donna Zaleski, Nicole M. Morris, JoAnn Polaconis, and Brenda Caruso for their filing, typing, and proofreading services.

Finally, eternal gratitude to my wife for her inspiration, patience, and motivation.

Part I
The Elderly as Victims

1

Exploitation and Abuse of Older Family Members: An Overview of the Problem

Nancy R. King

The most recent aspect of family violence to emerge into public view is abuse of the older person. In the 1960s child abuse received public recognition and response; spouse abuse followed in the 1970s. Now the exploitation and abuse of older persons, most often by younger family members responsible for their care, has been brought to light as a prevalent and serious form of family violence.

Elder abuse takes many forms. The most shocking is the physical battering of an older person by the family member who is responsible for providing care. Less flagrant but perhaps equally devastating forms are threats of physical assault, verbal assaults, and financial exploitation. Prescription and over-the-counter drugs such as tranquilizers or sleeping pills that are given to older persons in order to make them more manageable are sources of potential abuse. Excessive alcohol consumption may be overlooked by family members or even encouraged for the same reason. Involuntary constriction—tying an older person to a bed or chair—is sometimes inappropriately used to maintain control. In some instances sexual abuse has been inflicted upon older women. Unsanitary living conditions—the presence of vermin in the home, or inadequate ventilation or heat—can arguably be considered abusive in some situations.

Estimates of the national scope of elder abuse vary from 500,000 to 1 million persons a year. This chapter examines the bases for these estimates and summarizes major findings from recent research on elder abuse. The findings are drawn primarily from surveys of health-care and social-work professionals working with older people, review of case records, and mail surveys of older persons living in one metropolitan area.

Extent of Abuse

Suzanne Steinmetz, associate professor of Individual and Family Studies at the University of Delaware, estimates that at least 500,000 elder men and

Reprinted with permission of the Center for Women Policy Studies and Nancy R. King from *Response to Violence in the Family and Sexual Assault,* vol. 6, no. 2, March/April 1983.

women are abused each year throughout the country. The U.S. House Committee on Aging deduced from its national survey which was issued in 1981 that 4 percent or 1 million of the nation's elderly are victims of abuse each year. University of Maryland researchers Marilyn Block and Jan Sinnott (1979) reached a similar conclusion in their study of elders residing in Maryland. An actual incidence rate based on empirical evidence is not known at present. As with many other social problems, it is difficult to ascertain how much abuse of older individuals exists; there is no common definition, and the phenomenon often goes unreported.

O'Malley et al. (1979) of the Legal Research and Services for the Elderly in Boston used the following definition of elder abuse: "the willful infliction of physical pain, injury or debilitating mental anguish, unreasonable confinement or deprivation by a caretaker of services which are necessary to maintain mental and physical health."

Devi Lyon, in testimony before the California Assembly Committee on Aging in 1981, defined elder abuse as "the physical and/or psychological infliction of injury, neglect, monetary exploitation, or abandonment of a senior, primarily by a family member."

Composite categories of abuse that have been identified by others include:

physical abuse—conduct that results in bodily harm;

psychological abuse—threats or violence that result in mental distress, fright, and/or emotional disturbance;

negligence—breach of duty or careless conduct that results in injury to an older person or in a violation of his or her rights;

financial exploitation—theft or conversion of money or property belonging to the older person by relatives or caregivers, sometimes accomplished by threat, deceit, or battering.

These differences in definition are one reason for the wide variance in the estimates of abuse cited earlier. Another difficulty in determining the incidence of elder abuse is the reluctance of victims to report maltreatment. Many fear retaliation in the form of further abuse, abandonment, or institutionalization. To some, the thought of entering a nursing home is worse than knowing that they will be mistreated in their own home or the home of a family member. Another perhaps critical factor is the victim's feelings of protection for the abuser and of responsibility for his or her behavior.

It is not uncommon for elder victims to deny that abuse has occurred, even when confronted with its evidence. Outsiders are also reluctant to report elder abuse. Many outside observers are not willing to participate in an investigation or in finding a solution; they just want the situation ended. Professionals have been known to join the abuser and/or other family members in covering up the problem in order to protect themselves.

Unlike children who are in regular contact with teachers, doctors, and other adults, infirm elders are often isolated, and therefore, their mistreatment is less likely to be noticed by those who might be alert to symptoms of abuse. Bruises or welts may be thought to be the result of a fall, an illness, or the aging process. When evidence of abuse is detected, victim complaints may be dismissed as paranoia or senility.

Since the studies discussed here differ widely in their definition of abuse, methodology, and scope, only very tentative generalizations can be drawn from their results. Nevertheless, three of the four major studies found a significant level of physical and psychological abuse. The most common form seems to fall into categories of neglect rather than of physical violence. Abuse was likely to be a recurring or ongoing phenomenon, and often more than one type of abuse was present.

University of Michigan researchers Douglass, Hickey, and Noel (1981), who interviewed 228 professionals in five Michigan communities, found that although abuse and neglect of elders by their caregivers does exist, it is not pervasive. Passive neglect (being ignored, left alone, isolated, or forgotten) was the most prevalent form of abuse; verbal and emotional abuse followed. Active neglect—withholding of care such as medicine, food, exercise, or assistance to the bathroom—and physical abuse were found to a far less extent, although respondents in virtually every profession had some experience with physical abuse of elder persons.

When Elizabeth Lau and Jordan Kosberg (1979) reviewed all the case records of clients over age 60 being serviced at the Chronic Illness Center in Cleveland, Ohio, during one year, they found nearly 10 percent of all such persons to be victims of some form of abuse during the year. Physical abuse was found in nearly 75 percent of the cases of abuse. Within this category, the most common form was "lack of personal care." Direct beatings were found in 28 percent of the cases. Psychological abuse was found in 51 percent, and verbal assault in 33 percent of the cases. Material abuse, such as financial exploitation, occurred in 31 percent of the abuse cases. In each case, there was likely to be more than one form of abuse.

University of Maryland researchers Block and Sinnott (1979), whose results are based on 26 cases identified from a mail survey of a random sample of community-dwelling elders, agency records, and responses to a mail survey of selected professionals, found that psychological abuse was more common than physical abuse. Lack of personal care and supervision were factors in 38 percent of the cases reported; beatings were cited in 15 percent.

O'Malley et al. (1979) studied 332 responses to a survey of 1,044 professionals and paraprofessionals serving the elderly in Massachusetts in order to gain descriptive information on the extent of abuse of elders residing at home by their families, friends, or other caregivers. Fifty-five percent of those who responded cited an incident of elder abuse within the prior eighteen months. Over 41 percent of the reported cases were judged to be the result of physical trauma. Injuries included bruises, welts, cuts, punctures, bone fractures, dislocations, and burnings. Verbal harassment, malnutrition, financial mismanagement, unreasonable confinement, over-sedation, and sexual abuse were also observed but less frequently.

The Victim

The characteristics of the victims in the four studies were remarkably similar. Most were female and over age 75; most were physically and/or mentally impaired and lived with their abuser. They were physically, emotionally, and/or financially dependent upon their abuser. They were generally unaware of the community resources available to them and fearful of the alternatives.

Fifty-four percent of the victims in the Massachusetts study were over age 75, and 36 percent were over age 80; 80 percent were female, and 75 percent lived with the person who abused them. In 84 percent of the cases the abuser was a family member. Seventy-five percent of the victims were physically impaired and most were abused on a recurring basis.

The University of Maryland study found the abused elder to have a mean age of 84. Eighty-one percent were female, 61 percent Protestant, and 58 percent "middle class." Nearly half suffered from moderate to severe mental impairment, and 96 percent from some form of physical disability.

The Cleveland, Ohio, study revealed that 76 percent of the victims identified were women who had at least one major physical or mental impairment. Fifty-eight percent were widowed, 75 percent white, and 66 percent lived with their relatives.

These findings must be viewed against the profile of the typical older person. Most people over the age of 65 have at least one chronic illness or impairment, although most are not severely limited by it. Most elders are women; in fact, in the over-75 age group, women outnumber men two to one. Most older women are widowed (70 percent in the over-75 age group), and most older, widowed women are low-income (half live below the official poverty line).

The Abuser

The typical abuser was usually a close relative and primary caregiver for the abused elder. The abuser was likely to be under severe stress and may have suffered from alcoholism and/or mental illness.

The Massachusetts study revealed that 86 percent of the abusers were relatives and that in 75 percent of the cases the abuser lived with the victim. Three-quarters of the abusers were reported to be suffering from some form of stress, and alcohol or drug abuse was a problem for 28 percent. The elder victim was judged to be a source of stress to the abuser in 63 percent of the cases due to the high level of physical, emotional, and/or financial support required.

Data from the University of Maryland study showed that 81 percent of the abusers were relatives; 42 percent were children of the victim; 53 percent were in their 40s and 50s; 58 percent were female; 88 percent were white; and 65 percent were "middle class." Elder abuse was recurring in 58 percent of the cases and was judged to be the result of psychological problems of the abuser in 58 percent of the cases. Economic problems were a factor in 31 percent.

Although the Ohio study presented no complete profile of the abusers, over 90 percent of the abusers were relatives; they were most likely to be daughters.

Factors Contributing to Abuse

Longer Life

The changing demographic structure may be a contributing factor in any increase in elder abuse. The life expectancy for an infant born in 1900 was less than 50 years. In comparison, a baby girl born today can expect to life to age 84 and a baby boy to age 77. Older people have become the fastest-growing segment of the United States population. The over-60 population increased sevenfold between 1900 and 1977 in comparison to a threefold growth in the population at large. In addition, the older population group itself is getting older. In 1930, only 29 percent of the over-65 population was age 75 and over. By 1975, 38 percent were beyond this age.

Of the predicted 7 million increase in the size of the older population between now and the year 2000, almost three-quarters will be concentrated in the over-75 age group. The number of those over age 85 is expected to grow by 64 percent during this period. It is the persons in these groups who are likely to be physically and/or mentally impaired and, therefore, in need of assistance and care from family members. These Census Bureau projections indicate that the dependent element of the older population will increase at a significantly greater rate than those to whom they will turn for assistance.

Dependency

Dependency is the most common precondition in domestic abuse. Changes associated with aging along with changes produced by chronic disease often cause a loss of physical and emotional self-sufficiency. These losses are often sufficient to place an older person in a position of dependency on their children or other relatives at some point during their lives.

Financial dependence is also often associated with elder abuse. For the first time, a large group of people are living beyond their economically productive years, and their income, which may have seemed sufficient at retirement, has been eroded by economic forces beyond their control.

The studies indicate that elder-abuse victims are generally physically and/or mentally impaired and, therefore, dependent upon their families for care and, perhaps, survival, thereby increasing their vulnerability to abuse.

Stress

Most researchers who have explored the problem of elder abuse cite the stress inherent in the caregiving role as a factor in most abuse cases. Elaine Brody, director of the Philadelphia Geriatric Center, feels that elder abuse is an example of individual or family psyhopathology. Others argue that although this is sometimes the case, even psychologically healthy family members can become abusive as the result of the exhaustion and acute stress caused by overwhelming caregiving responsibilities.

Brody estimates that 80 percent of home care to the aged is provided by family members residing in the same household. About one-third of these older people need constant care of a medical and personal nature. It has been estimated that approximately two-fifths of adult children caring for parents in their homes spend an amount of time providing care equivalent to a full-time job.

Care of elder parents has customarily been the socially assigned responsibility of adult daughters and daughters-in-law. By the time their parents require assistance and care, these women may also be experiencing stressful age-related changes. These may include return to or retirement from the work force, widowhood, illness of self or spouse, and/or financial difficulties.

Many look forward to middleage as a time to enjoy financial independence and freedom from parental responsibilities. The progressive dependence of aging parents may conflict with their children's goals of personal fulfillment beyond traditional family roles.

Medical and pharmacological advances have prolonged disease states and, therefore, the duration of dependency on the family support system. It is increasingly likely that impaired elders will be dependent on their children for extended periods, perhaps longer than their children were dependent upon them. Physiological and psychological changes caused by illnesses such as diabetes and strokes, as well as certain medications or combinations of medications, can cause severe personality changes in older people. It is difficult for families to cope with these changes, especially when eruptions of aggressive, belligerent, and disoriented behavior occur. Even the most devoted and responsible caregiver may see feelings of love and respect erode into anger, guilt, and disappointment after years of tiring caregiving.

Financial aspects of caregiving must not be overlooked. Medical costs have skyrocketed in recent years, and neither public nor private health insurance policies have kept pace. Medicare, the public health insurance program for older Americans, covers less than 50 percent of their health-care costs.

Brian Langdon, director of the Family Services Association of Greater Lawrence Massachusetts, in testimony before the House Select Committee on Aging, observed that abuse and neglect of older people by their families seem to fall into several broad categories. First are those families whose emotional, physical, and financial resources are depleted in their efforts to care for a frail elder person. Most of these families were fairly well adjusted, but the burden became too much. Second were families with past unresolved family conflicts that became reactivated during the stress of caring for an elderly family member. Third are those families who have long histories of poor adjustment in the community. Fourth are those elders who are victims of abuse or neglect because of the failure of the community to provide sufficient support and help to their families.

Learned Violence

Some students of domestic violence hold that children learn violent behavior from experiencing abuse or observing abusive and violent parents. They see family violence as a potentially cyclical pattern of intergenerational abuse with parents and their children abusing each other throughout their lifetimes.

Straus, Gelles, and Steinmetz (1980) found a high correlation between personal experience with family violence as a child and later experience. Although that study did not specifically focus on elder abuse, other researchers reason that if such a pattern does exist, it is likely to be a factor in all forms of domestic violence. Steinmetz (1980) reports that children who were not treated violently while growing up abuse their parents later by a ratio of 1 to 400, and children who are treated violently by their parents, by a ratio of 1 to 2. An Ohio task force on domestic violence corroborated Steinmetz's findings. They found that children who abuse their parents were most likely to have been abused by them as children. Renvoise's (1978) study found, however, that most families who abused elders did not have a history of previous abuse.

University of Michigan researcher Tom Hickey agrees with the hypothesis that abused children are predisposed to becoming abusive adults. He suggests, however, that learned violence is not the only factor in domestic abuse. Life events and crises serve as "triggers" of existing developmental patterns and of previous learning.

Other theorists point to personal or pathological problems inherent in the abuser as a primary cause of abuse. Lau and Kosberg (1979) discuss the role of the "non-normal" caregiver who may be alcoholic or mentally ill or who may suffer from a form of organic brain deterioration. Such individuals are incapable of sustaining positive interfamily relationships or providing care for another. Renvoise found that drinking was associated with violence in almost half of the cases that she studied.

One out of five professionals who participated in the Michigan study concluded that personal problems, including alcohol abuse, contributed to neglect and abuse.

In Conclusion

Concern about elder abuse has already resulted in the enactment of mandatory reporting laws in sixteen states, which, in turn, has resulted in increased reports of elder abuse. The states that have mandatory reporting laws include Alabama, Arkansas, Connecticut, Florida, Kentucky, Maryland, Minnesota, Nebraska, New Hampshire, North Carolina, Oklahoma, South Carolina, Tennessee, Utah, Vermont, and Virginia.

Under state law, Connecticut's Department of Aging is now required to investigate any complaint of abuse, neglect, exploitation, or abandonment of any citizen age 60 or over. In the eight months after the law became effective, 600 reports of elder abuse were received. Of the 464 cases that were initially investigated, 87 involved physical abuse, 314 involved neglect, 65 exploitation, and 8 abandonment.

Within three years after a mandatory reporting law went into effect in Connecticut, 3,380 cases of elder abuse were reported in that state. Of those

2,500 involved neglect, 500 involved physical abuse, 330 exploitation, and 90 abandonment.

In 1974, South Carolina enacted a law to protect vulnerable elders from abuse, neglect, and exploitation. By 1976, a protective services program was fully operational. Over 2,000 cases were treated in the first six years, and the number of new reports increases by about 25 percent each year, cutting across all socioeconomic, racial, and geographic lines.

However, recognition of the phenomenon of elder abuse should not lend credibility to the myth that American families mistreat and/or abandon their elder members. Studies have demonstrated that this is not a valid generalization. In most families, ties between generations remain viable and strong.

One survey found that three-quarters of older persons lived within a half-hour journey of an adult child and had seen that child within the previous week. Other studies show that as individuals age, involvement with family members increases, especially during times of difficulty, illness, or crisis. These findings do not invalidate, however, the findings that ongoing caregiving responsibilities for impaired, dependent parents are placing a growing number of families under severe stress.

As discussed earlier, a number of factors combine to create or exacerbate abusive family situations. However, more research is needed if we are to understand clearly the phenomenon of elder abuse. Researchers need to move beyond the exploratory stage by choosing samples that are representative of the entire elder population and by clarifying the definitions of abuse. As our knowledge about elder abuse becomes more sophisticated, the strategies for prevention, invervention, and treatment will become more effective.

References

Block, Marilyn R., and J. Sinnott. *The Battered Elder Syndrome: An Exploratory Study.* Unpublished manuscript, University of Maryland, 1979.

Douglass, Richard L.; T. Hickey; and C. Noel. *A Study of Maltreatment of the Elderly and Other Vulnerable Adults.* Ann Arbor: University of Michigan, 1978.

Lau, Elizabeth, and J.I. Kosberg. "Abuse of the Elderly by Informal Care Providers." *Aging,* 1979, 299, 10–15.

Legal Research and Services for the Elderly. *Elder Abuse in Massachusetts: A Survey of Professionals and Paraprofessionals.* Boston, Mass.: LRSE, 1979 (available from LRSE, 2 Park Square, Room 311, Boston, Mass. 01116).

Renvoise, J. *Web of Violence: A Study of Family Violence.* London: Rout-
ledge and Kegan Paul, 1978.
Steinmetz, Suzanne. "Elder Abuse: Society's Double Dilemma." Testi-
mony before the Joint Hearing Senate Special Committee on Aging and
House Select Committee on Aging, June 11, 1980, 1–18.
Straus, Murray A.; R.A. Gelles; and S.K. Steinmetz. *Behind Closed Doors:
Violence in the American Family.* Garden City, N.Y.: Anchor Press,
1980.

Fear of Crime among the Aged

Frank Clemente and
Michael B. Kleiman

As Gubrium (1974) recently pointed out, one of the most neglected areas of empirical investigation in social gerontology is the impact of crime upon the aged. There have been very few attempts to examine the effect of crime, fear of victimization, or other aspects of criminal behavior on the elderly (see Goldsmith and Tomas 1974 for an important exception). In fact, even criminologists have generally ignored the problem. Our review of five years (1970–1974) of *Crime and Delinquency Abstracts* indicated that of literally thousands of studies on crime only a handful dealt specifically with the elderly.

Given this neglect of the impact of crime on the aged it is not surprising that discussions of the topic are laden with questionable assumptions and untested hypotheses (Gubrium 1974). Even more important, however, as Goldsmith and Tomas (1974) have noted, the paucity of research and data has severely inhibited the development of viable programs to reduce the effect of crime on the aged. Our research attempts to at least partially alleviate this situation by focusing on an important aspect of the problem—fear of crime among older people. Systematic research along these lines will provide an empirical background for practitioners seeking to control fear of crime among the aged segment of the population.

Fear as a Problem

While there are many facets to the impact of crime on the elderly, one of the most important relates to fear of victimization. In fact, it is reasonable to argue that for older people fear of crime is even more of a problem than crime itself. Despite popular assumptions to the contrary, the victimization rates for crimes against the person are *lower* for the elderly than for any other age group over age 12. This pattern holds regardless of whether vic-

An unidentified reader for *The Gerontologist* made helpful comments on an earlier version. Research supported by the College of Liberal Arts at Pennsylvania State. Data were collected under the direction of Professor James A. Davis for the National Data Program of the National Opinion Research Center (NORC) at the University of Chicago. Reprinted by permission of *The Gerontologist*, vol. 16, no. 3 (1976):207–210.

timization data come merely from crimes reported to the police or from surveys of the general population. We emphasize this point because some commentators have suggested that the lower victimization rates among the elderly are due to their reluctance to report crimes (cf. Goldsmith and Tomas 1974). All national survey data we have seen, however, clearly indicate that the aged have low victimization rates. For example, the most recent survey by the U.S. Department of Justice (1974), *Criminal Victimization in the United States,* indicated that for the age group 65 and over the victimization rate of crimes against the person was 4.4 per thousand. This compares with 10.9 in the 35–49 group and 31.3 in the 20–24 age category. These survey data demonstrate that even when the problem of nonreporting by the elderly is taken into account they have low victimization rates.

On the other hand, these low victimization rates notwithstanding, fear of crime among the aged is a harsh reality. Two recent statements from the social gerontology literature yield insight into the situation:

> criminal behavior has a chilling effect upon the freedom of older Americans. Fear of victimization causes self-imposed "house arrest" among older people . . . (Goldsmith and Tomas 1974).

> crime has . . . become increasingly a source of public fear. . . . I don't believe that such effects are anywhere more apparent than among the segment of aging persons in the United States . . . (Cunningham 1974).

Simply put, fear among the elderly is real and pervasive. It matters little whether this fear is out of proportion to the objective probability of being victimized. As Goldsmith and Tomas (1974) correctly point out, even though such fears may be largely unwarranted by local conditions, the effect is just as severe as when the fears are justified. The rate of elderly women being attacked on the street may be only one per thousand population. But if 80 percent of such women are afraid to leave their homes, fear of crime has become a major social problem.

In essence, then, there is solid documentation that the elderly suffer from a substantial fear of crime. To date, however, little empirical work has been done to assess which segments of the aged population are the most fearful. The elderly are not a uniform group with monolithic attitudes. Rather, they are a heterogenous aggregation. This diversity raises important questions in regard to fear. For example, are the black aged more afraid of crime than the white aged? Are the rural elderly less afraid than those who live in large cities? These and related questions demand careful attention before policy decisions can be made and effective programs can be developed and implemented. To this end, our analysis breaks down fear of crime among the aged by four variables that previous research has shown to be important for the general population. These four explanatory variables are (1) sex, (2) race, (3) socioeconomic status, and (4) size of community.

A National Data Set

Data were drawn from the 1973 and 1974 *General Social Surveys* conducted by the National Opinion Research Center (NORC) at the University of Chicago. Both were national multistage area probability samples designed to represent the noninstitutionalized adult population of the continental United States (see Davis 1973 and 1974 for details). We combined the samples in order to insure an analytically sufficient number of older people. This procedure yielded a total sample of 461 individuals age 65 and over. For comparative purposes we will present parallel data from the non-aged respondents (N = 2,488).

Fear of crime was ascertained via the question, "Is there any area right around here—that is, within a mile—where you would be afraid to walk alone at night?" Responses were dichotomized as either yes or no.

This question is useful for our analysis for several reasons. First, it was asked in identical form in both years. Second, it clearly gets at fear of crime rather than concern over the crime rate. As Furstenberg (1971) has emphasized, it is important not to confuse these phenomena. A person may be quite concerned over rising crime but not in the least afraid to walk about his own neighborhood. Third, the question has conceptual relevance because it brings the fear of crime down to the personal level. Our specific concern is whether or not people are afraid of crime. It seems reasonable that being afraid to walk about one's own neighborhood is a useful indicator of that concept.

Explanatory variables were operationalized along traditional lines. Sex and race are natural dichotomies. Socioeconomic status was measured along two dimensions. First, income (family dollar income per year), coded as either (1) less than $7,000 or (2) $7,000 and over. Second, education, coded as (1) less than high school, (2) high school, and (3) more than high school.

Community size was measured in the NORC surveys on the following five-category scale:

1. large city (250,000 plus),
2. medium size city (50,000–250,000),
3. suburb of large city,
4. small town (2,500–50,000),
5. rural (under 2,500)

The Fearful

The first task is to assess the difference in fear between the aged and non-aged. Our data strongly support the assumption that the elderly are more afraid of crime than their younger counterparts. While 51 percent of those respondents age 65 and over said they were afraid, only 41 percent of the under-65 group said so. Given this significant difference, we now turn to the disaggregation of the data by the explanatory variables.

Sex

Virtually all surveys on the fear of crime have indicated that women are far more likely to express fear than men (cf. Erskine 1974). This reluctance of men to admit fear is readily apparent in our data but is less prevalent among the elderly than among the non-aged. For example, while only 19 percent of the non-aged males said they were afraid, over one-third (34 percent) of the elderly men admitted fear. These figures compare to 60 percent of non-aged women and 69 percent of aged females. In other words, while men of all ages were less likely to express fear than women, this pattern was considerably less profound among elderly men.

Race

Blacks are more afraid of crime than whites. This holds true for all age categories and is especially evident in the aged. Our data indicated that about 47 percent of the white elderly were afraid to walk their neighborhoods alone at night. This compared to 69 percent of the black aged. More specifically, while less than half of the white aged expressed fear, over two-thirds of the black elderly did so.

Socioeconomic Status (SES)

People at the higher SES levels generally express less fear of personal crime than people at the lower levels (cf. Ennis 1967). In terms of income, our data fit this pattern for both age groups. Among the elderly with incomes less than $7,000 per year, 51 percent expressed fear. This compares to 43 percent of those with an annual income of more than $7,000.

A slightly larger difference by income existed in the under 65 group. For the non-aged, 47 percent of those with incomes under $7,000 said they were afraid as opposed to only 36 percent of those above $7,000. Thus, while in both age groups income emerges as a specifying factor, it is more important for the non-aged than the aged.

In regard to education and fear, however, there are minimal differences among the aged. For example, of elderly respondents with more than high school education 49 percent expressed fear. This compares to 53 percent of those with high school and 49 percent of those with less than high school. In short, for the aged, education makes little difference as to fear of crime.

For the non-aged, however, the situation is somewhat different. Of the respondents under age 65 with more than high school education only 37 percent said they were afraid to walk alone at night within a mile of their home. For the high school and less than high school groups this percentage was 44 and 43, respectively. Thus, while education did not emerge as an important specifying factor in regard to fear among the elderly, it did have a slight effect for the non-aged with the more educated respondents expressing less fear.

Community Size

Community size has typically been found to be directly related to fear of crime (cf. Erskine 1974). That is, residents of large cities tend to be more fearful of victimization than people in smaller towns and rural areas. Our data regarding the elderly parallel these findings. The percentages of the aged showing fear decrease in a clear step pattern as one moves from large cities to rural areas: 76 percent for large cities, 68 percent for medium-size cities, 48 percent for suburbs, 43 percent for small towns, and 24 percent for rural locations. In other words, while over three out of four elderly respondents were afraid, only one in four of the rural elderly indicated fear. This result provides strong support for the necessity of developing programs to reduce the effect of crime on aged residents of large metropolitan areas.

The poor position of the aged residents of large cities in regard to fear of crime is even further highlighted when we turn to responses of the non-aged. The percentages of respondents under age 65 who indicated fear are 57 percent in large cities, 47 percent in medium-size cities, 39 percent in suburbs, 40 percent in small towns, and 25 percent in rural areas. Note the large difference in fear between aged and non-aged residents of metropolitan cities (76 percent and 68 percent versus 57 percent and 47 percent). These findings dramatically underscore the deteriorating quality of life of the metropolitan elderly in the United States.

As noted above, low-income respondents in our national sample express substantially greater fear of crime than do respondents earning more than $7,000 annually. In addition, the NORC data indicate that such poor persons are disproportionately concentrated in urban areas. For example, while 26 percent of small-town respondents had an annual income of less than $7,000, 38 percent of large-city residents fell into this low-income category. To assess the effects of the disproportionate urban concentration of poor persons on the relationship between city size and fear of crime, we utilized income as a control variable in the analysis.

The results of partialing on income indicate that even when the fact that low-income respondents are more prevalent in cities is taken into account, the clear decrease in fear among the aged as one moves from large cities to rural areas remains in force. In other words, urban residents are more afraid than their rural counterparts regardless of income. For example, the percentages of low-income elderly showing fear in each of our size categories are: 71 percent for large cities, 70 percent for medium cities, 56 percent for suburbs, 48 percent for small towns, and 24 percent for rural areas. For the aged earning more than $7,000 a year, these respective figures are 77 percent, 75 percent, 27 percent, 26 percent, and 14 percent.

The extent of the metropolitan elderly's fear is further substantiated when we look at the results for the non-aged. The percentages of low-income respondents under age 65 who indicated fear are 62 percent in large cities, 54 percent in medium-size cities, 43 percent in suburbs, 38 percent in small towns, and 28 percent in rural areas. The corresponding percentages for the high-income non-aged are 55 percent, 46 percent, 38 percent, 38 percent, and 23 percent. Again, note the large differences in fear between aged and non-aged residents of cities over 50,000 (71 percent and 70 percent versus 62 percent and 54 percent for the less-than-$7,000 income bracket; 77 percent and 75 percent versus 55 percent and 46 percent for the $7,00-or-greater income group). These differences are yet another indication of the widespread fear of victimization among the urban elderly regardless of income.

In sum, then, the aged residents of cities over 50,000 show significantly greater fear of crime than either their younger counterparts or older inhabitants of suburbs, small towns, and rural areas. It is among these metropolitan elderly that fear of crime takes the heaviest toll. It is this group that stays behind locked doors subject to what Goldsmith and Tomas (1974) accurately term "house arrest." It is this group that is forced to curtail social activities, stay home from church, or abandon shopping trips for fear of being robbed. It is this group that is afraid of a strange adult, terrified of two or three youths on the street, and frightened by a dimly lit elevator. Clearly, it is this group that deserves and merits the development and implementation of programs designed to control the fear of crime.

Implications

Several important implications can be drawn from this analysis of a national data set. First, the results strongly support the argument that the aged are not a homogeneous group in regard to fear of crime (or, we suspect, most other attitudinal states). Rather, there are important specifying factors in regard to fear of victimization. It is not sufficient to merely conclude that the aged are more afraid of crime than the non-aged. Our findings, for example, indicated that sex, race, and city size were very important in specifying the relationship between age and fear. Socioeconomic status generally failed to emerge as an important factor for the aged.

Hopefully, our findings will serve as a useful point of departure of future research in the area. One line of investigation that would seem to merit careful consideration revolves around the socioenvironmental perspective advanced by Gubrium (1974). He has suggested, for example, that fear of crime among the aged is likely to be greater in age-heterogeneous housing than in age-concentrated housing. Unfortunately, the NORC data were not amenable to a test of this interesting hypothesis. There seems to be a surge of interest in social gerontology regarding the impact of crime on the aged (for example, the national conference held at American University in June, 1975). Further, various programs have been developed in several large cities to alleviate the fear of crime among the aged. In Philadelphia, for example, a pilot program of block organization to report crimes and quell rumors has received both federal and state funding.

References

Cunningham, C. The scenario of crimes against the aged. In N.E. Tomas (Ed.), *Reducing crimes against aged persons.* USDHEW, Philadelphia, 1974.

Davis, J.A. *National data program for the social sciences.* Univ. Chicago, Chicago, 1973.

David, J.A. *National data program for the social sciences.* Univ. Chicago, Chicago, 1974.

Ennis, P.H. *Criminal victimization in the United States.* USGPO, Washington, 1967.

Erskine, H. The polls: Fear of violence and crime. *Public Opinion Quarterly,* 1974, *38,* 131–145.

Furstenberg, F. Public reaction to crime in the streets. *American Scholar* 1971, *51,* 601–610.

Goldsmith, J., & Tomas, N.E. Crimes against the elderly: A continuing national crises. *Aging,* 1974, *236,* 10–13.

Gubrium, J. Victimization in old age. *Crime & Delinquency,* 1974, *29,* 245–250.

U.S. Dept. of Justice. *Criminal victimization in the United States.* USGPO, Washington, 1974.

**Crime against
the Elderly**

Experts in the area of elderly victimization tell us that older persons have varying degrees of concern about crime. Some make important changes in lifestyle and even deprive themselves because of fear. Others worry needlessly about being victims, even when there is a statistically low probability that anything will ever happen.

Street crimes such as mugging, holdup (when a weapon is used) and purse snatch are usually of particular concern to the older person.

You should know that the street criminal is an opportunist looking for an easy mark. Everything you do to make it difficult for him to strike reduces your chances of being a victim. You don't have to change your lifestyle or live in fear. But you should be "prevention conscious." Use caution and common sense.

When You Go Out

1. Try to arrange to have a companion with you when walking.
2. Plan your route in advance and be sure to use well-lit streets if you must go out at night.
3. Walk on the curbside away from buildings where an assailant could conceal himself.
4. Older women are often the victims of purse snatch. Our best advice is don't carry a purse if you can avoid it.
5. If you must carry a purse, hold it close to your body with a hand on the clasp. Don't dangle it.
6. If you have an armful of packages, tuck your purse in between the packages and your body.
7. Don't carry or flash large sums of cash.
8. Never leave a purse on a store counter or sitting on the floor of a restroom.
9. Be on the alert for suspicious-looking persons when you enter a public restroom.

Material prepared by the Pennsylvania Commission on Crime and Delinquency. Reprinted with permission.

10. When using the bus or other public transportation, sit near the driver if there aren't many passengers.
11. If a friend takes you home or you take a taxi, ask the driver to wait until you are safely inside before leaving.
12. Have your keys ready so you can get in the door with a minimum of fuss.

What If You Are Attacked?

If you develop good security habits, chances are slim that you will ever meet up with a street criminal. But if you are held up, don't resist. Give the criminal what he wants and try to get a good description for police. Never try to fight unless you are attacked. If you are attacked by an unarmed assailant, scream, call for help, kick, bite, struggle—anything that will help you break away to safety.

Your Home

Residential burglary is a serious problem everywhere. But since it's mostly a crime of opportunity, you can discourage the average burglar by making your home a tough target.

Use deadbolt locks on all exterior doors. Protect windows and other potential points of entry with good locks or other security devices. Keep the premises well lit at night. Make you home sound and appear occupied when you go out by using an automatic timer to turn on lights and a radio and asking a neighbor to keep an eye on things when you go on a trip.

Further details on residential security are contained in a booklet entitled "How to Make Crime More Trouble Than It's Worth," available from your local police department.

If you have taken precautions to make your home a bad bet for the burglar, you've made it tough on other types of intruders as well. Remember this: More serious crimes like rape and aggravated assault often occur when a burglar enters and finds an older woman alone.

Practice These Habits When You're at Home

1. Always keep your doors locked. Have a peephole in the door so you can see callers without opening it. Don't rely on security chains. They can be broken easily by a determined assailant.

2. Never let a stranger in. Insist on proper identification. If he can't show it or you're still suspicious, call whoever it is he represents for verification.
3. If a stranger asks to use the phone, don't let him in. Instead, offer to place the call for him.
4. Never give out information over the phone indicating when you will or won't be home. Don't let a caller know you're home alone.
5. Make sure you have a lock on your bedroom door.
6. Consider installing a phone in the bedroom, since it enables you to call for help if you wake up and hear an intruder.
7. Be sure your outside house number is displayed prominently so that it can be seen easily from the street by police responding to your call for assistance.

Fraud: The Con Game

According to the American Association of Retired Persons, older citizens are victims of fraudulent schemes far out of proportion to their population numbers. Con artists are slick, so you've got to keep your guard up. Be skeptical.

1. Be aware of what people are saying. Don't be rushed into any deal.
2. Know what you are signing. Carefully read all "receipts" or "minor contracts."
3. If you are being offered something for nothing, it's usually a phony deal. Allow yourself time to check things out.
4. Stay away from secret deals and plans. For example, there's a "bank examiner" scheme where a phony bank examiner tells you he's investigating a dishonest teller and wants you to help by withdrawing money from your account to use as a test. Don't fall for it.
5. Never turn over any sizable amount of cash to anyone, especially strangers offering to help you "get rich quick."

4 Victimization in Old Age: Available Evidence and Three Hypotheses

Jaber F. Gubrium

The subject of old age and the behavior of the elderly is not lacking its share of popular beliefs and sentiments.[1] Of particular note are common citations of the extent of criminal victimization experienced by the elderly as opposed to other age groups. Such discussions are often alarming, both to the elderly themselves and to the professional concerned with their well-being.

Certainly, this recent concern with victimization in old age is not completely unwarranted. The 1960s was a decade in which the issue of crime became paramount to many Americans. This is evident in the personal reactions of the public to crime as measured in a variety of opinion polls. What appears to be unwarranted, however, is the common belief and operating principle that the aged as a group are the greatest victims of crime.

In examining the available evidence on victimization by age categories, one should keep in mind that victimization statistics are figures on the number of reported *incidents* of various crimes in a certain period. These statistics do not reflect the relative impact of crime on the lives of persons with differing "recovery" resources—that is, health, income, and social support—markedly evident distinctions between age groups, particularly between the elderly and the younger.

Available Evidence

Two kinds of age-related data on rates of victimization are available. One provides statistics comparing age groups according to the relative incidence of victimization, with breakdowns by type of crime. The second kind of data is on variations in rates of victimization, within age groups, by such demographic variables as sex and race.

The evidence considered here is mainly confined to population surveys of victimization incidents. It does not include statistics available through

Reprinted from *Crime and Delinquency,* vol. 20, no. 3, (July 1974):245-250, with permission of Sage Publications, Inc. Copyright © 1974 by the National Council on Crime and Delinquency.

local and federal police agencies, the most extensive of which is the FBI's annual *Uniform Crime Reports* (UCR). Two levels of survey data are considered: (1) a national survey of 10,000 households conducted in 1966, reporting 2,098 vicitmizations[2] and (2) regional surveys of victimization, limited to a set of cities or to districts within a specific urban area.[3]

How does general victimization vary with age? Ennis's national survey data indicate that the relationship is curvilinear. Victimization is comparatively low among persons under age 20, rises to a peak in the age 20-to-50 categories, and declines after age 50.[4] Regional surveys show a more linear picture, with general victimization decreasing by age.[5] One fact is fairly clear from this evidence. Although the evidence on the extent of general victimization in the youngest age categories is contradictory, there is consensus on the relatively low degree of victimization in old age (age 60 and over).

Given that the risk of being victimized by any crime is less in old age than among younger persons, is the same true for specific kinds of crime? For instance, it is a popular notion that compared with persons of other ages the elderly are more often the victims of various kinds of fraud and malice. Survey data indicate that this belief may have some basis in fact. Ennis's data show that a woman over age 60 is more likely to be a victim of malicious mischief than is a female of any other age. Compared with females under age 40, elderly women are highly likely to be victims of counterfeiting and forgery.[6] From data gathered in the Minneapolis Model Cities area, Blyth and his associates conclude that persons over age 50 are more likely to experience such malicious mischief as obscene telephone calls and general harassment than are other age groups.[7]

The foregoing evidence on victimization and its relationship to age may be summarized as follows: Survey data do not support the popular belief that the aged as a group are the greatest victims of crime in general; also, they do not repudiate the probability that old people may have a greater risk than other persons of being the victims of certain minor crimes.

A second kind of age-related data on victimization is available. This pertains to the types of persons, within specific age groups, who are least likely and those who are most likely to be victims of crime. Since the concern here is with the elderly as a group, discussion of evidence focuses mostly on them.

Ennis's national survey report shows the percentages of persons—by race, sex, and age—who have been victimized by (1) any crime (except burglary) and by (2) aggravated assault and robbery.[8] The data indicate that among the aged, either white or nonwhite, males are more likely than females to be the victims of crime. Controlling for sex and comparing racial differences in victimization among the aged, we find some indications that white males have a slightly greater likelihood of being victimized than do nonwhite males. Among female respondents, the reverse is the case: Nonwhite elderly females are somewhat more likely than their white counterparts to be victims of crime, with the exception of aggravated assault and robbery. Race–sex differences in victimization are notably greater among younger persons (especially in the age 20-to-40 category) than among persons age 60 and over. Race–sex differences in general victimization tend to diminish as persons grow old.[9]

Three Hypotheses

The available survey statistics strongly suggest that differences in victimization are age-related and that victimization among the aged as a group shows demographic variations. I have reason to believe that victimization in old age also may be affected by at least one particular kind of social condition: the degree of "protectiveness" in the local housing environments of old people.

The argument about environmental protectiveness and victimization makes two kinds of distinctions:

First, local environments vary in the extent to which they protect the elderly from being victimized. In specific districts of urban areas, elderly persons reside in at least two sorts of housing environments: (1) single-family homes and (2) multiunit apartment buildings and high rises. The latter often provide supervisory protectiveness—entrance checks, periodic inspections of grounds, series of locked doors, and so forth—and thus are more likely than are self-maintained, single-family homes to shield residents from exposure to crime.

Second, distinctions are made among three types of victim-related behavior: (1) extent of victimization (that is, number of incidents), (2) concern about the seriousness and degree of crime committed, and (3) fear of crime.

What is generally being proposed is that the social conditions reflected in local housing environments of the elderly have a significant impact on their victimization and responses to crime. This proposition has three empirical sources. Reexamining data collected in Baltimore by Louis Harris, Furstenburg indicated recently that persons' responses to crime may vary, depending on whether one is focusing on concern about crime or fear of victimization.[10] He suggests that concern about crime is related to personal resentment of rapid change in social conditions, while fear of victimization is related to persons' definitions of their risks of being victimized, definitions being grounded in perceptions of safety in their local neighborhoods. Another kind of evidence underlying the above proposition is Reiss's analysis of Chicago statistics according to the place where various criminal offenses occurred.[11] His data show that regardless of type of crime, persons are less likely to be victims on the premises of public housing than in private residences.[12] Blyth and his associates record a similar relationship between kind of dwelling structure and the mean number of victim incidents per respondent over age 60 in Minneapolis.[13] The third source of the proposition is my study of 210 aged persons in Detroit, conducted to explore the effect of social life in various types of local housing environment on such psychological factors as morale, life satisfaction, and personal responses to crime.[14]

1. Protectiveness and Extent of Victimization

In constructing and testing a hypothesis on the relationship between local environmental protectiveness and extent of victimization in old age, we must consider at least two potentially confounding factors: First, the urban location of housing environments must be controlled for differential crime rates. Second, in testing a hypothesis relating the social conditions of local environments to extent of victimization, we must take into account the individual crime-vulnerability characteristics of persons in various environments.

One way to control for differential crime rates would be to examine protective and nonprotective housing environments for extent of victimization within the same area of the city. This would minimize the rival hypothesis that differential crime rates, which may be related in urban location to protectiveness, explain variations in extent of victimization between environments. Since the likelihood of being victimized varies also with income, sex, and race, some kind of matching procedure on these individual crime-vulnerability characteristics between protective and nonprotective housing environments would make less significant a second hypothesis that could rival protectiveness as an explanation for extent of victimization. This procedure would minimize the hypothesis that the relationship between protectiveness and extent of victimization is explained by a possible association between individual vulnerability and resident selection, on the one hand, with, on the other, housing environments having particular kinds of protectiveness.

With provision being made for the control of individual crime-vulnerability and area crime rate, the following hypothesis is suggested: *The extent of victimization of the elderly is greater in nonprotective than in protective housing environments.*

2. Protectiveness and Concern about Crime

The Detroit study referred to above suggests that concern about the extent of crime is related to variations in the degree of social interaction between persons within different housing environments.[15] Protective environments, which are often multiunit apartment complexes or high-rise residences, commonly house homogeneously aged populations. Nonprotective environments of one-family homes are characteristically composed of age-heterogeneous residents. This variation in local age composition is likely to have different effects on the social interaction and friendship of aged persons.[16] Elderly persons residing in protective, age-concentrated housing engage in more extensive social interaction than those in nonprotective, age-heterogeneous housing.

The relationship between differences in degree of social interaction among the elderly and concern about crime is contingent on the proposition that beliefs vary with the social conditions that perpetuate their diffusion among persons. Degree of social interaction is such a condition. As social interaction increases among persons and is sustained, they are likely to share a common concern about a particular subject. The current general interest in the subject of crime being what it is, each interacting person's concern with it tends to be corroborated by every other person's concern. This interactive and corroborating process makes it likely that a "concern-magnifying effect" will emerge.

Given that protective, age-concentrated housing is likely to induce more extensive social interaction between elderly persons than is nonprotective, age-heterogeneous housing, and assuming that concern is partially a function of social communication and corroboration, a second hypothesis is suggested: *Concern about the extent of crime is greater among aged persons residing in protective, age-concentrated housing than among those residing in nonprotective, age-heterogeneous housing.*

3. Protectiveness and Fear of Crime

Although it has been suggested that fear of crime is provoked by the risk of being victimized,[17] it also may be affected by the degree of social interaction of elderly persons in various environments.[18] This is tied to the relatively large number of friendships that are likely to emerge among the aged within age-concentrated, protective housing as opposed to age-heterogeneous, nonprotective housing.

In protective housing, the typical social concentration of aged persons has been hypothesized as leading to a magnification of concern about crime. It does not follow from this, however, that these same persons are necessarily more fearful than their nonprotected, elderly counterparts. The development of comparatively extensive friendships among socially concentrated aged persons suggests that they have socially sympathetic and supportive relationships that diffuse their fears. These relationships are scarce in age-heterogeneous housing. In the latter, whatever apprehensions an elderly person has about crime and whatever encounters he has with it are experienced in comparative isolation; he deals with them individually. Since he has few locally supportive relationships to help him cope with apprehensions, these feelings are likely to become magnified.

On the basis of this argument about the fear-diffusing character of supportive relationships, and controlling for Furstenburg's evidence that fear is a function of risk, a third hypothesis is offered: *Among the aged, fear of crime is likely to be greater in nonprotective, age-heterogeneous housing than in protective, age-concentrated housing.*

Conclusion

Although the hypotheses listed in this discussion are statements about the impact of protectiveness and the social effects of age concentration on victimization, concern about crime, and fear, there may be ways in which these variables interact. For instance, it has been hypothesized that protectiveness decreases the victimization of the elderly. However, it is conceivable that the concern-magnifying effect of social interaction within protective environments leads to greater precaution taken by the elderly against crime, which in turn increases protectiveness. The above hypotheses do not suggest that such interaction between variables does not occur; rather, they are hypothetical statements about specific aspects of social systems that involve the elderly with criminal acts.

Notes

1. See Jaber F. Gubrium, *The Myth of the Golden Years: A Socio-Environmental Theory of Aging* (Springfield, Ill.: Charles C. Thomas, 1973), ch. 7; and Carl Gersuny, "The Rhetoric of the Retirement Home Industry," *The Gerontologist,* Winter 1970, pp. 282–286.

2. Phillip H. Ennis, *Criminal Victimization in the United States: A Report of a National Survey,* President's Commission on Law Enforcement and Administration of Justice, Field Survey II (Washington, D.C.: U.S. Government Printing Office, 1967).

3. Albert D. Biderman et al., *Report on a Pilot Study in the District of Columbia on Victimization and Attitudes toward Law Enforcement,* President's Commission on Law Enforcement and Administration of Justice, Field Survey I (Washington, D.C.: U.S. Government Printing Office, 1967); D.A. Blyth, P.D. Reynolds, and T. Bouchard, "Victimization and the Aging Process," University of Minnesota, Center for Sociological Research (mimeo.); Robert Crosby and David Snyder, *Crime Victimization in the Black Community: Results of the Black Buyer II Survey* (Bethesda,

Md.: Resource Management Corp., 1970); and Albert J. Reiss, Jr., *Studies in Crime and Law Enforcement in Major Metropolitan Areas,* Vol. I, President's Commission on Law Enforcement and Administration of Justice, Field Survey III (Washington, D.C.: U.S. Government Printing Office, 1967).

4. Ennis, op. cit. supra note 2, pp. 34–35.

5. Blyth et al., op. cit. supra note 3; Crosby and Snyder, op. cit. supra note 3, p. 6.

6. Ennis, op. cit. supra note 2, p. 35.

7. Blyth el al., op. cit. supra note 3, p. 5.

8. Ennis, op. cit. supra note 2, p. 103.

9. Reiss indicates (using UCR data) that, at least for homicide, this may be true for race but not for sex. See Reiss, op. cit. supra note 3, pp. 14–18.

10. Frank Furstenburg, "Public Reactions to Crime in the Streets," *American Scholar,* Autumn 1971, pp. 601–610.

11. Reiss, op. cit. supra note 3, pp. 102–130.

12. We are assuming here that many high-rise residences for the elderly would fall into the "public housing" category and that single-family homes are generally "private residences."

13. Blyth et al., op. cit. supra note 3.

14. See Gubrium, op. cit. supra note 1, ch. 5; Jaber F. Gubrium, "Self-Conceptions of Mental Health in Old Age," *Mental Hygiene,* July 1971, pp. 398–403; and Jaber F. Gubrium, "Apprehensions of Coping Incompetence and Responses to Fear in Old Age," *International Journal of Aging and Human Development,* 1973, pp. 111–125.

15. Gubrium, op. cit. supra note 1, ch. 5.

16. See Irving Rosow, *Social Integration of the Aged* (New York: Free Press, 1967).

17. Furstenburg, op. cit. supra note 10.

18. Since both risk of being victimized and degree of social interaction have been suggested as having an impact on fear of crime, risk must be controlled in examining the effect of social interaction on fear. With respect to our hypotheses on the social effects of protectiveness, risk can be controlled while we vary social interaction by sampling protective environments with differing concentrations of elders.

The Future Elderly: Needs and Services

Sheldon S. Tobin

Whatever the uncertainties regarding the future, population projections for the future aging are relatively clear. Those who will be living through the end of the century are already alive. Thus Dr. Spengler's projections are quite believable. But what will be the future needs of this nation's aging population? More to the point, what will they want? Answers to both questions must begin with the distinction between the young old and the old old.

Because of the lowering of retirement age, 55 is beginning to be the demarcation for the young old. Although the trend toward earlier retirement depends upon the economy, our best prediction is that increasing numbers of Americans will leave the labor market earlier. Not only will they retire earlier, but they will also be healthier longer. Those between age 55 and 75, the future young old, will comprise 15 percent of the total population, and of them, Neugarten[1] has written: "A vigorous and educated young-old group can be expected to develop new needs with regard to the meaningful use of time. They will want a wide range of options and opportunities both for self-enhancement and for community participation." Moreover, they will want sufficient income to maintain their preretirement standard of living. Indeed, Leroy A. Shaver, in a survey for his AOA-funded doctoral dissertation at the University of Chicago, has discovered that already four of five business executives in their fifties would retire now if they could maintain their standard of living, particularly if their retirement income were inflation-proof. Also, more middle-aged and older people are seeking education. Because the next generation of elderly will average twelve years of school rather than eight, which is true for today's elderly, the demand for educational opportunities will increase dramatically. The elderly will also desire options for meaningful pursuits and particularly for community participation.

While they will pressure for improving their own quality of life, however, the young old will be parent-caring for old old family members. For many young old, parent-caring will begin at the very time that they expect to relax and enjoy retirement from the labor force but not from meaningful participation in life.

Reprinted from *Aging,* vol. 279–280(1978):22–26.

But what about the old old? If we choose to meet the needs of those over age 75, as many as 8 percent of the future population, it will indeed be costly! Although it is anticipated that future generations of older persons will not only live about five years longer than the present generation but will also stay healthier to a more advanced age, there is no evidence to suggest that they will be less incapacitated in the final phase preceding their death nor that the length of a preterminal phase will be shorter. Thus, it can be anticipated that at least one of every five Americans age 65 and over will need a combination of intensive and extensive social and health services.

This amount of need is reflected in current survey data: About 5 percent of older Americans currently reside in institutions, and for every older person in an institution there are close to two others (about 8 percent) who are homebound, one of four who is bedridden, and another 6 percent who are quickly becoming homebound.[2] Corroboration for this amount of need for social and health services comes from the planners of protective service programs for the elderly, who have estimated that about one of six older Americans who are not institutionalized are so impaired as to necessitate one or more types of direct social and health services. When this 16 percent or so of community-dwelling elderly who need services are added to the 5 percent who reside in institutions, the total again is about 20 percent—or about one of five older Americans. Most of these 20 percent are among the old old, those age 75 and over, who in successive decades will be increasingly older when they need social and health services.

Health Needs of the Elderly

One indicator of how health needs increase with age are the statistics on the elderly in long-term care facilities. Their average age is about 82, and one of five is over age 90. However, of all persons age 65 to 74, only 2 percent reside in institutions; of those age 75 to 84, 7 percent; and of those age 85 and over, 16 percent. People age 65 and over have only a one in four chance of ending their lives in a long-term care facility, but those age 80 and over, a one in two chance. If the delivery of health care to the future chronically ill elderly is the same as the care for the chronically ill of today, the average age of residents in long-term care facilities may be age 90, and one of five residents may be over age 100.

Before discussing the possible beneficial changes in the delivery of social health care for the elderly, it is sensible to begin by analyzing the current situation. For example, the long-term care institutions in which older people reside are likely to be proprietary—that is, run for profit. To be sure, some older people reside in state mental hospitals where half of the residential population may be elderly, but four of five institutionalized elderly reside in nursing and personal-care homes and three-fourths of these homes are proprietary. In spite of the many recent investigations of nursing-home abuse, these homes have increased by a third in the past ten years. Because of nursing-home scandals and the enormous cost that is reimbursed largely through Medicaid, there has been an effort to provide community alternatives to institutional care. Possibly a significant proportion of those now in institutions can return to the community—if appropriate supportive services were available. But as Pollak[3,4] has cautioned, it is erroneous to assume that beds would remain empty or that the cost would necessarily be less. Using supportive services appropriately, for example, could lead to the identification of as many candidates who need social health care in a protected and skilled nursing care environment as would be discharged. Regarding costs, a viable community social health system would be providing services to as many as one in six who now live in the community and suffer in silence with virtually no formal supportive services. Moreover, the provision of home care for the impaired elderly quickly becomes more costly than institutional care if even a small amount of home care is provided. In arriving at estimates of cost, Pollak very sensibly added the costs of rent, meals, and so forth that are provided to residents of an institutional setting.

Thus we are currently providing costly long-term care largely in proprietary nursing homes, and community alternatives to long-term care facilities may not be less costly. Indeed, home health services, which were legislated not to be proprietary, have become not-for-profit in name only because entrepreneurs now establish a home health program paying themselves an appreciable salary, which pushes up costs even further. Yet the benefit to the elderly of maintenance in the community is incontestable. Because the effect of becoming institutionalized is not simply a function of living in the institution but also a product of the feelings of abandonment that precede the relocation, the task is to develop community social and health services that limit the necessity for institutional care.[5]

We will develop community social health services? Legislation was first proposed by Kennedy and Mills in 1974 and then again by Kennedy and Corman in 1975 to develop community social and health organizations under one auspice that attempts to integrate service. This legislation included a modification of Medicare that would cover costs of providing those social and health services that would help older persons avoid institutionalization for as long as possible and that would also cover institutional care when such care becomes necessary. The proposed legislation incorporated the Morris proposal for local personal-care organizations to be developed and funded through nonprofit corporations that would purchase care for all beneficiaries within a substate area. The intent of the Morris proposal was to create for each beneficiary a package of social and health services that would be tailored to meet his particular needs. The fate of this type of legislation must await the arrival of national health insurance. Yet the concerns prompting national health insurance relate more to coverage and efficiency for curing acute illness than to care for the chronically ill. The proposal to modify Medicare, however, focused explicitly on care rather than cure, a rarity in this country when contrasted with other advanced technological societies.

Care for the chronically impaired is decidedly more difficult than cure for the acutely ill. While we shall keep people alive even longer in the future, as was noted earlier, we shall not do away with the frailties among the oldest of our citizens. Ben Franklin's adage will be as poignant then as it is now: "All would be long lived but none would grow old." Needed in the caring for the chronically impaired elderly is a case-management approach that is implied in the Morris proposal. Case managers are skilled professionals who have the ability to assess the need of the elderly client, which extends beyond interpreting functional deficits to at least evaluating the quality of family supports. They can thereby develop a service plan, monitor care, and evaluate the performance of service programs used for clients, including homemakers and home health providers. There must be available to professional case managers a variety of ancillary social and health services encompassing legal services, transportation, housing, mental health, physical health, and social services.

One way of understanding the potpourri of services is to consider three somewhat different ways of structuring the delivery of services. The three approaches to service delivery can be constructed to cover a range of needs, including services for the comparatively well elderly, services that provide alternatives to premature institutionalization, and services for those whose needs may demand institutional care or its equivalent. That is, for older people anywhere along the continuum, service can be organized around an individualized, home-delivered approach, a congregate-organized approach, or a congregate-residence approach.[5,6,7] In the first approach, older people living in their own homes or the homes of others have services delivered to them. In the second approach, the elderly are transported to congregate-organized services. The latter permits them to socialize with others and is both efficient and economical. Both of these approaches, of course, permit the older person to remain in his or her own residence. In the congregate-residence approach, older people reside together.

Congregate Services

For the less impaired, the young old, we could develop congregate-organized opportunities, particularly educational opportunities in the classroom, as well as less traditional settings. We could also develop congregate residences that enhance the development of self-help communities. For the most impaired elderly, on the other hand, we could develop an array of home-delivered services that assist the family in its caretaking efforts, whether the impaired elderly person lives with a child or in his (or more likely, her) own dwelling. Currently families strive, often through immense personal sacrifice, to help their oldest member remain in the community. Unfortunately, services are typically used only when families are exhausted rather than earlier when they are still actively struggling to reestablish a comfortable life for an impaired family member. A change in use of public service is obviously called for: from helping "only after the family no longer can" to helping the family when actively involved in parent-caring. In the future our attempts to help the family will be even more complicated because the children of 80- and 90-year-olds are increasingly likely to themselves be in their sixties or older.

Useful for families who wish to have a parent live with them, particularly when the octogenarian widow lives with her eldest young-old daughter, are congregate-organized services, specifically medically oriented day care (day hospital). Innovative congregate residence solutions can also be viable solutions. One example was reported by Judith Wax in the *New York Times Magazine.*[8] In her article, 'It's Like Home Here." she reported on a small group-living venture developed by the Chicago Council for Jewish Elderly. The Weinfield Group Living Residence houses twelve old people, who averaged 82 years of age. Each of the six units is shared by two residents, who have a bathroom, dining room, and kitchen. Communal dining was the norm. A caretaker lives on the premises, and the council provides counseling, homemaking, and health care. To be effective, this type of housing program requires social and health backup services from outside agencies. Bridging housing, health, and social services, however, is impossible with current categorical funding, which actively avoids using congregate housing as a service strategy.

Housing is particularly important to the elderly because as many as one of five elderly people may be living in housing that is inappropriate to their needs. Some live in substandard dwellings, others in homes with physical barriers to mobility and self-care. Still others reside in isolating apartments or homes where they often fear to venture out because of the possibility of criminal victimization and obviously many elder people live where there is a combination of these impediments to well-being. Using modern technology, the most impaired elderly could benefit from innovative prosthetic environments making use of sophisticated electronic devices that, for example, prepare and serve prepackaged foods, efficiently clean floors and other spaces, and telemetrically monitor vital physiological functions. These devices could decrease the burdens related to the tasks of everyday living and thus afford greater physical and emotional independence. One device now being adapted for hospital use permits an immobilized patient to dial a telephone, turn pages of a book or magazine, or change television channels by simply moving his or her eyes across a monitoring screen. The attitudes of the future elderly will make these innovations more feasible. In the future, aged people, who will have experienced the increased benefits of science and technology, are likely to be comfortable with sophisticated medical technology and advanced electronic gadgetry.

Thus the social and health needs of the future old old will indeed be great. Yet the services to meet their needs are not only known but also are in use in other countries. To be sure, developing these services in this country would entail a shift away from curing acute illness and toward caring for the chronically ill. In a caring society we would have a system encompassing services delivered into people's homes, those organized for groups, and congregate residential services. Professional case managers would have the responsibility for assessment of the need of individual elderly, development of service plans, assuring the delivery of services, and monitoring service delivery. Services would function to enhance the natural supporting efforts of family and peers. But will we achieve the care necessary to meet the needs of the future old old? Can we argue that their children, the young old, will tolerate anything but the best care for their eldest family members? Will the rising expectations among each future generation of the aging be translated into gains for the elderly? No. Judging from current evidence, older people have not acted as a cohesive political force.

Although the elderly have had a modicum of success in the past decade and in many ways have made impressive gains relative to other age groups, the amount of need, particularly among the old old, suggests that a wide gap exists between the needs of older individuals and services to meet the needs. We can probably anticipate, however, continuing support for alternatives to institutional care and a shift away from proprietary ownership of social health-care services. We may even achieve a sensible system of social and health services for the chronically impaired. But if we do, will we also allocate sufficient resources for those residual debilitated and confused elderly people whose very survival depends upon care in institutional settings? Many argue (as does Odin Anderson on my campus) that our society will never allocate sufficient funds for therapeutic institutional care for the most debilitated among the old because, among other reasons, it is very costly to provide sufficient personnel for more than minimal attention to the unpleasant task of caring for them. With health costs mounting to consume about 9 percent of our gross national product and likely to rise precipitously after the establishment of some form of national health insurance, we will be hard pressed to justify giving the best health service to everyone who needs it. Will we be willing to provide renal dialysis to everyone who needs this life-saving procedure? Will we put plastic hips in every octogenarian who could benefit from this prosthesis? Will we adopt an attitude more favorable than benign neglect for as many as 5 percent of the elderly whose survival needs dictate institutional care? These are questions we have not yet addressed. Will we address these questions in the near future? If we do, will we have a rational debate on the deployment of health dollars and the related ethical issues? Unfortunately, we have no evidence to suggest a rational discourse. We do have evidence, however, that business as usual will be as devastating to the future elderly as nursing home abuses have been to the current elderly.

Notes

1. Bernice L. Neugarten. "The Future and the Young Old." *The Gerontologist,* vol. 15. no. 1 (February 1975), pp. 4–9.

2. Ethel Shanas, et al. *Old People in Three Industrial Societies.* (New York: Atherton Press, 1968).

3. William Pollak. "Cost of Alternative Care Settings for the Elderly," in E. Powell Lawton, Robert J. Newcomer, and Thomas Byert (eds.), *Community Planning for an Aging Society.* (Stroudsbury, Pa.: Dowden, Hutchinson, and Ross, 1976a), pp. 128–142.

4. William Pollak. "Utilization of Alternative Case Settings by the Elderly," in E. Powell Lawton, Robert J. Newcomer, and Thomas Byert (eds.), *Community Planning for an Aging Society.* (Stroudsbury, Pa.: Dowden, Hutchinson, and Ross 1976b), pp. 106–127.

5. Sheldon S. Tobin, and Morton A. Lieberman. *Last Home for the Aged: Critical Implications of Institutionalization.* (San Francisco: Jossey–Bass 1976).

6. Sheldon S. Tobin. "Social Health Services for the Future Aged." *The Gerontologist,* vol. 15, no. 1, Part II (February 1975), pp. 32–37.

7. Sheldon S. Tobin et al. *Effective Social Services for Older Americans.* (Ann Arbor: Institute of Gerontology, 1976).

8. Judith Wax. "It's Like Home Here." *New York Times Magazine,* November 22, 1976.

Strategies to Reduce the Incidence and Impact of Crime That Victimizes the Elderly in Pennsylvania

This summary presents a compendium of the results of a research project conducted by staff of the Pennsylvania Commission on Crime and Delinquency to examine the problem of crime that victimizes the elderly in the Commonwealth of Pennsylvania. It has been condensed to provide the reader with pertinent background information, on a national and commonwealth level, on the subject of crime that victimizes the elderly. Further, it recommends a program to reduce the incidence of these crimes and their impact on senior citizens' quality of life.

Background on Need

The Pennsylvania Commission on Crime and Delinquency, in response to a growing perception among concerned officials that the elderly were suffering inordinately from the incidence of crime, directed staff in 1980 to study this problem and its ramifications. A research team, appointed by the commission's executive director, had four objectives: research and analyze available data on the incidence of crime as it affects the elderly; explore and study available data on the fear of crime and its consequences on the quality of life of Pennsylvania senior citizens; review currently available strategies and services, on a national and commonwealth level, that address the subject; and formulate an effective program that applies proven strategies to confront the problem.

The research team focused its efforts on the incidence of crime as it victimizes the elderly who reside in Pennsylvania. The team was limited in this respect by the lack of original research on this subject specifically focusing on Pennsylvania's senior citizens. Consequently, it was forced in many cases to draw conclusions based on related research conducted on the na-

This report was prepared by the Bureau of Regional Operations of the Pennsylvania Commission on Crime and Delinquency, Herbert C. Yost, director. The following staff assisted in the formulation of this document: Robert A. Akers (project coordinator); James L. Bubb; Keith L. Douglass; John P. Hannah; Rodney L. Kelley; and Lougwin E. Spencer. Reprinted with the permission of the Pennsylvania Commission on Crime and Delinquency.

tional level by a variety of sources. The materials presented in this report commence with a description of Pennsylvania's elderly and demographic trends and then proceeds to discuss their victimization problems as well as recommendations to overcome these problems.

Graphs in support of findings and recommendations follow narrative explanations.

Summary of General Findings

Demography

Finding: The elderly population in Pennsylvania is increasing in number and proportion of total residents. In 1900, as depicted in figure 6–1, 262,000 Pennsylvanians were 65 years of age or older. This segment of society increased in number to 1,272,000 persons or 11 percent of the population in 1970. By 1985, given current estimates, the trend should continue

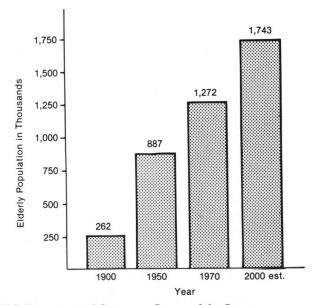

Source: U.S. Department of Commerce, Bureau of the Census.

[1]For this report, the term *elderly* will apply to age 65 and over.

Figure 6–1. Growth of Pennsylvania's Elderly[1] Population in the
                Twentieth Century

so that the elderly will constitute 12 percent of the population or 1,600,000 persons. By the year 2000, it is estimated that 1,743,000 elderly will reside in Pennsylvania.

Finding: The elderly constitute a major percentage of the total population in a significant number of Pennsylvania's counties. In general, the northeast region appears to have a higher concentration of senior citizens than the remainder of the commonwealth. It also should be pointed out that the southeast region, despite having the highest concentration of total population, has the lowest proportionate amount of elderly residents.

Finding: In Pennsylvania, there are significant concentrations of elderly who have an income that is below the poverty level. There are significant concentrations of elderly residents in many Pennsylvania counties who are experiencing poverty. This is especially true in the northeast and southwest regions of the commonwealth. The highest proportion of elderly poor resides in Sullivan County. In 1970, 4.9 percent of that county's population was elderly and received income that fell below the federal poverty level, with Bucks County having the lowest proportion in Pennsylvania at 1.0 percent. This is a significant problem caused in no small measure by the fixed incomes of many elderly.

Finding: Concentrations of the elderly residing alone are found in a significant number of Pennsylvania counties. Characteristic of the elderly population is a high number of persons who reside alone. In many cases these individuals are female since males on the average have a shorter life expectancy. The northeast and southwest regions of Pennsylvania have an especially high concentration of elderly living alone. Pike and Forest Counties each share the highest proportionate share of the total county elderly population residing alone, with 3.8 percent each. The suburban Philadelphia counties collectively have the lowest incidence of this characteristic. In particular, Bucks County has the lowest proportion of individuals, at 1.2 percent of the total population.

Finding: Pennsylvania's elderly who are members of a minority are concentrated around the urban centers of Philadelphia and Pittsburgh. This characteristic will have far reaching consequences in an anticrime program since a large proportion of the crime incidence in Pennsylvania occurs in urban areas.

Criminal Victimization

Finding: Incidence of crime is not directly related to percentage of elderly residents in a given Pennsylvania county. Incidence of crime is more a factor of total population concentration than elderly residency. This is especially so in the northeast region of Pennsylvania.

Finding: Elderly criminal victimization trends in Pennsylvania appear to be generally similar to national patterns. They indicate that the elderly are the least victimized of all age groups. Police agencies generally do not collect or publish data on the age, sex, or race of crime victims, except for the crime of murder. Recently, however, victimization surveys conducted by the Law Enforcement Assistance Administration, United States Department of Justice, and the Bureau of Census, United States Department of Commerce, have produced data that describes the extent of crime against the elderly for the nation generally and Pennsylvania in particular. According to one of these surveys, *Criminal Victimization in the United States, 1976,* persons age 65 and over constitute the least likely age group to be victimized by any of the four crimes of violence studied: rape, robbery, aggravated assault, and simple assault. Persons age 65 or older were also the least likely to become victims of theft, with the exceptions of pocket picking and purse snatching.

Victimization survey results for Pennsylvania tend to reflect national trends. *National Crime Survey Data for Pennsylvania,* published in 1975, shows that age group 65-plus is the *least* likely age group to be victimized. Figure 6-2 indicates that age group 65-plus has lower victimization rates than all other age groups for crimes of violence and theft. The only exceptions again are purse snatching and pocket picking. These crimes are age related and impact particularly on the elderly.

Finding: Crime's effects are far more devastating for the elderly than for other age groups. The consequences of victimization that leave the elderly devastated can be categorized as economic, physical, and emotional. Economic consequences are particularly devastating because so many older persons live on fixed incomes. Thus, a loss due to crime can have a severe impact on an elderly person's budget.

A three-year study that assessed the patterns of elderly criminal victimization in Kansas City conducted by the Midwest Research Institute (1976) indicated that elderly purse-snatching victims had lost on the average 93 percent of a month's income when victimized. The study noted that given the low median incomes of the elderly, they were losing vital necessities when victimized by a crime. This included money for rent, doctor bills, and food. Consequently, when the elderly were victims of even relatively minor

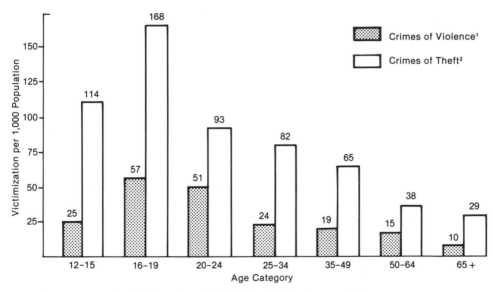

Source: Pennsylvania Subsection of the National Crime Survey, 1975.
[1]Includes rape, robbery, and assault.
[2]Includes personal larceny both with and without contact.

Figure 6–2. Personal Crimes: Pennsylvania Victimization Rates for
Age 12 and Over, 1975.

crimes, the results can be life threatening given the limited resources of the elderly.

Due to their frailty, the elderly are more likely than other age groups to suffer broken bones and other injuries due to criminal victimization. In addition, they require a longer recovery period due to their physical makeup. Tragically, many elderly persons are unlikely ever to recover fully from a severe injury due to physical assault.

Finally, criminal victimization of older people can manifest some social and psychological consequences. These can be as severe as economic deprivation and physical impairment, which often results in the elderly seeking isolation from their community due to fear of crime.

Finding: A significant number of Pennsylvania's elderly population limit or change activities due to a fear of crime. Fear of crime among the elderly in Pennsylvania tends to mirror national trends. A 1975 Louis Harris poll sampled 4,000 persons over age 65 throughout the nation, and the results showed that fear of crime was perceived by the respondents as the elderly's most serious concern. In fact, in this poll fear of crime was ranked by 23 percent of the elderly respondents as the most serious concern, outranking even health problems (21 percent) and financial problems (15 percent).

Studies by the Law Enforcement Assistance Administration conducted in Pennsylvania and other areas of the country report the same findings. A survey conducted in 1975 in thirteen American cities reported that 64 percent of respondents age 65 and over felt either somewhat unsafe or very unsafe when out alone in their neighborhoods at night. Similar surveys conducted by the Law Enforcement Assistance Administration in Pittsburgh and Philadelphia found that fear of crime particularly effects the elderly. As illustrated in figure 6-3, in Pittsburgh 75 percent of elderly nonwhite females felt somewhat or very unsafe when out alone at night. Further, nearly seven out of ten white elderly females expressed a similar fear. Both nonwhite and white elderly males expressed considerably less fear than elderly females of either race.

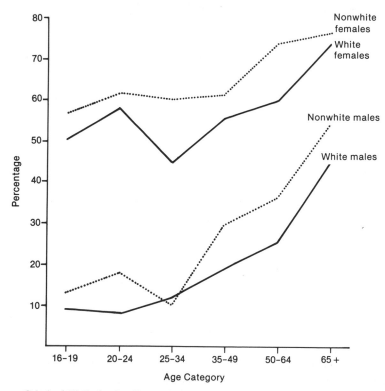

Source: Criminal Victimization Survey in Pittsburgh, 1973.

Figure 6-3. Percentage of Pittsburgh Survey Respondents Who Felt Somewhat Unsafe or Very Unsafe When Out Alone in Their Neighborhoods at Night

Although the elderly, particularly the poor, black, and female, experience high levels of fear in urban areas, the problem is not limited to large cities. According to testimony presented to the Select Committee on Aging, United States House of Representatives, in February 1978 by Professor Wesley Skogan, fear of crime is not distinctively a big city problem. Professor Skogan's data, taken from a national survey by the National Opinion Research Center, reports that "fully one-half of the fearful elderly in that national survey lived in towns, villages and rural areas and another twenty percent in suburban areas."

The high fear levels of the elderly can easily be reconciled with the low crime rates. Part of this is due to the lower visibility of the elderly, who frequently do not venture out of doors thus avoiding victimization. The elderly have a life style that is naturally self-protective. Elderly citizens are rarely auto theft victims because they own fewer cars and infrequently show up in assault cases because they are involved in fewer conflicts.

Finding: Fear of crime impairs significantly the quality of life for the Commonwealth's elderly residents. Surveys conducted on a national and commonwealth level report that nearly half of the elderly respondents changed or limited their activities because of their fear or crime. This is evidenced in figure 6–4, where 56 percent of the female elderly and 47 percent of the male senior citizen respondents stated that they had limited or changed their activities because of crime. A heavy toll is exacted on many elderly for their self-imposed confinement. The Law Enforcement Assistance Administration in its booklet *We Can Prevent Crime* states that many poor elderly who reside in inner-city neighborhoods with high crime are actually under "house arrest" because they "virtually imprison themselves in their homes." Dr. Barry D. Lebowitz of the National Institute of Mental Health in testimony before the Select Committee on Aging, United States House of Representatives, stated that "decades of research have consistently shown that social isolation has deleterious mental health consequences of the most serious kind."

Strategies

Based on analysis of the incidence and effect of crimes that victimize the elderly in Pennsylvania, this section identifies a number of strategy recommendations for implementation. They are based upon successful precedents in other states and are designed for implementation primarily by existing social services agencies across Pennsylvania.

The foundation of the program is the existing social service networks system, made up of the Pennsylvania Department of Aging and the forty-

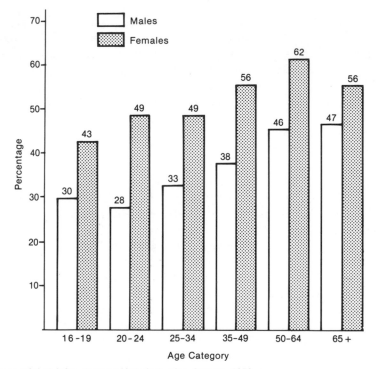

Source: Philadelphia Criminal Victimization Survey, 1972.
Figure 6-4. Percentage of Philadelphia Survey Respondents Who Limited
    or Changed Their Activities Because of a Fear of Crime

nine Area Agencies on Aging located at the county level. The Area Agencies
on Aging are charged with providing comprehensive community services to
the elderly. In addition, many other organizations providing services to
senior citizens at the local level, such as the more than 2,000 senior centers
and clubs, can aid in the delivery of services.

    Also available to deal specifically with community crime prevention is
the commonwealth-wide program known as Pennsylvania Crime Watch.
Pennsylvania Crime Watch involves state and local law enforcement agencies in a coordinated effort to educate the public in crime-prevention techniques and assist local police agencies to identify specific crime problems
and effectively counteract them. Pennsylvania Crime Watch, coordinated
by the Pennsylvania Commission on Crime and Delinquency, can easily be
geared to focus special attention on the elderly. Through the commission's
regional offices and its network of over 600 trained crime-prevention officers in local police departments, positive follow-through on elderly crime
prevention strategies can be assured.

Through a coordinated effort at the state, county, and municipal levels, an effective, inexpensive program to combat the problem of crime victimization of Pennsylvania's elderly can be achieved.

Recommendation: The Pennsylvania Uniform Crime Report should be modified to include the age, sex, and race of crime victims. Currently there exists no systematic process of collecting, aggregating, reporting, and analyzing data on crimes that victimize the elderly population in Pennsylvania. Many local police departments collect the data on individual cases but do not aggregate it in periodic reports. All departments should be advised by the Pennsylvania State Police to report this information for incorporation in the annual Pennsylvania Uniform Crime Report. Implementation of this recommendation would result in valid figures on the extent of crime, which not only victimizes the elderly but all age groups. This would contribute to more effective planning, monitoring, and evaluation of anticrime programs by state and local elderly service providing agencies.

Recommendation: An interagency task force should be appointed to marshal available resources and insure coordination of effort in combating crimes that victimize Pennsylvania's senior citizens. Through coordination of resources, various agencies of the commonwealth collectively possess the capability to effectively assist the elderly in anticrime programs. For example, the Department of Community Affairs, Bureau of Consumer Protection, Crime Victim's Compensation Board, Department of Banking, Insurance Department, State Police, Commission on Crime and Delinquency, and others have in-house expertise and resources that can contribute to reducing elderly crime incidence and assisting elderly crime victims. The State Police, Insurance Department, and Bureau of Consumer Protection could initiate educational programs designed to reduce the incidence of consumer fraud among the elderly. To insure maximum resource utilization and coordination of effort, the governor should consider the appointment of an interagency task force. The task force, composed of representatives from the aforementioned agencies, should develop a timely plan of action outlining programs that each agency should undertake in order to reduce elderly crime risks. The lead role in formulating the task force should be jointly assigned to the Commission on Crime and Delinquency and the Department of Aging. The Secretary of Aging should serve as chairman of the task force.

Recommendation: A crime-prevention training program should be developed and administered to the elderly service providers. Throughout the nation in recent years, crime prevention training has been an effective means of combating both the incidence of crime and its ramifications on the elderly community. The National Council of Senior Citizens' Criminal Justice and the Elderly Program has proven in a series of demonstration projects in such major urban areas as Chicago, New York, New Orleans, Los Angeles, Milwaukee, and Washington, D.C., that crime prevention training helps the elderly in a number of significant ways to avoid both victimization and fear of crime. Training provides the opportunity to orient social networks to the needs of the elderly and strengthen neighborhoods to be more crime-prevention conscious. Furthermore, training expands public awareness of the problem of the crime against the elderly and in the activities needed to effectively combat it. Formulation of a specific training program for elderly-service providers utilizing the expertise of the National Council on Senior Citizens' program would be an effective and efficient means of educating Pennsylvania's social service network on elderly crime problems and the means to reduce both their incidence and impact. The Commission on Crime and Delinquency in conjunction with the National Council of Senior Citizens should formulate this anticrime program. The commission's field staff after completing training of its own should conduct throughout the commonwealth sessions for elderly-service-providing agencies to increase their sensitivity and awareness of the impact crime has on Pennsylvania's senior citizens. Coordination of these sessions on the local level should be made by the local Area Agency on Aging. Service providers who participate in the anticrime training workshop could then be able to present crime prevention training to the elderly either in a group or individual setting.

It should be emphasized that coordination with the crime-prevention officers of the municipal police departments throughout the commonwealth will be an important factor in this program's long-term success.

Recommendation: A training program should be developed to sensitize law enforcement officers to understand and deal more effectively with older persons. Everyday law enforcement officers deal with the problems of crime and its effect on the elderly. An understanding of the aging process can improve law enforcement officers' relationships with older persons. Such understanding helps officers avoid regarding the elderly in the same stereotypical fashion as does much of the rest of the society, thus greatly assisting their delivery of services to protect senior citizens.

A training package has been developed by the American Association of Retired Persons to specifically deal with this subject. Commission on Crime and Delinquency staff should contact the American Association of Retired Persons and make arrangements for utilization of this curriculum to instruct Pennsylvania's local law enforcement personnel. The same training method utilized in the service-providers program will be applied.

Field staff of the Pennsylvania Commission on Crime and Delinquency will receive instruction from the American Association of Retired Persons and, in turn, present instruction to law enforcement personnel throughout the commonwealth. This program will improve communication between the police community and the growing elderly population and will help individual officers relate more effectively to older citizens.

Recommendation: Residential security services should be provided to Pennsylvania's Elderly. The National Council on Senior Citizens, in their demonstration projects throughout the country, found that the most popular crime-prevention services provided were home security surveys and hardware installations.

Security surveys include assessments of the vulnerability of property protection and a prescription of measures for exterior lighting, entry protection including locks on doors and windows, adequate interior lighting, and key control. These services are "tangible," as the elderly can take part in the survey of their residences. It has been found that this service reduces fear of crime and chances of victimization. When followed by assistance from local police crime prevention officers this service has been found to be extremely effective.

Elderly-service-providing agencies can also perform or coordinate this service after completing crime-prevention instruction offered from police crime-prevention units established under Pennsylvania's Crime Watch Program. Commission on Crime and Delinquency field staff can provide backup assistance and referral as needed.

Recommendation: Community-based crime prevention programs should be established in areas of high elderly resident concentration. For several years, the Pennsylvania Crime Watch Program has been actively involved in the formation of crime-prevention programs in residential areas. This effort has been based on successful precedents in communities throughout the country. Community-based crime-prevention programs have proven successful in reducing crime risks, reducing community fear, and increasing clearance of criminal incidents. Local police should continue to be encouraged through Pennsylvania Crime Watch to target areas of high elderly residential concentration for community crime-prevention programs.

Such programs should include block watch, escort, lobby monitor, and telephone assurance services. This approach, fostered by active local police, would stimulate the elderly community to assist itself in helping reduce criminal incidence and ease the atmosphere of fear of crime.

Recommendation: Police should establish anticrime units designed to apprehend perpetrators of crimes that victimize the elderly. It has been established that law enforcement authorities should be aware of the nature of crime that preys on elderly citizens. Developing such awareness includes the continuous analysis of the nature, location, and scope of criminal activity in areas housing high concentrations of senior citizens. Where appropriate, police should establish high-visibility patrol units disguised as decoys to operate in determined areas of high criminal incidence. As an additional measure, the use of auxiliary police in areas of high elderly population concentration should be considered.

Recommendation: Senior citizens with suitable expertise should be utilized by Area Agencies on Aging to reduce incidence of consumer fraud among the elderly. It is an accepted sociological fact that peer pressure is an effective method in changing behavior. Peer pressure can be an effective tool in alerting senior citizens of the ever-increasing problem of consumer fraud.

Studies have revealed that consumer-fraud victimization is due to the elderly victims' getting the impression that they can "get something for nothing." Antifraud committees composed of senior citizens with trade and legal skills should be developed by Crime and Delinquency field staff. Retired contractors, plumbers, roofers, and so forth, could serve on these committees and offer practical ideas for reducing the incidence of confidence swindles. However, such panels should be created only with the full cooperation and endorsement of the local police authorities.

Recommendation: The direct deposit program should be endorsed and actively advocated by the Pennsylvania elderly service system for use by Pennsylvania's senior citizens. The direct deposit of income in the form of checks from the federal government or pension funds is critical to the reduction of theft of income from the elderly. A senior citizen's loss of income, even for a short period of time, has devastating consequences and often causes irreparable harm. A public-awareness program monitoring the direct deposit program would be extremely beneficial.

Staff of senior centers should receive training in direct-deposit regulations and procedures and assist the elderly with enrolling in this program. This can be done as part of the aforementioned anticrime public education program.

Recommendation: The extent and nature of crime victimizing the elderly in public housing projects should be researched and appropriate anticrime programs formulated. Pertinent information on crime against the elderly in public housing areas is not currently available. This is a problem that must be addressed, as an increasing number of the commonwealth's elderly population reside in these projects. To prevent housing-project crime, authorities should consider age-integrated housing in both urban and rural areas. Further, public housing authorities for the elderly should incorporate "defensible space" concepts into design features in order to reduce criminal opportunities. If appropriate, the Department of Community Affairs should assume a lead role in assuring that all future elderly facilities incorporate design features that tend to reduce crime by means of environmental design.

Recommendation: The basic municipal police course should include instruction in crime against the elderly with emphasis on the aging process. As noted in an earlier recommendation, law enforcement officers need to be sensitized to the nature of crime against the elderly. Therefore, all local police in their qualification training should be made aware of this situation so that they may better serve Pennsylvanians over age 65. The appropriate training module can be drawn from the American Association of Retired Persons police instructional material.

Recommendation: Security surveys should be conducted of local senior center facilities by police crime-prevention officers. The elderly center much of their public life around service facilities. In the commonwealth there are approximately 2,000 senior centers and clubs. Many such centers are located in crime areas. In these areas, municipal police crime-prevention officers and service providers should conduct standardized security surveys of the centers. These surveys should include a review of the area surrounding the facility, such as location of bus stops, parking areas, and so forth, in order to reduce criminal opportunities. Local communities should routinely request comments on site planning for future elderly facilities from police crime-prevention officers.

Recommendation: Parent abuse is a growing problem and should be researched to determine its scope and incidence. The extent of parent abuse is not known, since there has been no original research undertaken in Pennsylvania. However, authorities believe this offense to be increasing rapidly. Studies in Ohio and Massachusetts suggest that the problem may be of considerable magnitude. The Department of Aging should conduct research on this problem, and existing legislation should be reviewed in order to determine whether current statutes are adequate concerning the reporting of this problem by social service agencies, physicians, and so forth.

Recommendation: District attorneys should be encouraged to provide assistance to elderly victims of crime to reduce trauma and fear. As this report notes, crime victimization is an especially unnerving experience for the senior citizen. District attorney's offices can provide a variety of services to assist the elderly crime victim, especially when a person is participating as a prosecution witness. Case-scheduling and witness-notification procedures that minimize the time that the elderly need to wait in court should be adopted. Information on court proceedings, including a clear presentation on court process, should be provided to minimize fear and confusion. Where the elderly victim/witness does not have convenient means of transportation to and from court, coordinated arrangements with local aging service centers and the county area agency on aging should occur to provide transportation. A special waiting area for the elderly to avoid contact with the accused would be beneficial. Procedures expediting payment of fees to elderly witnesses should be implemented. Victim-impact statements could be incorporated into presentence reports, especially for the elderly victims.

Recommendation: Area Agencies on Aging should designate a staff member to assist elderly victims of crime. In spite of the prescribed victim-assistance services provided by the district attorney's offices, trauma incurred by elderly victims impacts on all aspects of their lives. Basic services required to help the elderly cope with trauma include crisis intervention and management, criminal justice services, crime-prevention services and compensation, property repair, and restitution assistance. Most of these services are not available in Pennsylvania at this time.

A staff member of the local Area Agency on Aging should be given the responsibility for identifying and coordinating agencies who can assist elderly crime victims. The staff member could establish interagency procedures and protocol to insure that the service delivery system is responsible to elderly crime victims. Liaison with local police should also be the responsibility of this person.

Recommendation: Staff of senior centers should be instructed on the crime victims compensation program and how to assist the elderly victim. The commonwealth has a compensation program that provides assistance to victims of violent crimes. Victims may be eligible for medical expenses, loss of earnings, and support, and reimbursement for burial expenses is available for their families.

Recent legislation mandates that police officers provide written advice to victims about the compensation program. However, many elderly may need assistance in making application for compensation. Processing of awards can take six months to a year, but time can be reduced if proper documenation is submitted. To fill their assistance void, elderly-service providers can be instructed by the Pennsylvania Commission on Crime and Delinquency in the intent and mechanics of the compensation program and how to assist the elderly with filing claims.

Recommendation: Staff of the Pennsylvania Commission on Crime and Delinquency and Department of Aging should review on an annual basis the status on implementation of recommendations contained in this report and the continuing need for services to the elderly. As noted in this report, the proportion of elderly citizens is growing in Pennsylvania, with special needs in the area of crime prevention and victim assistance. In this regard, it is essential that the needs of this segment of the population be assessed yearly in order that services for the elderly be provided in a timely and effective manner.

Closing Statement

Governor Dick Thornburgh at a conference on Crime and the Elderly in Philadelphia, on May 15, 1980, stated, "Crime against older persons cannot be tolerated—for it spreads fear among those of our citizens who are most vulnerable, and those who, after a lifetime of work, are most entitled to be free of the physical and psychological effects of fear." It is hoped that this report has laid the groundwork for an effective program to alleviate this problem.

The strategies recommended band together Pennsylvania's government, law enforcement organizations, business, and citizens in an alliance based on the common theme of combating a problem which, according to Governor Thornburgh, "reduces the luster of these golden years."

Elder Abuse in Massachusetts: A Survey of Professionals and Paraprofessionals

Introduction and Methodology

This report presents a preliminary analysis of information on the abuse of elders in Massachusetts within the period of October 1977 through March 1979. This information was collected through a survey of medical, legal, police, and social-work professionals and paraprofessionals during March and April 1979. The survey yielded five types of data:

1. *professions that see elder abuse* (for example, visiting nurses, home-care-corporation staff, hospital staff);
2. *characteristics of the abused person* (for example, age, sex, race, religion, physical and mental functioning, household composition);
3. *characteristics of the abuser* (for example, relation to abused, stressful situations affecting the abuser);
4. *description of the incident* (for example, types of injuries sustained by the abused elder, narrative description of the incident);
5. *response to the incident(s)* (for example, emergency action taken, referrals, barriers to service delivery).

The report text and summary tables present the major findings.

Purpose

Little organized knowledge exists to date of the problem of elder abuse, defined as the physical abuse of elderly persons at the hands of their chil-

This report was prepared by Helen O'Malley, Howard Segars, Ruben Perez, Victoria Mitchell, and George M. Kneupfel. Project staff (James Bergman, project director; Karen Myers, staff attorney; Helen O'Malley, researcher/planner; Howard Segars, staff psychologist) wish to acknowledge the assistance given them by the following individuals and organizations: Julia Herskowitz, Massachusetts Commission for the Blind; Janice Roundy, Massachusetts Hospital Association; Martin Lawsine, Massachusetts Criminal Justice Training Council; Carolyn Davis, Massachusetts Association of Community Health Agencies; Peg Monroe, Massachusetts Department of Mental Health; Christine Spurgeon, Legal Research and Services for the Elderly.

This project was funded through a contract from the Department of Elder Affairs of the Commonwealth of Massachusetts. Without this support this project would not have been possible. Project staff wish to express our sincere appreciation to the department for both its financial and personal support.

Reprinted with permission of Legal Research and Services for the Elderly.

dren, other relatives, friends, or caretakers. Child battering has received considerable attention over the past fifteen to twenty years since Kempe et al. described the "battered child syndrome,"[1] Spouse battering has now been identified as another form of familial violence occurring in staggering proportions (estimates of as many as 2 million cases per year of wife battering have been made by Steinmetz et al.)[2]

Current literature on violence within the family focuses almost exclusively on these two forms of abuse. The bulk of this literature describes studies that attempt to identify the causal antecedents to abuse, trying to answer the question "Why does it happen?" A handful of researchers however, such as Suzanne Steinmetz and Marilyn Block, are beginning to relate their findings to another population: elderly residing at home.[3]

While abuse of elderly living in institutions, such as nursing homes or rest homes, is a phenomenon that receives sporadic attention from the media and government agencies, the problem of elderly who are abused in their own or their families' homes has gone largely undetected and unrecognized. Little information exists on the extent of the problem, what this form of abuse looks like, who sees it, or what can be done about it.

The purpose of this survey is, therefore, to provide *preliminary* data on the nature of elder abuse. Does the phenomenon "elder abuse" exist, and if so, what professions see it, what does it look like, what are some characteristics of the abuser and the victim, and what action do people take when they recognize or suspect that abuse has occurred?

Data gathered in this type of survey yield *descriptive* information that will, we believe, be useful in designing more analytical studies on the extent of elder abuse in the population at large and the variables associated with the abusive situation. It should be emphasized that data generated from this preliminary survey are a first step in the study of elder abuse and should be viewed as part of the design phase for other, more controlled and hence generalizable studies.

A second purpose for conducting this survey is to raise the awareness of professionals and paraprofessionals regarding elder abuse as a potential differential in their diagnosis of elderly clients. The elder who "falls down a lot" could just as easily be a vicitm of abuse as he or she could be experiencing the frailities of advanced age. Until workers with elders add abuse to their vocabulary, the problem may continue to go undetected.

Methodology

Definitions. For the purpose of the survey, *abuse* is defined to mean:

> the willful infliction of physical pain, injury, or debilitating mental anguish, unreasonable confinement, or willful deprivation by a

caretaker of services that are necessary to maintain mental and physical health.

Elder is defined as:

any person age 60 or older and residing in a noninstitutional setting, including persons living alone, with family or friends, or with a caretaker.

The definition of abuse selected for this survey is a broad one. While the definition clearly eliminates self-neglect, willful neglect by a caretaker (relative or nonrelative) is included. In its most severe form, willful neglect is difficult to distinguish from physical abuse. For example, a person who is confined to bed and intentionally deprived of proper diet or medication is suffering from what some would call neglect and others abuse. The survey attempts to capture information on this type of case by stipulating that the neglect must be willful—that is, intended. Because "intentions" are difficult for an observer (in this case the survey respondent) to determine, however, the broadening of the definition increases the likelihood that survey responses will include other, less willful forms of neglect.

By including "debilitating mental anguish" in the definition, the survey includes as abused elders persons who are suffering anxiety or fear of another person so great as to impair physical or mental functioning. The fear of being beaten or punished, whether that punishment actually occurs, may be as serious a form of abuse as the actual act of striking the elder. Again, as with neglect, the interpretation of "debilitating" when left to the respondent may result in some citings that are only remotely related to physical abuse and would more properly fall into some other category of mistreatment or injury, such as "intimidation."

The broadening of the definition to include "willful neglect" and "debilitating mental anguish" may therefore inflate the citings of abuse elicited through the survey. Because this is an exploratory survey, however, a broad definition encompassing many aspects of trauma seems an appropriate first step in identifying various models or types of abuse. The analysis of data does not distinguish between these models.

In the discussion of one question, however (What does elder abuse look like?), data are separately analyzed in order to provide figures on the relative number of physical-abuse citings (beating and kicking) versus other forms of mistreatment (confinement, verbal harassment, and so forth).

Instrument Design and Pretest. In February 1979, project staff conducted a literature search on violence in the family, including in particular readings on child abuse and spouse abuse. Survey forms developed by the University of Maryland Center on Aging for its study on elder abuse were also reviewed.[4] Based on this literature search, staff developed a survey that consists primarily of multiple-choice questions. Some open-ended questions (for example, describing the abusive incident or action taken) were also included.

The survey includes items requiring primarily factual answers, although certain judgmental decisions are requested (such as, Was the abused person a source of stress to the abuser?). Because instructions did not stipulate that responses be based on written agency case records, reconstruction from memory may have been relied on by an undetermined number of respondents, thus increasing the opportunities for inaccurate reporting of data.

The survey attempts to elicit information along two primary dimensions that are cited in child-abuse literature as possible variables relating to abuse:

impairment of the abused person;

stressful situations affecting the abuser.

A third type of variable, psychological traits of the abused person and abuser, was judged too difficult to capture in this type of survey. The survey focuses rather on the more observable characteristics of the abuser and abused person, data likely to be available in case records of those professions that were surveyed.

While this type of descriptive survey is not designed to test hypotheses, researchers had two theories in mind as they developed the survey:

1. The person being abused is likely to be very old *or* physically or mentally disabled and is likely to be dependent on the abuser for his or her care (impairment of the abused person).
2. The person committing the abusive act is likely to be experiencing some form of stress other than the abusive situation (such as job loss, medical problem, or alcoholism) to which has been added the care of the elder (stressful situations affecting the abuser).

Questions selected for the survey, therefore, tend to elicit data along these two dimensions. There are many other theories of abuse (pathological individual behavior, culturally determined behavior, learned role model, intergenerational model) that may apply to certain cases of abuse. These and the above two hypotheses can neither be confirmed nor disproved by the current survey. Survey results should indicate, however, potentially fruitful areas for further investigation, particularly along the two dimensions cited above.

Professions to be surveyed were selected because of their degree of contact with the elderly population and/or their likelihood of seeing abused elders.

A pretest was conducted at the Massachusetts General Hospital Chelsea Health Center, Chelsea, Massachusetts, among five staff members (nursing, social work, and psychological professions) who had previously reported citings of elder abuse. The instrument was also reviewed by state agency research staff familiar with survey technique. Instrument revision resulted from both the pretest and review.

Data Collection. Stamped, self-addressed surveys were sent to 1,044 professionals and paraprofessionals during the month of March, according to the schedule in table 7-1.

Mailing lists were compiled with the assistance of state-wide organizations representing these professions. Although duplicate addresses were eliminated whenever possible, approximately twenty-nine agencies received the survey twice.

Persons receiving the survey were asked to complete the form within three weeks, making additional copies of the blank survey for each case of elderly abuse being reported. No surveys were accepted after May 4, 1979.

Completion Rate. Three hundred fifty-five surveys were returned; this represents a completion rate of 34 percent. Of the 355 surveys returned, nineteen were eliminated because more than one citing of elder abuse was reported on each form, making data tabulation difficult. Four additional surveys were eliminated because information was too unclear to be tabulated. Of the remaining surveys, 183 (55 percent) reported a citing of elder abuse within the past eighteen months. When multiple count surveys (those that were eliminated from analysis) are taken into account, the percentage of returned surveys citing abuse rises to 57 percent. One hundred forty-nine returned surveys (42 percent) reported seeing no abuse during the past eighteen months.

Unit of Analysis. Each survey reporting on one abused elder is considered to be one *citing* of abuse. This survey has uncovered 183 such citings, in addition to nineteen citings of abuse cases involving more than one elder (for example, a couple being abused by their son).

Citings *do not* represent unduplicated counts of cases of elder abuse. That is, several survey respondents could have reported on the same case of abuse. It is important to remember that 183 citings of abuse do not represent 183 elder persons who have been abused. This survey does not lend itself, therefore, to estimating the incidence of elder abuse in Massachusetts. Additional, more controlled studies will be required before estimates of incidence can be made.

Because single cases of abuse may have been counted several times, data may be skewed; interpreting survey results, especially in those

Table 7–1
Recipients of Survey on Elder Abuse in Massachusetts

Profession/Agency	Schedule	Number Sent	Method
Accredited visiting nurses associations	Statewide mailing	132	Survey sent to all agency directors
Certified homemaker and home-health-aid agencies	Statewide mailing	50	Survey sent to all agency directors
Hospital social-service directors and	Statewide mailing	163	Survey sent to all hospital administrators who are members of the Massachusetts Hospital Association with instructions to forward survey to (1) directors of social services and (2) nursing supervisors
Hospital emergency-room nursing supervisors	Statewide mailing	163	
Home care corporations	Statewide mailing	28	Survey sent to all agency directors
Department of Public Welfare regional protective services managers	Statewide mailing	6	Survey sent to all regional managers
Legal aid agencies, lawyers and paraprofessionals	Selected mailing	109	Survey sent to agencies and individuals included in the Elderly Legal Coalition mailing list
Police	Selected mailing	163	Survey sent to crime-prevention officers and graduates of "crime and elderly" training sessions for police personnel
Private social-service agencies (includes Councils on Aging and Senior Centers)	Selected mailing	168	Survey sent to agencies included on United Way listings of Massachusetts social services agencies
Other (that is, other health-agency staff, nutrition programs)	Selected mailing	62	Survey sent to other agencies and individuals included on Elderly Legal Coalition Mailing list and Massachusetts Hospital Association's mailing list

categories in which a relatively small number of responses were coded, is made more tenuous because of this factor. In general, therefore, analysis of survey data concentrates on the grossest findings: those in which one data element is overwhelmingly selected by most respondents when answering a particular question.

Validity and Generalizability. This survey permits the respondent, abuser, and victim to remain anonymous. This was done in order to protect the confidentiality of client identity and to encourage a higher response rate on the part of survey recipients. Anonymity does mean, however, that survey results are not verifiable.

This survey does not represent a random sampling of any population. Hence, survey results are not generalizable beyond this particular data set. This is especially important to keep in mind in reviewing the findings.

Analysis of Survey Results

A. Does Elder Abuse Exist?

Initial results indicate that professionals who were surveyed are encountering cases of abuse. One hundred eighty-three of the 332 surveys returned (55 percent) stated that the respondent knew of at least one case of elder abuse occurring during the past eighteen months. The abuse cases described ranged from inability or unwillingness of a caretaker (relative or nonrelative) to provide essential services to that of repeated physical battering by a family member. The types of mistreatment uncovered by the survey include financial mismanagement, confinement, physical trauma, malnutrition, threats of physical harm, abandonment, sedation (overmedication), and sexual abuse.

Perhaps one of the most significant findings of this survey is that incidents of abuse tend to be recurring events and not single occurrences. Of the 183 surveys citing abuse, 70 percent indicated the abuse occurred more than twice. Another 8 percent reported that the abuse happened at least twice.

While the data do not permit us to estimate the incidence of elder abuse, demographic trends toward an increasing elderly population and the recurrent nature of abuse make it likely that we will see more rather than less of the problem.

Tables 7–2 and 7–3 display data on citings and recurrence of abuse.

B. Who Sees Elder Abuse?

Table 7–4 discusses surveys sent to each professional/paraprofessional group, surveys returned by each profession, number of abuse citings per profession, and response rate per profession.

These data indicate that within the past eighteen months, elder abuse was cited by all but one of the professional/paraprofessional groupings that were surveyed. Some professions, such as visiting nurses, hospital social-services directors, and private social-service agency staff were responsible for large numbers of citings of abuse. One hundred nine of the 187 citings are attributed to these three professional groups. We must bear in mind,

Table 7-2
Does Elder Abuse Exist?

Type of Survey	Number of Surveys	Percentage of Total Surveys Returned	Percentage Citing Abuse	Percentage Eliminated	Percentage of Analyzed Surveys
Surveys citing abuse	202	57%	—	—	—
Citing single cases (coded)	183	—	52%	—	55%
Citing multiple cases (not coded)	19	—	5%	5%	—
Surveys citing no abuse	149	42%	—	—	45%
Surveys eliminated for unclear data (not coded)	4	1%	—	—	—
Total surveys returned	355	100%	57%	6%	—
Total surveys analyzed (coded)	332	94%	—	6%	100%

Table 7–3
Does Elder Abuse Tend to Recur?

Abuse Has Happened:	Number of Citings	Percentage of Citings
Once	14	8%
Twice	15	8%
More than twice	128	70%
No answer	26	14%
Total	183	100%

however, that these professions also received a proportionately large number of the surveys that were sent out (47 percent) and that this may account for the high number of citings attributed to them.

For this reason, we cannot rely solely on absolute numbers of citings per profession in order to understand who sees abuse. Columns C and D are useful in helping us examine our data more carefully.

We see, for example, in column D that certain professions have a much higher response rate than others. For example, home-care-corporation staff received twenty-eight surveys and returned twenty-two. This professional group also reported twenty citings of abuse out of the twenty-eight surveys distributed to them (column C). This means that 80 percent of the surveys sent to them were returned and 71 percent of the surveys sent to them were returned citing abuse. This is a much higher response and citing rate than any other profession, even though the absolute number of citings reported is much less for home-care corporations than for some other professions.

Similarly high response and citing rates are found in the professional category labeled "other," which consisted of a small number of health-oriented professionals (such as nurses and medical social workers), probation officers, and other persons who primarily provide services to elders. Visiting nurses, hospital social-services directors, and homemaker or health-aide staff also displayed relatively high rates of response to the survey (63 percent, 34 percent, and 34 percent, respectively) and as professional groups had reasonably high abuse-citing rates with reference to the number of surveys sent to them.

These data would indicate that as future studies or responses to elder abuse are developed, the professions specifically mentioned above should play a key role both as potential sources of research data and as professions most likely to see and hence deal with abuse.

The data displayed in table 7–4 are also interesting in their negative findings. Surveyed groups that produced the lowest citings of abuse were emergency-room nursing supervisors, police, and welfare protective-service

Table 7-4
Professions Seeing Abuse

Profession	Surveys Sent		Surveys Returned		Abuse Citings per Profession		Response Rate
	Number	Percentage	Number	Percentage of Total Returned	Number	Percentage	Percentage
Visiting nurse	132	13%	83	24%	46/132	35%	63%
Hospital social-services director	163	16%	56	16%	33/163	20%	34%
Homemaker and home-health-aide staff	50	5%	17	5%	10/50	20%	34%
Home-care-corporation staff	28	3%	22	6%	20/28	71%	79%
Emergency-room nursing supervisor	163	16%	22	6%	5/163	3%	13%
Public welfare protective-services manager	6	1%	4	1%	0/6	0%	67%
Private social-service agency staff/social worker[a]	195	19%	49	14%	30/195	15%	29%
Lawyer/paralegal	109	10%	24	7%	18/109	17%	22%
Police officer	163	15%	33	10%	6/163	4%	20%
Other	35	3%	27	8%	18/35	51%	44%
No answer	0	0%	7	2%	1	0%	0%
Total	1,044	101%	344[b]	99%	187/1,044	18%	32%

[a]Includes mental-health-center staff.

[a]This total is greater than the number of surveys returned (332) because several surveys indicated dual professions.

managers at the regional level; yet one might expect each of these professions to know of cases of elder abuse in their role as obvious mediators of family violence. This survey can only raise the obvious question of why these key professions cite so few instances of elder abuse.

While these data provide us with some interesting findings, we remind the reader that in no instance were *all* members of a profession surveyed. In some cases, only agency directors received surveys; in others (police, for example), a self-selected and nonrepresentative segment of the profession was surveyed. Additional research will be required, therefore, in order to more accurately determine the relative involvement of each profession in abuse reporting and treatment and to explain the variables that shape this involvement, such as professional awareness of abuse, degree of contact with elderly clients, completeness of reporting and case-record forms, levels of abuse in the profession's case load, and access to home environments.

Table 7–5 displays raw data on the number of abuse citings reported by each professional group.

C. How Were Cases of Abuse Brought to the Respondent's Attention?

The need for direct contact with the victim of abuse is indicated by the findings that describe how abuse citings were made. Only 24 percent of the abuse citings were brought to the respondent's attention by the victim. A major portion of the citings were obtained either from personal observation by the respondent (24 percent) or by a co-worker (19 percent). Equally remarkable is the small number of referrals made by the legal profession, police, and medical doctors as a means of uncovering abuse. As in our previous discussion on who sees elder abuse, we ask why certain professions that might be expected to be called in cases of domestic violence or trauma account for such a small percentage of reports of elder abuse. Is it that these professions do not see abuse, do not recognize it when they see it, or tend to deal with the problem in isolation from other professions? A survey or study more specifically designed to elicit data on these professions might clarify this question.

Perhaps our most interesting finding in this area was that in at least 70 percent of the abuse citings, involvement of a third party (someone other than the victim or his or her family) was required before the case was brought to the attention of concerned professionals or paraprofessionals. This suggests the need for some form of outside (third-party) observation as a means of identifying abuse cases.

Data also indicate that one in every five citings of abuse was reported to the respondent at least twice. Additional analysis of survey data could yield

Table 7-5
Who Sees Elder Abuse?

Profession	Number of Surveys Sent to Profession	Number of Surveys Returned (coded)	Abuse Citings		No Citings	
			Number	Percentage of Surveys Returned by Profession	Number	Percentage of Surveys Returned by Profession
Visiting nurse	132	83	46	55%	37	45%
Hospital social-services director	163	56	33	59%	23	41%
Homemaker and home-health-aide staff	50	17	10	59%	7	41%
Home-care-corporation staff	28	22	20	91%	2	9%
Emergency-room nursing supervisor	163	22	5	23%	17	77%
Public welfare protective-services manager	6	4	0	0%	4	100%
Private social-service agency staff/social worker	168	49	30	61%	19	39%
Lawyer/paralegal	109	24	18	75%	6	25%
Police officer	163	33	6	18%	27	82%
Other	62	27	18	67%	9	33%
No answer		7	1	14%	6	86%
Total	1,044	344[a]	187	54%	157	46%

[a]This number is greater than our number of 332 coded surveys because some surveys indicated dual professions.

Table 7-6
How Were Cases of Abuse Brought to the Respondent's Attention?

Sources of Abuse Citings	Number	Percentage of Total Sources (n = 226)	Percentage of Citings (n = 183)
Personal observation	43	19%	24%
Co-worker	35	15%	19%
Subject (self-report)	43	19%	24%
Member of subject's family	10	4%	5%
Subject's friend or neighbor	13	6%	7%
Private agency	38	17%	21%
Public agency	8	4%	4%
Hospital or clinic	18	8%	10%
Police	4	2%	2%
Private medical doctor	5	2%	3%
Lawyer/paralegal	0	0%	0%
Other	4	2%	2%
No answer	5	2%	3%
Total Sources	226	100%	—
Total Citings	183	—	124%[a]

[a]Indicates that some respondents checked multiple sources who brought abuse to their attention.

information on the ways in which abuse citings are brought to the attention of each profession. Do home health aides become aware of abuse in different ways than visiting nurses or private social services staff? Time did not permit this analysis for this report.

Table 7-6 presents data on how respondents became aware of instances of elder abuse.

D.   What Does Elder Abuse Look Like?

The most frequently cited injury inflicted on the abused elder was bruises and/or welts (44 percent of all citings). Debilitating mental anguish followed (40 percent), with other types of injuries being recorded less frequently. Multiple injuries were frequently cited by respondents. These data are displayed in table 7-7.

Table 7-8 aggregates injury data into six major categories and more clearly distinguishes between the instances in which the elder suffered some

Table 7-7
What Does Elder Abuse Look Like?

Injuries	Number	Percentage of All Injuries (n = 309)	Percentage of Total Citings (n = 183)
Bruises, welts	81	26%	44%
Debilitating mental anguish	74	24%	40%
Other	32	10%	17%
Malnutrition	30	10%	16%
None apparent	25	8%	14%
Wounds, cuts, punctures	12	4%	7%
Bone fractures	12	4%	7%
Abrasions, lacerations	10	3%	5%
Sprains, dislocations	8	3%	4%
Sexual abuse	6	2%	3%
Freezing	4	1%	2%
Skull fractures	2	1%	1%
Burns, scalding	1	0%	1%
No answer	12	4%	7%
Total	309	100%	168%[a]

[a]Indicates respondents checked multiple injuries.

Table 7-8
Injuries Sustained by the Abused Elder

Injuries	Number	Percentage of of All Injuries (n = 309)[a]
Physical trauma: (bruises and welts; wounds, cuts, and punctures; bone fractures; abrasions and lacerations; sprains; dislocations; skull fractures; burns, scalding)	126	41%
major (bone fractures; sprains, dislocations; skull fractures)	22	7%
minor (bruises, welts; wounds, cuts, punctures; abrasions, lacerations; burns, scalding)	104	34%
Debilitating mental anguish	74	24%
Malnutrition	30	10%
None apparent	25	8%
Sexual abuse	6	2%
Freezing	4	1%

[a]This table does not present data on all categories of injuries; therefore, column totals have been omitted.

physical trauma primarily related to battering and other categories of abuse or neglect, such as malnutrition or freezing.

We see that physical trauma constituted 41 percent of all reported injuries: 34 percent of the injuries are minor trauma such as bruises, welts, cuts or punctures, while 7 percent are major trauma including skull or other fractures and dislocations. The categories labeled "None apparent" (no apparent injury) and "Other" tended to be used to describe incidents in which no apparent physical injury could be identified but in which the respondent felt that "neglect" had taken place. "Neglect" was sometimes of a serious nature (for example, permitting an elder to remain in his or her own feces) but more often than not was left unclarified by the respondent.

In addition to analyzing the injuries sustained by the abuse victim, research staff reviewed narrative descriptions of the abuse situation provided by respondents. In reading these brief narratives, staff attempted to classify abuse into the most frequently ocurring types or models. Each abuse citing was classified into one of seven categories. The primary presenting problem was unclear in thirty-three of the 183 citings of abuse, but in ninety-six citings, *physical trauma* in which the elder had been battered in some manner was the presenting condition. Twenty citings were primarily *verbal harassment* situations, sixteen were citings in which *malnutrition* was the chief complaint, eight constituted *financial mismanagement* (such as withholding rent and food monies from the elder), and seven were primarily citings of *unreasonable confinement. Oversedation* and *sexual abuse* occurred in one citing each.

These data clearly indicate that *visible* injury to the elder may be present in a large proportion of abuse cases and may serve as a clue in helping practitioners identify such cases.

B. Characteristics of the Abused Person

Age. In the survey, "elder" was defined as anyone age 60 or older. The survey divided age categories into: under 65, 65–69, 70–74, 75–79, and over 80. Results indicate that the largest single age group represented in the survey were elders over age 80, with sixty-six citings (36 percent of all abuse citings). The next largest category, ages 75–79, contained 19 percent of the citings. The smallest age group represented in the abuse citings was the under age 65 category with 9 percent. These data are presented in table 7–9.

One reason for examining the abused person's age is to see if abuse occurs or is cited more frequently in one age group than another. Survey results appear to indicate that this may be true for the over-80 age group.

The number of abuse citings in any age group can, however, simply be a reflection of the relative size of that age group with reference to the total elder population. That is, we may have uncovered more citings of abuse in

Table 7-9
Age Distribution of Abused Persons Compared with Age Distribution of General Population

Age	Number of Citings	Percentage of Total Citings (n = 183)	National Population[a] (in thousands)	Percentage of Total Population
Under 65	17	9%	9,362	28%
65–69	33	18%	8,446	26%
70–74	32	17%	6,137	19%
75–79	34	19%	4,068	12%
80 and over	66	36%	4,842	15%
No answer	1	1%	—	—
Total	183	100%	32,855	100%

[a]National population 1977 U.S. census report.

the over-80 population because that population represents a proportionately large segment of all elders over age 60.

In order to correct for this, we have compared the ratio of abuse citings in each age group over total abuse citings with national census statistics on the proportion of elders over age 60 who fall within each of our five age categories. This comparison is depicted in figure 7-1.

If abuse occurs in all age groups over age 60 with the same frequency, we would expect our findings to mirror the composition of the general population over age 60: Two relatively parallel lines would emerge in figure 7-1. This is not the case. Figure 7-1 shows that for ages below 70, elder abuse was cited less frequently than population figures would suggest. We also find a proportionately greater number of abuse citings in the over-75 age groups than population figures would suggest.

These data, while by no means definitive, tend to support the conclusion that victims of abuse are more likely to be very old (age 75 and over) rather than younger (age 60–75).

Sex. Table 7-10 shows that in 80 percent of the 183 citings of abuse the person who had been abused was female. National census figures indicate, however, that women account for only 58 percent of the population age 60 or older. Survey data seem to indicate that women may represent a proportionately larger share of the abused population than their numbers in the general population would suggest.

In order to examine these data more carefully, the ratio of male to

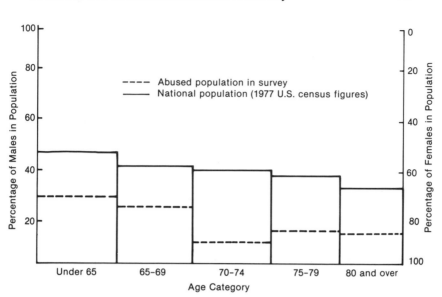

Figure 7–1. Comparison of the Proportion of Abuse Citings within Each
Age Group with the Proportion of National Population in
each Age Group.

Table 7–10
Sex of Abused Persons Compared with General Population

Sex	Number of Citings	Percentage of Total Citings (n = 183)	National Population[a] (in thousands)	Percentage of Total Population
Female	146	80%	18,906	58%
Male	29	16%	13,950	42%
No answer	8	4%	—	—
Total	183	100%	32,855	100%

[a]National population 1977 U.S. census report.

female in the national population was compared with the ratio of male to
female in our abuse citings *within each* of the five age categories listed in the
survey. Figure 7–2 depicts these data. Table 7–11 displays raw data from
which this figure was constructed.

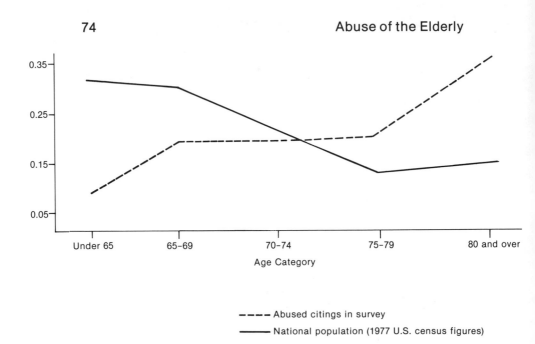

Figure 7-2. Comparison of the Ratio of Male to Female in the National
Population with Ratio of Male to Female Abuse Citings

The figure illustrates that within each age group the proportion of
females cited as abuse victims exceeds the proportion that general population statistics would suggest.

Our survey results thus indicate that women may be more likely to be
abused than men across all age categories.

In interpreting both age and sex data, readers are cautioned to remember that:

This survey was not a random sampling of the abused or elder population nor did it produce an unduplicated count of individual cases.
Results may therefore be skewed in some undetermined way.

It may be that women are more likely to seek assistance or report abusive behavior than men, thus increasing the number of citings in which
women appear as the victim of abuse.

The client population of the professions surveyed may be composed
largely of women and/or "very old" elderly, thus skewing our results
in these directions.

Additional research will be needed to confirm these findings.

Table 7-11
Sex of Abused Persons across Age Distribution

	Males				Females			
	Abuse Citings		National Population		Abuse Citings		National Population	
Age	Number of Citings	Percentage of Citings in Age Category	Number (in thousands)	Percentage	Number of Citings	Percentage of Citings in Age Category	Number (in thousands)	Percentage
Under 65	4	29%	4,381	47%	10	71%	4,981	53%
65–69	8	24%	3,739	44%	25	76%	4,708	56%
70–74	4	9%	2,597	42%	29	91%	3,540	58%
75–79	5	16%	1,589	39%	27	84%	2,479	61%
80 and over	8	15%	1,644	34%	55	85%	3,198	66%
Total	29	17%	13,950	42%	146	83%	18,906	58%

Physical or Mental Disability. In 75 percent of the abuse citings, the respondent stated that the abused person had a mental or physical disability that prevented him or her from meeting daily needs. It is difficult, however, to draw a conclusion from this data regarding the role that disability may play in the abusive situation. As with age and sex, national or state statistics on disability of the elder population might have been helpful in analyzing these data. Because these statistics are difficult to obtain, a different analysis was attempted. A comparison was made of the number of times disability was indicated within each of the five age categories. One would expect disability to increase with age. Our findings, however, indicate a relatively equal proportion of disability across abuse citings in all five age groups. (See tables 7–12A and 7–12B).

Table 7–12
Does the Abused Person Have a Mental or Physical Disability That Prevents Him or Her from Meeting Daily Needs?
A. Disability

Disability	Number	Percentage of Total Citings (n = 183)
Yes	138	75%
No	33	18%
No answer	12	7%
Total	183	100%

B. Disability across age groups

	Abuse Citings		Physical of Mental Disability	
Age	Number	Percentage of Total Citings (n = 183)	Number	Percentage of Total Citings in Each Age Category
Under 65	17	9%	14	82%
65–69	33	18%	20	61%
70–74	32	17%	25	78%
75–79	34	19%	23	68%
80 and over	66	36%	56	85%
No answer	1	1%	—	—
Total	183	100%	138	75%

This would indicate that our data could be a function of the client population served by the professions that we surveyed. One would expect that these agencies would see a high proportion of disabled rather than self-sufficient elders.

Significant disability does appear to be present, however, in a much higher percentage of the abused survey population than in the elderly population as a whole. We do not know if this is due to sampling artifact (that is, agency case loads having a much higher percentage of disabled patients) or whether disability is independently and significantly correlated with abuse. This issue needs further investigation.

Race/Religion. Issues similar to those described above affect data collected on the race and religion of abused persons. We have therefore eliminated this analysis. Raw data are included in tables 7–13 and 7–14, however.

Table 7–13
Race of Abused Persons

Race	Number of Citings	Percentage of Total Citings (n = 183)
Native American	13	7%
Black	8	4%
Latino/Latina	1	1%
Asian	0	0%
White	156	85%
Other	0	0%
No answer	5	3%
Total	183	100%

Table 7–14
Religion of Abused Persons

Religion	Number of Citings	Percentage of Total Citings (n = 183)
Catholic	67	37%
Protestant	46	25%
Jewish	5	3%
None	2	1%
Other	7	4%
No answer	56	31%
Total	183	100%

Degree of Isolation. Survey data indicate that the majority (75 percent) of the victims lived with someone else. In only 19 percent (thirty-five out of 183) of the citings of abuse was the abused person described as living alone. The remaining 6 percent failed to answer the question. Of those living with someone else, at least 83 percent (151) lived with a relative, and 13 percent (twenty-three) lived with nonrelatives. Most surveys (72 percent) also stated that the abused person had family, friends, or relatives outside his or her immediate household. Tables 7–15, 7–16, and 7–17 display these data.

Income of Household. The surveys indicated that 27 percent of the households where elder abuse had occurred received annual incomes of less than $5,200. This question appeared to be the most difficult question for professionals to answer, with a very high no response rate: Sixty-eight surveys (37 percent) failed to respond.

Income findings are supported by the latest census information on income. In the 1977 U.S. census report over 60 percent of those over age 65 earned less than $5,000 per year. Census information also showed that the average income of elderly women was significantly lower than the income of elderly men. An interesting hypothesis might be whether the greater financial dependence of women on their families could be a factor that helps to explain the higher proportion of abused women to men that our survey found. The results of the survey do not lend themselves to this conclusion but at best indicate that further research may be warranted.

It is possible that many of the professionals who responded to the survey serve primarily low-income clients. If that is the case, our findings on income would merely represent the income classes reached by the survey and not the true population of abused elders. It is important then that the result not be construed to mean that poor elderly are most likely to be abused. Such a conclusion requires more controlled and precise research into this question.

Table 7–18 displays data on income of the abused person's household.

Table 7–15
Does Subject Live with Others?

Response	Number of Citings	Percentage of Total Citings (n = 183)
Yes	137	75%
No	35	19%
No answer	11	6%
Total	183	101%

Table 7–16

Does Subject Have Family, Friends, or Relatives outside the Household?

Response	Number of Citings	Percentage of Total Citings (n = 183)
Yes	131	72%
No	34	19%
No answer	18	10%
Total	183	101%

Table 7–17

Who Resides at the Same Address as Subject?

Residents	Number of Citings	Percentage of Total Citings (n = 183)
Husband	31	17%
Wife	15	8%
Son	35	19%
Daughter	26	14%
Son-in-law	5	3%
Daughter-in-law	15	8%
Other relative	85	46%
Nonrelative	23	13%
No answer	9	5%
Total	244	133%[a]

[a]Indicates multiple persons living with subject.

Table 7–18

Approximate Income of Household

Annual Income	Number of Citings	Percentage of Total Citings (n = 183)
Less than $5,200	49	27%
$5,200–$9,000	42	23%
$10,000–$14,000	14	8%
$15,000–$19,000	7	4%
$20,000 and over	3	2%
No answer	68	37%
Total	183	101%

F.   Information on the Abuser

Living Arrangement and Relationship of Abuser to the Abused. In 75 percent (137) of the abuse citings the abuser lived with the person he or she was abusing. In 86 percent of the citings, the abusing person was a relative of the abused. Sons, husbands, and daughters were the largest categories of abusing relatives, accounting for 24 percent, 20 percent, and 15 percent of all abusers. Nonrelatives accounted for only 14 percent of abusing persons. In approximately one in every ten citings of abuse, the abuse was inflicted by more than one person.

While these data indicate that relatives are more likely to be abusers than nonrelatives, it may be that living arrangement is a more pertinent variable than relationship in explaining the abusive situation. In that case, results indicating that a high proportion of abusers tend to be relatives may only reflect the fact that elders, especially elders requiring care, tend to live with their families.

Certainly, however, data collected from this survey indicate that elders living with their relatives may constitute a significant portion of the abused population. Tables 7-19 and 7-20 display these data.

Stress. The survey also indicated that the abuser was usually experiencing some form of stress when the abuse occurred. Twenty-eight percent of the abuse citings indicated that the abuser was experiencing alcoholism or drug addiction at the time the abusive act occurred. Long-term medical complaints and long-term financial difficulties were also leading categories of stress checked by the respondents. Table 7-21 displays data on stress being experienced by the abuser.

Because duplicate reporting of individual cases of abuse may have skewed responses to this question, the frequency with which each stress category was checked is less significant than the fact that stress, as we

Table 7-19
Does the Abuser Live with the Subject?

Response	Number of Citings	Percentage of Total Citings (n = 183)
Yes	137	75%
No	35	19%
No answer	11	6%
Total	183	100%

Table 7–20
Relation of Abuser to Subject

Relation	Number of Citings	Percentage of Total Citings (n = 183)	Percentage of Abuses (n = 203)
Husband	36	20%	18%
Wife	11	6%	5%
Son	44	24%	22%
Daughter	28	15%	14%
Son-in-law	5	3%	2%
Daughter-in-law	10	5%	5%
Other relative	40	22%	20%
Nonrelative	25	14%	12%
No answer	4	2%	2%
Total	203	111%[a]	100%

[a]Indicates that respondents identified multiple abusers in some citings of abuse.

Table 7–21
Was the Abuser Experiencing any of the Following Symptoms of Stress?

Stress	Number of Citings	Percentage of Total Citings (n = 183)
Alcohol/drug abuse	52	28%
Long-term medical complaint	33	18%
Recent medical complaint	14	8%
Recent loss of spouse	11	6%
Recent birth of child	3	2%
Recent death in immediate family	3	2%
Past suicide attempt	3	2%
Long-term financial problem	30	16%
Recent financial problem other than loss of job	8	4%
Recent loss of job	6	3%
Limited education	24	13%
History of mental illness	26	14%
Lack of needed services	17	9%
Other	31	17%
No answer	47	26%
Total	308	178%[a]

[a]Indicates that respondents checked more than one category.

Table 7–22
Was the Elderly Subject a Source of Stress to the Abuser?

Response	Number of Citings	Percentage of Total Citings (n = 183)
Yes	116	63%
No	42	23%
No answer	25	14%
Total	183	100%

defined it, was present in 74 percent of the abuse citings. While the relative ranking of stressful conditions remains unclear, stress itself appears to be a potential factor in the abusive situation.

Was the Elderly Person a Source of Stress? Table 7–22 shows that in 116 (63 percent) of the surveys that cited abuse, the elderly subject (the person being abused) was a source of stress to the abuser. When asked to explain *how* the subject was a source of stress, 48 percent of these surveys indicated that the elderly victim required a high level of physical and emotional care from the abuser (such as personal care, preparing meals, administering medication). In addition, another 13 percent of the surveys indicated that the elderly victim was either financially dependent on the abuser or had severe physically debilitating conditions that acted as a source of stress for the abuser. Table 7–23 displays these findings.

We also know (see the discussion above on characteristics of the abused person) that 75 percent of the surveys citing abuse described the victim as having a mental or physical handicap that impaired daily functioning. These two pieces of data would indicate that impairment of the elderly victim *as it impacts on the abuser* may be a relevant variable for further analysis.

Other ways were cited in which the elder contributes to the stress of the abuser: nagging, demanding, manipulative behavior on the part of the elder; previous family history of arguments over specific issues (such as gambling or alcoholism); control of financial assets within the family; and arguments over placement or services for the elder. Each of these types of behavior may constitute variables that are at work in the abusive situation.

Other Forms of Violence. Eighty-four percent of the respondents either did not know whether other types of violent behavior were present in the abuser's family or stated that no other violence was known to them. This question was ambiguously worded and does not yield itself to interpretation. Table 7–24 presents raw data on this question.

Table 7–23
If So, How Was the Subject a Source of Stress?

Types of Stress	Number of Citings	Percentage of Total Citings of Elder-Related Stress (n = 116)
Needs care from abuser	56	48%
Financially dependent on abuser	2	2%
Severe physical or mental disability	13	11%
Subtotal	71	61%
Other	42	36%
No answer	3	3%
Total	116	100%

Table 7–24
Does the Respondent Know of Any Other Incidence of Violence or Abuse within the Immediate Family of the Abuser?

Response	Number of Citings	Percentage of Total Citings (n = 183)
Yes	28	15%
Child abuse	7	
Spouse abuse	3	
Assault and battery	7	
Other	11	
No	61	33%
No answer	94	51%
Total	183	99%

G. Action Taken When Elder Abuse Is Encountered

Action Taken. Most of the 183 surveys citing abuse indicated that more than one type of action had been taken by the respondent in dealing (or attempting to deal) with the abusive situation. In 62 percent of the citings, some form of direct action was taken. Twenty-two percent of the surveys stated that emergency action was taken, and 48 percent of the surveys indicated that a referral was made. Data was further analyzed to identify

Table 7-25
What Action Did the Respondent Take?[a]

Action Taken	Number of Surveys	Percentage of Total Surveys (n = 183)	Percentage within Each Type of Action
Direct action	114	62%	
Placement or hospitalization	41		36%
Arranged in-home services	25		22%
Interagency response	18		16%
Spoke with or counseled abuser	17		15%
Spoke with or counseled abused	15		13%
Spoke with or counseled family	8		7%
Emergency action	41	22%	
Medical treatment or hospitalization	16		39%
Other placement	5		12%
Crisis team or support team	3		7%
Police	2		5%
Nursing-home placement	2		5%
Referral action	88	48%	
Social services	63		48%
Legal services	26		20%
Other	23		17%
Police	20		15%
No answer	16	9%	

[a]This table illustrates only the major categories and subcategories of action taken by respondents. Because some data do not appear on the tables, subcategories do not add up to the number displayed under each major action heading. Because respondents often checked multiple types of action, percentages also do not add to 100 percent. We have therefore eliminated totals on this table.

specific action or recommendations made by the respondent, whether those recommendations were accepted by the abused person or his or her family. Tables 7-25 and 7-26 display this information.

Under "direct action" the single step most often taken or recommended was described as placement in a nursing home, hospital, temporary housing, or mental health facility. Thirty-six percent of all direct action included placing or attempting to place the victim elsewhere. Arranging for in-home services (homemakers, chore, meals on wheels, visiting nurses, or home health aides) constituted 22 percent of all direct action. Coordination of interagency treatment plans (16 percent, counseling or speaking with the abuser (15 percent), and speaking with the victim (13 percent) were also cited as forms of direct action.

One half (56 percent) of all "emergency action" included removal or

Table 7–26
Additional Analysis of Referrals

Referral	Number of Times Cited by Respondents
Social services	63
Other/not specified	17
Mental-health staff	11
Home-care corporation	8
Hospital social services	6
Family services	6
Visiting nurses	5
Welfare	5
Legal	26
Legal services agency	11
Other/not specified	8
Private attorney	5
Court/probation	2
Other	23
Other family or agency	10
Placement (hospital or nursing home)	8
Physician	5

recommended removal of the victim from the home. Reasons for removal included medical treatment in a hospital emergency room or hospitalization (39 percent of all emergency action), nursing home placement (5 percent), or other placement, such as public housing (12 percent). Other types of emergency action included calling the police, calling a crisis team or support team, and arranging for the household to be monitored.

In surveys that cited "Referral" as the type of action taken, referral to social services agencies was the most frequently checked category, with 48 percent of referrals being made to these agencies. Social-services agencies cited include mental-health-clinic staff, home-care corporations, hospital social services, family services, visiting nurses, and public welfare.

Legal services (including legal-services agencies, private attorneys, courts, and probation departments) represented 20 percent of all referrals. Police represented 5 percent of referrals.

Perhaps the most interesting feature of these data is what they tell us about the wide variety of responses that elder abuse elicits in the professionals who see abuse. Referral to social-services agencies, counseling, arrangements of in-home services, and removal of the victim appear to be the most frequently used intervention strategies. It would be interesting to know whether these responses were appropriate to the specific cases being discussed, a function of what services were available in a given area, or a function of the respondent's professional bias or "style." This is a question that our survey cannot answer.

The wide disparity in skills, approaches, and attitudes among respondents is also indicated by the range of responses that we received. Confronting the abuser and telling him or her to stop abusing the victim was one respondent's approach; others called in crisis teams to evaluate the victim and establish interdisciplinary treatment plans for the victim, abuser, and family. One wonders, again, whether this wide range of responses to abuse is due to the variables at work in the abuse case itself or to the skills and services available to the respondent who is dealing with the case.

A second interesting finding is the degree to which placement (temporary or permanent removal of the victim from the abusive situation) is cited as a response to abuse. This survey does not permit us to assess the appropriateness of these placements, but in some instances respondents themselves indicate their frustration in finding suitable alternatives to hospitals and nursing homes as places of refuge or respite for the victim.

Barriers to Service. One hundred twenty-nine (70 percent) of surveys reporting elderly abuse indicated that some barrier to service provision was experienced by workers. Forty-eight surveys responded with a "No answer" to this question. Four surveys said no barriers existed.

Of those surveys that reported barriers, the greatest percentage (36 percent) indicated that the refusal of the victim to acknowledge the problem constituted the barrier. This refusal was variously attributed to "fear of retaliation" from the abuser, feelings of kinship and love for the abuser, or simply as a refusal to accept services.

Fourteen percent of the surveys indicated that a legal problem constituted the barrier to care. Legal problems included:

1. lack of legal protection for workers who intervene in the family situation;
2. lack of eyewitnesses to the abusive act (lack of proof) when abused person refuses to file complaint;
3. lack of appropriate person to accept guardianship for the elder (this was cited four times);
4. requirement of a formal complaint from the abused individual before police can act;
5. unwillingness of witnesses to testify;
6. lack of formalized statutes protecting elders from manipulation or exploitation.

Thirteen percent of the surveys indicated that lack of cooperation of the abuser and/or family with whom the elder was residing was the principal barrier to services provision. An additional 11 percent stated that lack of services were the barrier. Needed services that were unavailable included protective services for adults, respite care facilities, temporary shelters that can care for persons requiring assistance in activities of daily living, emergency foster care for elders, and nursing-home placements. Lack of coordination among service providers was also cited in this category.

In 9 percent of the surveys, access to the elder was cited as the barrier to services provision—that is, the worker was barred from entering the home by the abuser or family. An additional 3 percent of the surveys stated that agency attitudes were a barrier to service. Examples include a worker deciding that the abuser is "not reachable by counseling," an agency dropping the client because of an obstructive family, a doctor refusing to acknowledge the problem and take some form of action, time demands of the case making a worker reconsider his or her involvement in the case.

Table 7-27 present data on barriers to service provision.

H.   Has the Problem Been Resolved?

Forty-five percent of the respondents indicated that the problem of abuse had been resolved, and another 4 percent said that resolution was in process. Thirty-six percent said the problem was not resolved. These data are presented in table 7-28.

Table 7-27
Barriers to Service Provision

Response	Number of Responses	Percentage of Total Barriers Cited (n = 129)	Percentage of Total Citings (n = 183)
Responses citing barrier	129	100%	71%
Refusal of services by abused	46	36%	
Legal	18	14%	
Family's or abuser's lack of cooperation	17	13%	
Lack of services	14	11%	
Access refused	11	9%	
Agency or staff attitudes	7	5%	
Other	16	12%	
No barriers cited	4	—	2%
No answer	48		27%
Total	181	—	100%

Table 7-28
Has the Problem Been Resolved?

Response	Number of Citings	Percentage of Total Citings (n = 183)
Yes	82	45%
No	65	36%
No answer	29	16%
In process	7	4%
Total	183	101%

Five of the 82 "resolved" citings indicated that the abused elder had died. It is not known whether these deaths resulted from the abuse or were due to failing health and old age.

These data tell us very little about the actual status of the abuse situation. Additional information is needed on the appropriateness of the intervention and the potential for recurrence of abuse in order to describe the status of cases with any degree of confidence.

Notes

1. Newberger, Eli H. "Child Abuse and Neglect: Toward a Firmer Foundation for Practice and Policy." *American Journal of Orthopsychiatry* 47 (3) (July 1977), pp. 374–376.

2. ———. "Beating Up Hubby." *Human Behavior* 7 (November 1978), p. 60.

3. O'Malley, Helen. "Elder Abuse: A Review of Recent Literature." Legal Research and Services for the Elderly, Elder Abuse Project, Boston, Massachusetts, May 1978.

4. ———. "Study on Elderly Abuse." Center on Aging, Division of Human and Community Resources, University of Maryland, College Park, Maryland, 1978.

Appendix 7A:
Original Survey

Legal Research and Services for the Elderly

Sponsored by: National Council of Senior Citizens

2 Park Square ■ *Boston, MA 02116*

Telephone: (617) 426-3401

March 6, 1979

Dear Colleague:

Legal Research and Services for the Elderly is conducting a study on elder abuse within Massachusetts. This study is sponsored by the Massachusetts Department of Elder Affairs and runs through June 30, 1979.

Your response to this survey is very important to the solution of this growing problem and we urge you to take the time to fill out the attached forms. We are interested in your description of cases of abuse in which the victim is sixty years old or older and residing in a non-institutional setting. This would include persons living alone, with family or friends or with a caretaker. We are interested only in abuse which has occurred within the past eighteen months.

For the purposes of this survey, we are defining abuse to mean: the willful infliction of physical pain, injury or debilitating mental anguish, unreasonable confinement or willful deprivation by a caretaker of services which are necessary to maintain mental and physical health.

Of course, no names or addresses of the abused person or abuser are requested. Please respond even if you know of no abuse cases. If you know of more than one case of abuse, we ask that you make additional copies of the blank survey forms and complete one set of forms for each case. If you do not have sufficient information to answer a question, please go on to the next question. Answer as many questions as you can, even if this means answering only one or two.

-2-

The survey should be returned to Legal Research and Services
for the Elderly (LRSE) within three weeks. The survey has been
stamped and addressed for your convenience. Please call Helen
O'Malley or Howard Segars at LRSE, (617) 426-3401, if you would
like additional information about this survey or the elderly abuse
project.

Sincerely yours,

James A. Bergman

JAB/HCO'M/vm
Enclosure

1. I am a:

_____ community mental health
      center staff
_____ visiting nurse
_____ hospital social services   _____ public welfare protective
      director   services manager
_____ homemaker/home health   _____ private social service agency
      aide staff   staff/social worker
_____ home care corporation   _____ lawyer/paralegal
      staff   _____ police officer
_____ emergency room nursing   _____ other (specify) _____
      supervisor   _____

2. _____ I know of no cases of   3._____ I do know of at least one
         elder abuse   case of suspected elder
                                            abuse.

                                     Please continue to respond.
----

4. Who brought this case to your   5.Check injuries sustained by the
   attention: subject:

_____ personal observation   _____ none apparent
_____ co-worker   _____ bruises, welts
_____ subject (self-report)   _____ sprains, dislocations
_____ member of subject's   _____ malnutrition
      family   _____ freezing
_____ subject's friend or   _____ burns, scalding
      neighbor   _____ abrations, lacerations
_____ private agency   _____ wounds, cuts, punctures
      (specify) _____   _____ bone fractures
_____ public agency   _____ skull fractures
      (specify) _____   _____ debilitating mental anguish
_____ hospital or clinic   _____ sexual abuse
_____ police   _____ other (specify) _____
_____ private medical doctor   _____
_____ lawyer/paralegal
_____ other (specify)   6. Give brief description of abuse:
      _____   _____
      _____   _____
                                           _____
                                           _____

____ INFORMATION ON SUBJECT (ABUSED PERSON) ____

7. Age: _____ under 65   8. Race: _____ Native American
          _____ 65-69   _____ Black
          _____ 70-74   _____ 80   _____ Latino/Latina
          _____ 75-79   and   _____ Asian
                         over   _____ White
                                         _____ Other (specify)

9. Religion: _____

_____ Catholic   _____ None   10. Sex:
_____ Protestant _____ Other
_____ Jewish   (specify)   _____ Male
                       _____   _____ Female

                    -1-

11. Does the subject have a physical or mental disability which prevents him or her from meeting daily needs: _____ yes _____ no

12. Does the subject have family, friends or relatives outside the household: _____ yes _____ no

13. Has the abuse happened more than once: _____ once _____ twice _____ more than twice

14. Does the subject live with others: _____ yes _____ no

15. If YES, who resides at the same address:

        Relationship   Age   Sex

    1.
    2.
    3.
    4.
    5.

16. What is the approximate income of the household:

    _____ $5,200 or less   _____ $15,000 - 19,000
    _____ $5,300 - 9,000   _____ $20,000 and over
    _____ $10,000 - 14,000

INFORMATION ON ABUSER

17. Does the abuser live with the subject: _____ yes _____ no

18. Relation of abuser to subject:

    _____ husband   _____ other relative (specify) _____
    _____ wife   _____ non-relative (specify) _____
    _____ son
    _____ daughter
    _____ son-in-law
    _____ daughter-in-law

19. Was the abuser experiencing any of the following:

    _____ alcohol and/or drug abuse
    _____ long term medical complaint (self or family)
    _____ recent medical complaint (self or family)
    _____ recent loss of spouse through death or divorce
    _____ recent birth of child
    _____ recent death in immediate family
    _____ past suicide attempt
    _____ long term financial problems
    _____ recent financial problems other than loss of job
    _____ recent loss of job
    _____ limited education
    _____ history of mental illness
    _____ lack of needed services (self or family)
    _____ other (specify) _____
          _____
          _____

-2-

20.   Was the elderly subject a source of stress to the abuser: ___ yes ___ no

21.   If YES, in what way was the subject a source of stress:

_____
_____
_____

22.   Do you know of any other incidence of violence or abuse within the
      immediate family of the abuser:

       ____ child abuse   ____ documented assault and/or battery
       ____ spouse abuse   on others
                           ____ other (specify) _____

ACTION TAKEN

23.   What action did you take:

       ____ direct action (specify) _____

_____

       ____ emergency action (specify) _____

_____

       ____ referral to: police
                       social services agency (specify) _____
                       legal services agency (specify) _____
                       other (specify) _____

24.   Barriers to provision of service:

_____
_____
_____

25.   Has the problem been resolved: ____ yes ____ no

****

Thank you for your help.

If you would like to be interviewed at a later time about the case which
you have described (in confidence), please write your name, address, and
telephone number below. It is not necessary to give this information
if you do not want to be interviewed.

I want to be interviewed to talk more about the case I described. I
understand that this is voluntary on my part and I may withdraw my
consent at any time.

NAME:_____

ADDRESS:_____

TELEPHONE:_____

Part II
Resources and Services

**State and Area
Agencies on Aging**

The Emerging Aging Network, 1978
Select Committee on Aging
U.S. House of Representatives
Washington, D.C.

Alabama (*Federal Region IV*)

Commission on Aging
740 Madison Avenue, Montgomery 36104
Emmett Eaton, Director, (205) 832–6640

Northwest Alabama Council of Governments
P.O. Box 2603, Muscle Shoals, 35661
Elliot Conway, Sr., (205) 383–3861

West Alabama Planning and Development Commission
P.O. Box 28, Tuscaloosa 35401
Carole Hill, (205) 345–5545

Birmingham Regional Planning Commission
2112 11th Avenue, South Suite 220, Birmingham 35203
Thomas B. Holmes, (205) 251–8139

East Alabama Regional Planning and Development Commission
1001 Leighton, P.O. Box 2186, Anniston 36201
Porter Benefield, (205) 237–8623

South Central Alabama Development Commission
2815 East South Boulevard, Montgomery 36116
Sylvia Alexander, (205) 281–2196

Alabama–Tombigee Rivers Regional Planning and Development
    Commission
Clifton Street, P.O. Box 269, Camden 36726
C. Emmett McConnell, Jr., (205) 682–4234

Southeast Alabama Regional Planning and Development Commission
P.O. Box 1406, Dothan 36301
William Cathell, (205) 794-4092

South Alabama Regional Planning Commission
International Trade Center, 250 North Water Street, P.O. Box 1665,
    Mobile 36601
Joan B. McMillan, (205) 433-7417

Central Alabama Aging Consortium
808 South Lawrence Street, Montgomery 36104
Brenda Kirk, (205) 262-7316

Lee County Council of Government
P.O. Box 1072, Auburn 36830
Linda Conway Adams, (205) 821-7845

North Central Alabama Area Agency on Aging
City Hall Tower, 5th floor, 402 Lee Street, P.O. Box 1069, Decatur 35601
Viki Gonia, (205) 355-4515

Top of Alabama Regional Council of Governments
Central Bank Building, Suite 350, Huntsville 35801
Bob Gonia, (205) 533-3335

Alaska (*Federal Region X*)

Alaska Office on Aging
Pouch H-OIC, Juneau 99811
M.D. Plotnick, Coordinator, (907) 465-4903

Arizona (*Federal Region IX*)

Bureau on Aging, Department of Economic Security
P.O. Box 6123, Phoenix 85005
John B. Fooks, Chief, (602) 271-4446

Area Agency on Aging Region 1
1802 East Thomas Road, Suite 8, Phoenix 85016
Alice Drought, (602) 264-2255

Pima County Council on Aging
100 East Alameda, Suite 406, Tucson 85701
Marion Lupu, (602) 624–4419

Northern Arizona Council of Governments
P.O. Box 57, Flagstaff 86002
Jackie Sweet, (602) 774–1895

District 4 Council of Governments
377 South Main Street, No. 202, Yuma 85364
Irene Six, (602) 782–1886

Southeastern Arizona Governments Organization
P.O. Box 204, Bisbee 85603
Tim Welsh, (602) 432–2237

Arkansas *(Federal Region VI)*

Office on Aging, Department of Human Services
1200 Westpark Drive, Little Rock 72204
Delores Martin, Acting Director, (501) 371–2441

Northwest Arkansas Area Agency on Aging
P.O. Box 190, Harrison 72601
Lloyd Kennedy, (501) 741–5404

White River Area Agency on Aging
P.O. Box 2396, White River Regional Services Center, Highway 25 North,
   Batesville 72501
Jon Looney, (501) 793–5270

East Arkansas Area Agency on Aging
P.O. Box 5035, Jonesboro 72401
Herb Sanderson, (501) 972–5980

Southeast Arkansas Area Agency on Aging
P.O. Box 6806, 1108 Popular Street, Pine Bluff 71601
John White, (501) 536–1971

Central Arkansas Area Agency on Aging
1700 West 13th Street, Little Rock 72202
Dixie Matthews, (501) 372–5566/5497/5498

West Central Arkansas Area Agency on Aging
P.O. Box 1558, 2814 Malvern Street, Hot Springs 71901
Darrell Smith, (501) 321-2214

California (*Federal Region IX*)

Department of Aging
918 J. Street, Sacramento 95814
Janet J. Levy, Director, (916) 322-3887/5290

Area 4 Agency on Aging
1832 Tribute Road, Sacramento 95815
Deanna Lea, (916) 929-6802

North Bay Senior Planning Council
1302 Holm Road, Petaluma 94952
Henry Mattimore, (707) 763-2295

Marin County Area Agency on Aging
Marin City Civic Center, Room 279, San Rafael 94930
Michael Bradney, (415) 479-1100

San Francisco City and Country Commission on Aging
1095 Market Street, No. 700, San Francisco 94103
Glenn B. McRibbin, (415) 558-2126

Area 7 Area Agency on Aging
2450 Stanwell Drive, Suite 220, Concord 94520
Jane McClelland, (415) 671-4233

San Mateo County Area Agency
617 Hamilton Street, Redwood City 94063
Thomas J. Jordan, (415) 364-5600

Alameda County Department on Aging
1755 Broadway, 5th floor, Oakland 94612
Eddie J. James, (415) 874-7233/5741

Council on Aging of Santa Clara County, Inc.
277 West Hedding Street, San Jose, 95110
Richard Fisher, (408) 287-7111

Area 11A Agency on Aging
1100 Kansas Avenue, Suite E, Modesto 95350
Beverly Carr, (209) 521-7066

San Joaquin County Area Agency on Aging
222 East Weber, Room 144, Stockton 95202
Charlotte Humphrey, (209) 944-2504/2420

Tri-County Area Agency on Aging
1270-A Coast Village Circle, Montecito 93108
Joan Tadeo, (805) 969-5080

Los Angeles County Department of Senior Citizens Affairs
601 South Kingley Drive, Los Angeles 90005
Leon Harper, (213) 385-4221

Office on Aging, San Bernadino County
602 South Tippecanoe, Room 1320, Building No. 3, San Bernadino 92415
Phil Nathanson, (714) 383-3673

County of Riverside Office on Aging
3601 University Avenue, Suite 201, Riverside 92501
Fred Hubbard, (714) 787-6557

Senior Citizens Program Office
801-C North Broadway, Santa Ana 92701
Walter Scales, (714) 834-6017

San Diego County Office of Senior Citizens Affairs
1955 4th Avenue, San Diego 92101
Lola Hobbs, (714) 236-3269

Aging Division Community Development Department
City Hall, Suite 2100, 200 North Spring Street, Los Angeles 90012
Jerry C. Cimmarusti, (213) 485-4402

Colorado (*Federal Region VIII*)

Division of Services for the Aging, Department of Social Services
1575 Sherman Street, Denver 80203
Dorothy Anders, Director, (303) 839-2651

Northeastern Colorado Area Agency on Aging
P.O. Box 1782, Sterling 80851
(303) 522-0040

Larimer-Weld Area Agency on Aging
201 East 4th Street, Room 201, Loveland 80537
Gary Houser, (303) 667-3288

Region III Office on Aging
2480 West 26th Avenue, Denver 80211
Wendy Snow, (303) 758-5166

Pikes Peak Area Agency on Aging
27 East Vermijo, Colorado Springs 80904
Jeremy Huffman, (303) 471-7080

East Central Council of Governments
P.O. Box 28, Stratton 80836
Shelley Hornung, (303) 348-5562

Lower Arkansas Valley Area Agency on Aging
Bent County Courthouse, Las Animas 81054
Jerry Garcia, (303) 456-0061

District 7 Area Agency on Aging
1 City Hall Place, 3d floor, Pueblo 81003
Manuel Esquibel, (303) 544-4307

Department of Aging
Box 28, Adams State College, Alamosa 81101
Modesto Salazar, (303) 589-7927

San Juan Basin Area Agency on Aging
1911 North Main Street, Durango 81301
Lawrence Marsh, (303) 259-1967

Rocky Mountain Area Agency on Aging
P.O. Box 351, Rifle 81650
Dave Norman, (303) 243-9322

Upper Arkansas Area Agency on Aging
1310 East Rainbow Boulevard, No. 17, Salida 81201
Betty Cook, (303) 275-3342

Connecticut (*Federal Region I*)

Department on Aging
90 Washington Street, Room 312, Hartford 06115
Marin Shealy, Director, (203) 566–2480

Northwestern Connecticut Agency on Aging, Inc.
20 East Main Street, Room 344, Waterbury 06702
Barbara Grant, (203) 753–2145

Community Council of the Capitol Region, North Central Connecticut
   Agency on Aging
999 Asylum Avenue, Hartford 06115
James Gaito, (203) 278–2044

Eastern Connecticut Agency on Aging
317 Main Street, Norwich 06360
Linda Eckert, (203) 887–3561

Southwestern Connecticut Area Agency on Aging
328 Park Avenue, Bridgeport 06604
Clifford Laude, (203) 333–9288

South Central Connecticut Agency on Aging
15 June Street, Woodbridge 06525
Daro Quiring, (203) 389–9541/9543

Delaware (*Federal Region III*)

Division of Aging, Department of Health and Social Services
1901 North Dupont Highway, New Castle 19720
Eleanor L. Cain, Director, (302) 421–6791

District of Columbia (*Federal Region III*)

District of Columiba Office on Aging
1012 14th Street NW, Suite 1106, Washington 20005
D. Richard Artis, Director, (202) 724–5622

Florida (*Federal Region IV*)
Program Office of Aging and Adult Services, Department of Health and
   Rehabilitation Services
1323 Winewood Boulevard, Tallahassee 32301
E. Bentley Lipscomb, Director, (904) 488–2650

Area Agency on Aging of North Florida
2639 North Monroe Street, Suite 145–B/Box 12, Tallahassee 32303
Margaret Lynn Duggar, (904) 385-2133

Area Agency on Aging
3008 Northwest 13th Street, Gainesville 32601
Virgie H. Cone, (904) 378-6716/6749

Northeast Florida Area Agency on Aging
1045 Riverside Avenue, Suite 250, Jackson 32204
David Adkins

Tampa Bay Regional Planning Council
3151 3d Avenue, North, 5th floor, 300 Center West, St. Petersburg 33713
Julia Greene, (813) 821-2811

Area Agency on Aging
W.T. Edwards Hospital, 4000 West Buffalo Avenue, Tampa 33614
Grace Ganley, (813) 877-3053

East Central Florida Regional Planning Council
1011 Wymore Road, Suite 105, Winter Park 32789
James Mowbray, (305) 645-3339

South Central Florida Area Agency on Aging
P.O. Box 2258, 3049 Cleveland Avenue, Fort Myers 33901
Maeve Foster, (813) 332-2211

Gulfstream Areawide Agency on Aging
Indian River Community College, 3209 Virginia Avenue, Fort Pierce 33450
George Tsismanakis, (305) 464-2000

Area Agency on Aging of Broward County, Inc.
5950 Park Drive, Margate 33063
Nan Hutchison, (305) 973-1350/51

United Way of Dade County
955 Southwest Second Avenue, Miami 33130
Carl Dahl, (305) 854-8311

Georgia (*Federal Region IV*)

Aging Section, Department of Human Resources
618 Ponce De Leon Avenue N.E., Atlanta 30308
Troy Bledsoe, Director, (404) 894-5333

Atlanta Regional Commission
230 Peachtree Street, Suite 200, Atlanta 30303
Cheryll Schramm, (404) 656-7767

Central Savannah River Area Planning and Development Commission
P.O. Box 2800, 2123 Wrightsboro Road, Augusta 30904
Sister Elizabeth Ann Ney, (404) 828-2356

Coastal Area Planning and Development
P.O. Box 1316, Brunswick 31520
Christine Long, (912) 264-7363

Coastal Plains Area Planning and Development Commission
P.O. Box 1223, Valdosta 31601
Pauline Carter, (912) 247-3454/3459

Coosa Valley Area Planning and Development Commission
P.O. Drawer H, Rome 30161
Ralph Peters, (404) 295-6485

Georgia Mountains Area Planning and Development Commission Aging
   Program
P.O. Box 1720, Gainesville 30501
Pat Viles, (404) 536-3431

Middle Georgia Area Planning and Development Commission
711 Grand Building, Macon 31201
Nancy Thompson, (912) 744-6160

North Georgia Area Planning and Development Commission
212 North Pentz Street, Dalton 30720
Lawrence Besel, (404) 226-1670

Northeast Georgia Planning and Development Commission
305 Research Road, Athens 30601
Claire Hamilton, (404) 548-3141

Southwest Georgia Area Planning and Development Commission
P.O. Box 346, Camilla 31730
Ted Heiland, (912) 439-4315

Hawaii (*Federal Region IX*)

Executive Office on Aging
1149 Bethel Street, Room 307, Honolulu 96813
Renji Goto, Director, (808) 548-2593

Kauai County Office of Elderly Affairs
4396 Rice Street, Lihue 96766
Eleanor J. Lloyd, (808) 245-4737

Honolulu Area Agency on Aging
51 Merchant Street, Honolulu 96813
Horace E. Maclaren, (808) 523-4361

Maui County Committee on Aging
200 South High Street, Wailuku 96793
Robert Yokoyama, (808) 244-7838

Hawaii County Office of Aging
34 Rainbow Drive, Hilo 96720
William Takaba, (808) 961-3794

Idaho (*Federal Region X*)

Idaho Office on Aging
State House, Boise 83720
Kenneth Wilkes, Acting Director, (208) 384-3833

Panhandle Area Council
P.O. Box 880, Coeur d'Alene 83814
Katie Salo, (208) 667-1556

Community Action Agency, Inc.
1032 Bryden Avenue, Lewistown 83501
Bessie Lotze, (208) 746-3351

Idaho-Oregon Regional Planning and Development Association
P.O. Box 331, Weiser 83672
Elwin Grout, (208) 549-2411

College of Southern Idaho
P.O. Box 1238, Twin Falls 83301
Phil Sampson, (208) 733-9554

Southeast Idaho Council of Governments
P.O. Box 4169, Pocatello 83201
Sister Anthony Marie, (208) 233-4032

Eastern Idaho Special Services Agency
P.O. Box 1098, Idaho Falls 83401
Mike Kormanik, (208) 522-5391

Illinois (*Federal Region V*)

Department on Aging
Monadnock Building, Room 731, 53 West Jackson Boulevard,
   Chicago 60604
David Munson, Acting Director, (217) 785-3340

Northwest Illinois Area Agency on Aging
Eastmoor Building, 4223 East State Street, Rockford 61108
Janet B. Ellis, (815) 226-4901

Region Two Area Agency on Aging
P.O. Box 809, River Road, Kankakee 60901
Charles Johnson, (815) 939-0727

Western Illinois Area Agency on Aging
2201 11th Street, Rock Island 61201
Sid L. Granet, (309) 797-4319

Central Illinois Area Agency on Aging
300 East War Memorial Drive, Room 300, Peoria 61614
Frank G. Blumb, (309) 676-4312

East Central Illinois Area Agency on Aging
2714 McGraw Drive, Bloomington 61701
Phyllis H. Pinkerton, (309) 662-9393

West Central Illinois Area Agency on Aging
112 North 7th Street, P.O. Box 428, Quincy 62301
Lynn Niewohner, (217) 223-7904

Project LIFE Area Agency on Aging
1029 South 4th Street, Springfield 62704
Dorothy Kimball, (217) 522-8954

Southwestern Illinois Area Agency on Aging
8787 State Street, Edgement Building, Suite 107, East Street, Louis 62203
Nancy C. Silvers, (618) 397-4118

Midland Area Agency on Aging
140 South Locust Street, Room 413, Centralia 62801
David P. Seibert, (618) 532–1853

Southeastern Illinois Area Agency, Inc.
425 Market Street, Mount Carmel 62863
Barbara Poshard, (618) 262–8001

Egyptian Area Agency on Aging, Inc.
John A. Logan College, Carterville 62918
William F. Price, (618) 985–4011

Mayor's Office for Senior Citizens and Handicapped
180 North LaSalle Street, Suite 500, Chicago 60601
Robert J. Ahrens, (312) 744–4016

Suburban Cook County Area Agency on Aging
223 West Jackson Boulevard, Suite 1200, Chicago 60606
Lynne Brenne, Acting Director, (312) 341–1400

Indiana (*Federal Region V*)

Commission on Aging and Aged
Graphic Arts Building, 215 North Senate Avenue, Indianapolis 46202
Maurice E. Endwright, Director, (317) 633–5984

Area Agency on Aging
5518 Calumet Avenue, Hammond 46320
Jerry Long, (219) 937–3500

Area 2 Agency on Aging, REAL Services of St. Joseph County, Inc.
P.O. Box 1835, 622 North Michigan, South Bend 46634
Jim Oleksak, (219) 233–8025, (800) 522–2916

Northeast Area 3 Council on Aging
Foellinger Center, 277 East Washington Boulevard, Fort Wayne 46802
L. Joyce Smith, (219) 423–7491, (800) 522–3662

Area 4 Council on Aging
1001 South Street, Lafayette 47901
Fay B. Ebrite, (317) 742–0061, (800) 382–7666

Area 5 Council on Aging, Inc.
912 East Market Street, Logansport 46947
Terrence R. McGovern, (219) 722–4801, 753–4311

Area 6 Council on Aging
1968 West Main Street, Muncie 47303
Karen Gardner DeHart, (317) 289–1121, (800) 382–8683

Area 7 Agency on Aging, West Central Indiana Economic Development
  District
P.O. Box 627, 700 Wabash Avenue, Terre Haute 47808
Jean Cox, (812) 238–1561, (800) 742–0804

Central Indiana Council on Aging, Inc.
146 East Washington Street, 2d floor, Indianapolis 46204
John Riggle, (317) 633–6191

Area 9 Agency on Aging
Indiana University East, 2325 Chester Boulevard, Richmond 47374
L. Jane Rice, (317) 966–1795

Area 10 Agency on Aging
2295 Bloomfield Road, Bloomington 47401
A. Louis Bridgewaters, (812) 334–3383

Area 11 Agency on Aging
P.O. Box 904, 2756 25th Street, Columbus 47201
Thomas A. Ross, (812) 372–9989

Area 12 Agency on Aging
P.O. Box 177, Dillsboro Manor, Lenover Street, Dillsboro 47018
Sally Dobson, (812) 432–5000

Area 13A Agency on Aging
P.O. Box 336, Community Service Center, 2d and Indianapolis Streets,
  Vincennes 47591
Gerald Wibert, (812) 882–6370

Area 13 B Agency on Aging, Southeastern Indiana Regional Council
  on Aging, Inc.
528 Main Street, Evansville 47708
Robert Patrow, (812) 425–6128

Area 14 Agency on Aging, South Central Indiana Council for the Aging
    and Aged, Inc.
317 East 5th Street, New Albany 41150
Thelma Bertrand, (812) 948-9161

Area 15 Agency on Aging
P.O. Box 128, Orleans Airport, Orleans 47452
Gene Purlee, (812) 865-3033

Iowa (*Federal Region VII*)

Commission on Aging
415 West 10th Street, Jewett Building, Des Moines 50319
Glenn R. Bowles, Director, (515) 281-5187

Area 1 Agency on Aging
Area One Vocational-Technical School, Calmer 52132
George Pfister, (319) 562-3263

North Central Iowa Area Agency on Aging
500 College Drive, Mason City 50401
Donald Ryerkerk, (515) 421-4339

Area 4 Agency on Aging
SIMPCO, P.O. Box 447, 626 Insurance Exchange Building,
    Sioux City 51102
Rick Motz, (712) 279-6220

Hawkeye Valley Area Agency on Aging
210 East 5th Street, Box 2576, Waterloo 50706
Chris Harshbarger, (319) 233-5214

Great River Bend Area Agency on Aging, Bi-State Metropolitan Planning
    Commission
1504 Third Avenue, Rock Island 61201
Dottie Seyfried, (309) 788-6338

Heritage Area Agency on Aging
Kirkwood Community College, 6301 Kirkwood Building SE,
    Cedar Rapids 52406
Russ Proffitt, (319)398-5559

Area 11 Agency on Aging, Central Iowa Regional Association of Local
  Governments
104½ East Locust Street, Des Moines 50309
Carolyn Bayreder, (515) 244-3257

Area 14 Agency on Aging
201 West Mills Street, Creston 50801
Lois Houston, (515) 782-4040

Area 15 Agency on Aging
SIEDA, Building No. 17, Ottumwa Industrial Airport, Ottumwa 52501
Shirley Baird, (515) 682-8741

Iowa Western Area 13 Agency on Aging
Iowa Western Community College, 2700 College Road, Kanesville Center,
  Room 203, Council Bluffs 51501
Frank Kowal, (712) 328-2540

Iowa Lakes Area Agency on Aging
P.O. Box 1533, 2328 Highway Boulevard, Spencer 51301
Richard Ambrosius, (712) 262-1775

Southeast Iowa Area Agency on Aging
Memorial Auditorium, 3rd floor, Front and Jefferson Streets,
  Burlington 51601
William F. Holvet, (319) 753-2191

Area 8 Agency on Aging
469 Emmett Street Dubuque 52001
Marguerite Carter, (319) 583-3547

Kansas (*Federal Region VII*)

Kansas Department on Aging
610 West 10th Street, Topeka 66612
Max M. Mills, Secretary, (913) 296-4986

Wyandotte-Leavenworth Area Agency on Aging
5th floor, City Hall, 701 North 7th Street, Kansas City 66101
Anita Favors, (913) 371-3142

Central Plains Area Agency on Aging
455 North Main Street, Wichita 67202
Irene Hart, (316) 268-4661

Northwest Kansas Area Agency on Aging
208 East 7th Street, Hays 67601
Merlin Sizlove, (913) 628-8204

Jayhawk Area Agency on Aging
444 Southeast Quincy, Suite 170, Topeka 66603
Donna Kidd, (913) 235-1367

Southeast Kansas Area Agency on Aging
Box 269, Chanute 66720
Jerry D. Williams, (316) 431-2980

Southwest Kansas Area Agency on Aging
1107 6th Avenue, Dodge City 67801
Mary Stuecker, (316) 225-0510

Mid-America Council on Aging
132 South Main Street, Ottawa 66067
Shirley Higdon, (913) 782-1900

North Central/Flint Hills Area Agency on Aging
217 South Seth Childs Road, Manhattan 66502
John Churchill, (913) 776-9294

Northeast Kansas Area Agency on Aging
107 Oregon West, P.O. Box 56, Hiawatha 66434
Anna Mae Shaffer, (913) 742-7324

South Central Area Agency on Aging
P.O. Box 1122, Arkansas City 67005
Betty Londeen, (316) 442-0268

Kentucky (*Federal Region IV*)

Aging Program Unit, Department for Human Resources
275 East Main Street, 5th floor west, Frankfort 40601
Thomas S. Cathell, Director, (502) 564-6930

Purchase Area Development District
P.O. Box 588, Mayfield 42066
Rebecca Blaine, (502) 247-7171

Pennyrile Area Development District
609 Hammond Plaza, Fort Campbell Boulevard, Hopkinsville 42240
Agnes Davis, (502) 886-9484

Green River Area Development District
P.O. Box 628, Owensboro 42301
Nelda Barnett, (502) 926-4433

Barren River Area Development District
P.O. Box 2120, Bowling Green 42101
Bill Guthrie, (502) 781-2381

Lincoln Trail Area Development District
305 First Federal Building, Elizabethtown 42701
Becky McMahan, (502) 769-2393/2002

Kentuckyiana Regional Planning and Development Agency
505 West Ormsby Street, Louisville 40203
Betty Rulander, (502) 587-3804

Northern Kentucky Area Development District
7505 Sussex Drive, Florence 41042
Deanna Skees, (606) 283-1885

Buffalo Trace Area Development District
State National Bank Building, Maysville 41056
Beth Hillemmayer, (606) 564-6894

Gateway Area Development District
P.O. Box 107, Owingsville 40360
Jim Templeton, (606) 674-6355

Fivco Area Development District
P.O. Box 636, Catettsburg 41129
Bob Haight, (606) 739-5191

Big Sandy Area Development District
552 Southlake Drive, Prestonsburg 41653
Phyllis Stanely, (606) 886-6869/6897

Kentucky River Area Development District
P.O. Box 986, Hazard 41701
Kenneth Blair, (606) 436-3158

Cumberland Valley Area Development District
Route 2, Box 4A, London 40741
Phillip Martin, (606) 864-7391

Lake Cumberland Area Development District
P.O. Box 377, Jamestown 42629
Bob Bowe, (502) 343-3154

Bluegrass Area Development District
120 East Reynolds Road, Lexington 40503
Peggy Chadwick, (606) 272-6656

Louisiana (*Federal Region VI*)

Bureau of Aging Services, Office of Human Development, Department of
   Health and Human Resources
P.O. Box 44282, Capitol Station, Baton Rouge 70804
O.B. Butler, Director, (504) 342-2744

Area Agency on Aging, District 1
4915 Magazine Street, New Orleans 70115
Margaret Roman, (504) 899-9376

Capitol Area Agency on Aging, District 2
P.O. Box 66638, Baton Rouge 70806
Sandra Adams, (504) 343-9278

Area Agency on Aging, District 3
402 West 5th Street, Lafourche Parish Agricultural Building,
   Thibodaux 70301
Irwin Joubert, (504) 446-3714

Area Agency on Aging, District 4, Acadiana Humanitarian Health
   Planning Council
P.O. Box 52223, Lafayette 70501
Al Edwin Thierry, (504) 234-4558

Area Agency on Aging, District 5
P.O. Box 6505, Pioneer Building, Lake Charles 70606
Orriene Fender, (318) 439-6113

Area Agency on Aging, District 6, Kisatchie-Delta Regional Planning and
   Development District
1220 MacArthur Drive, Alexandria 71301
Kristin Duke, (318) 448-5454

Area Agency on Aging, District 7
425 Milam Street, Ricou-Brewster Building, Suite 427, Shreveport 71101
Olivia Whitehurst, (318) 425-1559

Area Agency on Aging, District 8, North Delta Regional Planning and
   Development District, Inc.
2115 Justice Street, Monroe 71201
Jeanne Williams, (318) 387-2572

Maine (*Federal Region I*)

Bureau of Maine's Elderly
State House, Augusta 04333
Patricia Riley, Director, (207) 289-2561

Aroostook Regional Task Force of Older Citizens
457 Main Street, P.O. Box 1288, Presque Isle 04769
Stephen Farnham, (207) 764-3396

Eastern Task Force on Aging
153 Illinois Avenue, Bangor 04401
Willis Spaulding, (207) 947-0561

Central Maine Senior Citizens Association
P.O. Box 484, Augusta 04330
William Inlow, (207) 622-9344

Western Maine Older Citizens Council
65 Central Avenue, Lewiston 04240
Robert Armstrong, (207) 784-8797

Cumberland York Senior Citizens Council
142 High Street, Suite 401, Portland 04101
Donald Sharland, (207) 775-6503

Maryland (*Federal Region III*)

Office on Aging
State Office Building, 301 West Preston Street, Baltimore 21201
Matthew Tayback, Director, (301) 383-5064

Western Maryland Area Agency
Algonquin Motor Lodge, Room 510, Cumberland 21502
Joel Shoap, (301) 777-2167

MAC, Inc.
1504 Riverside Drive, Salisbury 21801
Joseph Eberly, (301) 742-0505

Baltimore City Area Agency
Waxter Center, 861 Park Avenue, Baltimore 21201
Eugene Bartell, (301) 396-4932

Central Maryland Area Agency on Aging
Johnsville School, 5745 Bartholow Road, Eldersburg 21784
Carolyn Del Giudice, (301) 795-8606

Baltimore County Aging Programs and Services
32 West Susquehanna Avenue, Towson 21204
Tim Fagan, (301) 494-2594

Montgomery County Area Agency on Aging
14 Maryland Avenue, Rockville 20850
Donald Wassmann, (301) 279-1480

Prince Georges County Area Agency on Aging, Division of Programs for
   the Elderly
9171 Central Avenue, Capitol Heights 20027
Magan Pathik, (301) 350-6666

Massachusetts (*Federal Region I*)

Department of Elder Affairs
110 Tremont Street, 5th floor, Boston 02108
Stephen G. Guptill, Director, (617) 727-7751/7752

Berkshire Home Care Corp.
246 North Street, Pittsfield 01201
Frederick H. Whitham, (413) 499-1353

Franklin County Home Care Corp.
Central Street, Turner Falls 01376
Margaret O. Keane, (413) 774-2994

Highland Valley Elder Service Center, Inc.
42 Gothic Street, Northampton 01060
Robert V. Gallant, (413) 586-9020

Holyoke/Chicopee Regional Senior Services, Inc.
198 High Street, Holyoke 01040
Priscilla Chalmers, (413) 538-9020

Home Care Corp. of Springfield, Inc.
1414 State Street, Springfield 01109
James Piscioneri, (413) 781-8800

Region 2 Area Agency on Aging, Inc.
697 Main Street, Holden 01520
James McNamera, (617) 829-5364

Senior Home Care Services, Inc.
94 Main Street, Gloucester 01903
Guntis Licis, (617) 281-1750

Northshore Elder Services, Inc.
Northshore Shopping Center, Peabody 01960
William Carney, (617) 523-0330

Greater Lynn Senior Services, Inc.
25 Exchange Street, Lynn 01902
Janet McAveeney, (617) 599-0110

Chelsea/Revere/Winthrop Home Care Center, Inc.
385 Broadway, P.O. Box 189, Revere 02151
James Cunningham, (617) 284-8375

Mystic Valley Elder Home Care, Inc.
341A Forest Street, Malden 02148
Elyse Salend, (617) 324-7705

Somerville/Cambridge Home Care Corp.
249 Elm Street, Somerville 02144
Lewis Levenson, (617) 628-2601/2602

Minuteman Home Care Corp.
365 Waltham Street, Lexington 02173
Jon Pynoos, (617) 862-6200

West Suburban Elder Services, Inc.
51 Spring Street, Watertown 02172
Grace Newman, (617) 926-3311

Baypath Senior Citizens Services, Inc.
5 Edgell Road, Framingham 01701
Bruce Hausch, (617) 620–0840

South Shore Home Care Services
c/o Hershey House, 229 North Street, Hingham 02043
Eileen Kirby, (617) 749–6832

Bristol County Home Care
178 Pine Street, Fall River 02720
Elizabeth Bielawski, (617) 675–2101

Coastline Elderly Services, Inc.
13 Welby Road, New Bedford 02745
David Alves, (617) 998–3016

Elder Services of Cape Cod and the Islands, Inc.
146 Main Street, Hyannis 02601
James Peace, (617) 771–4248

Elder Services of the Merrimack Valley
420 Common Street, Lawrence 01840
George Moran, (617) 683–7747

Commission on Affairs of the Elderly
1 City Hall Square, Room 271, Boston 02201
Ina Resnikoff, (617) 725–4366

Michigan (*Federal Region V*)

Office of Services to the Aging
300 East Michigan, P.O. Box 30026, Lansing 48909
Elizabeth J. Ferguson, Director, (517) 373–8230

Detroit–Wayne County Area Agency on Aging
3110 Book Building, 1249 Washington Boulevard, Detroit 48226
Fred C. Ferris, (313) 224–0960

Area Agency on Aging 1B
29508 Southfield Road, Suite 100, Southfield 48076
Sandra K. Reminga, (313) 569–0333

Region 2 Commission on Aging
611 South Center, Adrian 49221
Charles L. Anson, (517) 265-7881

Southcentral Michigan Commission on Aging
Room 127, Connor's Hall, Nazareth College, Nazareth 49074
Sarah Renstrom, (616) 343-4996

Region 4 Area Agency on Aging
Peoples State Bank Building, Room 8, 517 Ship Street, St. Joseph 49085
Robert L. Dolsen, (616) 983-0177

Valley Area Agency on Aging
708 Root Street, Room 110, Old Sears Building, Flint 48503
Valaria Conerly, (313) 239-7671

Tri-County Office on Aging
500 West Washtenaw, Lansing 48933
Roxanna O'Connor, (517) 487-1066

Region 7 Area Agency on Aging
971 Midland Road, Saginaw 48603
Richard Catalino, (517) 793-1416

Area Agency on Aging of Western Michigan, Inc.
Room 1108, Peoples Building, 60 Monroe Street NW, Grand Rapids 49503
Lawrence L. Murray, Jr., (616) 456-5664

Northeast Michigan Community Services Agency, Inc.
275 Bagley Street, Alpena 49707
Christine Baumgardner, (517) 356-3474

Northwest Michigan Planning and Development Services, Inc.
2334 Aero Park Court, Traverse City 49684
Ronald W. Crummel, (616) 947-8920

Region 2 Area Agency on Aging, UPCAP Services, Inc.
118 North 22nd Street, Excanaba 49829
Kathryn Kumkoski, (906) 786-4701

Region 14 Council on Aging
1111 4th Street, Muskegon 49441
James Peliotes, (616) 722-7811

Minnesota (*Federal Region V*)

Minnesota Board on Aging
Suite 204, Metro Square Building, 7th and Robert Streets, St. Paul 55101
Gerald A. Bloedow, Director, (612) 296-2544

Region 1 Area Agency on Aging
425 Woodland Avenue, Crookston 56716
Gerald Berglin, (218) 281-1396

Headwaters-Northwest Area Agency on Aging, Headwaters Regional
    Development Commission
Box 584, Bemidji 56601
Marcia Nottingham, (218) 751-3108

Region 3 Area on Aging, Arrowhead Regional Development Commission
200 Arrowhead Place, Duluth 55802
Steven Krasner, (218) 722-5545

Region 4 Area Agency on Aging, West-Central Regional Development
    Commission
Administration Building, Fergus Falls Community College,
    Fergus Falls 56537
Laurel Sorlie, (218) 739-3356

Tri-Regional Area Agency on Aging, Region 5 Regional Development
    Commission
102 6th Street, North Staples 56479
John Fellerer, (218) 894-3233

Southwestern Area Agency on Aging, Southwest Regional Development
    Commission
2711 Broadway, Slayton 56172
Fred DeJong, (507) 836-8549

Region 9 Area Agency on Aging, Region 9 Development Commission
120 South Broad, Mankato 56001
Connie Noterman, (507) 387-5643

Region 10 Area Agency on Aging, Southeastern Regional Development
    Commission
301 Marquette Bank Building, South Broadway at 2d Street SE,
    Rochester 55901
Gil Wilkins, (507) 285-2585/2550

Region 11 Area Agency on Aging, Metropolitan Council
300 Metro Square, 7th and Robert Streets, St. Paul 55101
Jane Whiteside, (612) 291-6305

Mississippi *(Federal Region IV)*

Mississippi Council on Aging
P.O. Box 5136, Fondren Station, 510 George Street, Jackson 39216
Norman Harris, Director, (601) 354-6590

North Delta Area Agency on Aging
P.O. Box 1244, Clarksdale 38614
Gloria Dear, (601) 627-3401

South Delta Area Agency on Aging
Route 1, Box AB 52, Greenville 38701
Sylvia Jackson, (601) 378-3831

North Central Area Agency on Aging
P.O. Box 668, Winona 38967
Carl Cooper, (601) 283-2675

Golden Triangle Area Agency on Aging
P.O. Drawer DN, Mississippi State 39762
Bobby Gann, (601) 325-3855

Trace Regional Area Agency on Aging
P.O. Box 7, Belden 38826
Jane Mapp, (601) 844-4081

Northeast Mississippi Area Agency on Aging
P.O. Drawer 6D, Booneville 38829
Billy Moore, (601) 728-6248

Central Mississippi Area Agency on Aging
2675 River Ridge Road, Jackson 39216
Joe S. Patterson, (601) 981-1511

East Central Mississippi Area Agency on Aging
410 Decatur Street, Newton 39345
Jenifer Buford, (601) 683-2401

Southern Mississippi Area Agency on Aging
1020 32d Avenue, Gulfort 39501
Jane Kennedy, (601) 868-2311

Southwest Mississippi Area Agency on Aging
P.O. Box 429, Meadville 39653
John W. Waid, (601) 384-5881

Missouri (*Federal Region VII*)

Office of Aging, Division of Special Services, Department of Social
  Services
Broadway State Office Building, P.O. Box 570, Jefferson City, 65101
E.C. Walker, Director, (314) 751-2075

Southwest Missouri Office on Aging
317 St. Louis Street, Springfield 65804
Winston W. Bledsoe, (417) 862-0762

Southeast Missouri Area Agency on Aging
1915 north Kings Highway, Cape Girardeau 63701
Vearl Caid, (314) 333-3331

District 3 Area Agency on Aging
P.O. Box 556, 604 North McGuire, Warransburg 64093
Leonard W. Westphal, (816) 726-3800

Northwest Missouri Area Agency on Aging
Box 207, County Courthouse, Albany 64402
Ronald Rauch

Northeast Missouri Area Agency on Aging
P.O. Box 1067, 400 North Baltimore, Kirksville 63501
Earl Welty, (816) 665-4682

Central Missouri Area Agency on Aging
Room 209, Professional Building, 909 University Avenue, Columbia 65201
Alan DeBerry, (314) 443-5823

Mid-America Regional Council Aging Program
20 West 9th Street, Kansas City 64105
Jean Bacon, (816) 474-4240

Mid-East Missouri Area Agency on Aging
Kimberly Building, Suite 212, 2510 South Brentwood Boulevard,
    Brentwood 63144
Floyd D. Richards, (314) 889-3050

Mayor's Office for Senior Citizens
560 Delmar Boulevard, St. Louis 63101
Lucius F. Cervantes, S.J., (314) 621-5600

Montana (*Federal Region VIII*)

Aging Services Bureau, Department of Social and Rehabilitation Services
P.O. Box 4210, Helena 59601
Holly Luck, Acting Director, (406) 449-5650

Area Agency 1 on Aging
306 North Kendrick, Glendrive 59330
Earl Hubley, (406) 365-3364

Area 2 Agency on Aging
202½ Main Street, Roundup 59072
Betty Stockert, (406) 323-1320

Area Agency 3 on Aging
94th Avenue SW, Conrad 59425
Earline Zoeller, (406) 278-5662

Area Agency on Aging 4
P.O. Box 721, Helena 59601
(406) 422-1552

Area 5 Agency on Aging
115 East Pennsylvania Street, Anaconda 59711
Jane Anderson, (406) 563-3310

Western Montana Agency on Aging
723 5th Avenue East, Kalispell 59901
Polly Nikolaisen, (406) 755-5300

Tribal Elders Program
R.R. 1, Box 58, Harlem 59526
Cynthia LaCounte, (406) 323-2205

Nebraska (*Federal Region VII*)

Commission on Aging
P.O. Box 95044, 301 Centennial Mall South, Lincoln 68509
David Howard, Director, (402) 471-2037

Eastern Nebraska Office on Aging
884 South 72nd Street, Omaha 68114
J. Kenton Fancolly, (402) 444-6540

Lincoln Area Agency on Aging
100 North 9th Street, Lincoln 68508
James E. Zietlow, (402) 475-7640

Northeast Nebraska Area Agency on Aging
North Stone Building at Regional Center, P.O. Box 1447, Norfolk 68701
Tim Austin, (402) 371-7454

South Central Nebraska Area Agency on Aging
2000 Central Avenue, Kearney 68847
Dennis Loose, (308) 234-1851

Midland Area Agency on Aging
P.O. Box 905, Hastings 68901
Jerry Ryan, (402) 463-4565

Blue Rivers Area Agency on Aging
Beatrice National Bank Building, Room 23, 109½ South 6th Street,
   Beatrice 68310
Fred Holtz, (402) 223-3124

West Central Nebraska Area Agency on Aging
Craft, State Office Building, 200 South Silber, North Platte 69101
James E. Lowe, (308) 534-6780

Western Nebraska Area Agency on Aging
P.O. Box 54, Scottsbluff 69361
Rena Mackrill, (308) 635-0851

Nevada (*Federal Region IX*)

Department of Human Resources, Division of Aging
505 East King Street, Kinkead Building, Room 101, Carson City 89710
John B. McSweeney, Director, (702) 885-4210

New Hampshire (*Federal Region I*)

Council on Aging
P.O. Box 786, 14 Depot Street, Concord 03301
Claira P. Monier, Director, (603) 271–2751

New Jersey (*Federal Region II*)

Division on Aging, Department of Community Affairs
P.O. Box 1768, 363 West State Street, Trenton 08625
James J. Pennestri, Director, (609) 292–4833

Atlantic County Office on Aging
Atlantic City Social Service Building, 1601 Atlantic Avenue, 6th floor,
    Atlantic City 08410
Stephen J. Bruner, (609) 348–4361

Bergen County Office on Aging
355 Main Street, Hackensack 07601
Mildren Kransnow, (201) 646–2625

Burlington County Office on Aging
Lumberton Road, County Office Building, 49 Rancocas Road,
    Mount Holly 08060
Linda Coffey, (609) 267–0610

Camden County Office on Aging
129 White House Pike, Audubon 08106
Edward L. Donohue, (609) 546–0044, 784–7744

Cape May Office on Aging
Social Service Building, Box 222, Rio Grande 08242
Ann Zahora, (609) 886–2784/2785

Cumberland County Office on Aging
29 Fayette Street, Bridgeton 08302
Dale Finch, (609) 451–8000

Essex County Office on Aging
520 Belleville Avenue, Newark 07109
Bernard J. Gallagher, (201) 751–6050

Gloucester County Office on Aging
44 Delaware Street, Woodbury 08096
Margaret Mendoze, (609) 845–1600

Hudson County Office on Aging
Murdock Hall, 114 Clifton Place, Jersey City 07340
Michael F. Reilly, (201) 434-6900

Hunterdon County Office on Aging
Community Building, Flemington, Route 31 North, Box 49A, RD6,
    Flemington 08611
Mary Housel, (201) 782-4300

Mercer County Office on Aging
640 South Broad Street, Trenton 08611
Carl West, (609) 989-6661

Middlesex County Office on Aging
Middlesex County Office Annex, 841 Georges Road,
    North Brunswick 08902
Thomas E. Hamilton, (201) 246-6293/6295

Monmouth County Office on Aging
10 Lafayette Place, Freehold 07728
Gloria Filippone, (201) 431-7450

Morris County Office on Aging
Court House, Morristown 07960
Norman Van Houten, (201) 285-6393

Ocean County Office on Aging
Court House, Toms River 08753
Philip Rubenstein, (201) 244-2121

Passias County Office on Aging
Rea House, 675 Goffle Road, Hawthorne 07506
Raymond Fink, (201) 525-5000

Salem County Office on Aging
94 Market Street, Salem 08079
Constance Undy, (609) 935-7510

Somerset County Office on Aging
36 Grove Street, Somerville 08876
Jean Siiberg, (201) 725-4700

Sussex County Office on Aging
46 Trinity Street, Newton 07860
Robert Callahan, (201) 383-5098

Union County Office on Aging
208 Commerce Place, Elizabeth 07201
Peter M. Shields, (201) 353-5000

Warren County Office on Aging
Court House Annex, Oxford Street and Hardwick, Belvidere 07823
Anne B. Schneider, (201) 475-5361

New Mexico (*Federal Region VI*)

Commission on Aging
Pera Building, Room 515, Santa Fe 87501
Willie Vigil, Director, (505) 827-2802

District 1 Area Agency on Aging
309 South 3d Street, Gallup 87301
Peggy Folk, (505) 722-4327

North Central New Mexico Area Agency on Aging
P.O. Box 4248, Santa Fe 87501
Gene Varela, (505) 827-2014

Middle Rio Grande Area Agency on Aging
505 Marquette Avenue NW, Suite 1320, Albuquerque 87102
Gloria Bruno, (505) 766-7836

Eastern Plains Area Agency on Aging
Curry County Courthouse, Clovis 88101
Ruby Goforth, (505) 762-7714

Southwestern New Mexico Area Agency on Aging
109 East Pine Street, Deming 88030
Mark Rogers, (505) 546-8816

Southeastern New Mexico Area Agency on Aging
P.O. Box 6639 RIAC, Roswell 88201
Lupe Mendez, (505) 347-5425

Southern Rio Grande Area Agency on Aging
P.O. Box 216, Socorro 87801
J. Lester Rigby, (505) 835-2475

New York (*Federal Region II*)

Office for the Aging
New York State Executive Department, Empire State Plaza, Agency
    Building No. 2, Albany 12223
Lou Glasse, Director, (518) 474-5731

Albany County Department for Aging
600 Broadway, Albany 12207
Richard Healy, (518) 445-7511

Allegany County Office of the Aging
17 Court Street, Belmont 14813
Diane Bollman, (716) 593-5460

Broome County Office for the Aging
County Office Building, Government Plaza, Binghamton 13902
Kevin Tobin, (607) 772-2821

Cattaraugs County Department of the Aging
116 South Union Street, Olean 14760
Kathleen Horner, (716) 372-0303

Cayuga County Office for the Aging
County Office Building, 160 Genesee Street, Auburn 13021
Joan Gallo, (315) 253-1226

Chautauqua County Office for the Aging
County Office Building, Room 341, Mayville 14757
Sven Hammar, (716) 753-4417

Chemung County Office for the Aging
214 West Grey Street, Elmira 14901
Sister Juliana O'Hara, (607) 737-2914

Chenango County Office for the Aging
12 Henry Street, Norwich 13815
William J. Fiorello, (607) 335-4624

Clinton County Office for the Aging
137 Margaret Street, Plattsburgh 12901
(518) 561-8800

Columbia County Office for the Aging
70 North 3d Street, Hudson 12534
Helen Montag, (518) 828-4258

Cortland County Office for the Aging
Court House, Cortland 13045
Helen Anderson, (607) 756-5691

Delaware County Office for the Aging
6 Court Street, Delhi 13753
Neal E. Lane, (607) 746-6333

Dutchess County Office for the Aging
236 Main Street, Poughkeepsie 12601
Patricia Pine, (914) 485-9920

Erie County Office for the Aging
Rath Building, Room 1329, Buffalo 14202
Clifford Whitman, (716) 846-8522

Essex County Office for the Aging
Maple Street, Elizabethtown 12932
(518) 873-6301

Franklin County Office for the Aging
County Courthouse, 63 West Main Street, Malone 12953
William O'Reilly, (518) 483-1610

Fulton County Office for the Aging
County Office, Johnston 12095

Genesee County Office for the Aging
Batavia-Genesee Senior Center, 2 Bank Street, Batavia 14020
Roger Tiede, (716) 343-1611

Greene County Department for the Aging
153 Jefferson Heights, Catskill 12414
Philip Schlenker, (518) 943-5332

Herkimer County Office for the Aging
County Office Building, Mary Street, Herkimer 13350
Douglas Brewer, (315) 866-4010

Jefferson County Office for the Aging
175 Arsenal Street, Watertown 13601
Douglas C. Gleason, (315) 785-3191

Lewis County Office for the Aging
Lewis County Courthouse, Lowville 13367
Randy Streeter, (315) 376-7753

Livingston County Office for the Aging
Livingston County Campus, Building 2, Mt. Morris 14510
Gloria Harrington, (315) 658-2881

Madison County Office for the Aging
20 Eaton Street, Morrisville 13408
Margaret Williams, (315) 684-9424

Monroe County Office for the Aging
375 Westfall Road, Rochester 14620
Gary Merritt, (716) 442-6350

Montgomery Countywide Office for the Aging
23 New Street, Amsterdam 12010
Carmela Simiele, (518) 843-2300

Nassau County Department of Senior Citizen Affairs
One Old Country Road, Carle Place 11514
Adelaide Attard, (516) 535-4414

Niagara County Office for the Aging
Civil Defense Building, Lockport 14094
Victor Cooke, (716) 433-2614

Oneida County Office for the Aging
County Office Building, 800 Park Avenue, Utica 13501
Anthony Montoya, (315) 789-5771

Metropolitan Commission on Aging
Onondaga County Civic Center, 10th floor, 421 Montgomery Street,
   Syracuse 13203
Roslyn Bilford, (315) 425-2362

Ontario County Office for the Aging
120 North Main Street, Canadaigua 14424
Rita Condon, (716) 394-7070

Orange County Office for the Aging
60 Erie Street, 3d floor, Goshen 10924
Anne Cortese, (914) 294-5151

Orleans County Office for the Aging
151 Platt Street, Albion 14411
Carole Blake, (716) 589-7743

Oswego County Office for the Aging
River Front Office Building, East 1st Street, Oswego 13126
Mary King, (315) 349-3231

Otsego County Office for the Aging
County Office Building, Cooperstown 13326
Patricia Leonard, (607) 547-4233

Putnam County Office for the Aging
County Office Building, Carmel 10512
Marion Hayes, (914) 225-6441

Rensselaer County Department for the Aging
8 Winter Street, Tory 12180
Paul Tazbir, (518) 270-5343

Rockland County Office for the Aging
Building B, Health and Social Services Complex, Pomona 10970
Virginia Weil, (914) 345-0200

St. Lawrence County Office for the Aging
County Office Building, Canton 13617
Joseph Sears, (315) 379-2204

Saratoga County Office for the Aging
40 Church Avenue, Ballston Spa 12020
Susan Baird, (518) 885-9761

Schenectady County Office for the Aging
101 Nott Terrace, Schenectady 12308
Virginia H. Pigott, (518) 382-3258

Schoharie County Office for the Aging
1 Lark Street, Cobleskill 12043
Ethel Benninger, (518) 234-4219

Seneca County Office for the Aging
P.O. Box 480, Seneca Falls 13148
Robert L. Lindner, (315) 539-9285

Steuben County Area Agency on Aging
Senior Center, Hornell 14843
Judy Herman, (607) 324-4891

Suffold County Office for the Aging
County Center, North Complex, 65 Jetson Lane, Hauppauge 11787
Elizabeth Taibbi, (516) 234-2622

Sullivan County Office for the Aging
New County Government Center, Monticello 12701
James J. Galligan, (914) 794-1404

Tioga County Office for the Aging
231 Main Street, Oswego 13827
Jean Hefft, (607) 687-4120

Tompkins County Office for the Aging
225 South Fulton Street, Ithaca 14850
(607) 274-5427

Ulster County Office for the Aging
17 Pearl Street, Kingston 12401
Antoinette Tennant, (914) 331-9300

Warren-Hamilton Counties Office for the Aging
Warren County Municipal Center, Lake George 12845
Louis Spelman, Jr., (518) 792-9951

Washington County Office for the Aging
P.O. Box 56, Whitehall 12887
Kenneth Ducharme, (518) 499-2468

Wayne County Office for the Aging
County Office Building, Lyons 14489
John C. Perry, (315) 946-4163

Westchester County Office for the Aging
County Office Building, White Plains 10601
Joseph A. Tortelli, (914) 682-2669

Wyoming County Office for the Aging
76 North Main Street, Warsaw 14569
May Lou Felton, (716) 786-3144

Yates County Area Agency for the Aging
218 Liberty Street, Penn Yan 14527
Foster Van Dusen, (315) 536-2368

New York City Department for the Aging
250 Broadway, New York 10007
Janet Sainer, (212) 577-0848

Akwesasne Office for the Aging
St. Regis–Mohawk Indian Reservation, Hogansburg 13655
(518) 358-2272

North Carolina (*Federal Region IV*)

North Carolina Division of Aging, Department of Human Resources
708 Hillsborough Street, Suite 200, Raleigh 27603
Nathan H. Yelton, Director, (919) 733-3983

Land of Sky Regional Council—B
P.O. Box 2175, Asheville 28802
Joan B. Tuttle, (704) 254-8131

Isotherman Planning and Economic Division
P.O. Box 841, Rutherfordton 28139
Myra Lynch, (704) 287-2281

Region D Council of Governments
Executive Arts Building, Furman Road, Boone 28607
Kim Dawkins, (704) 264-5558

Western Piedmont Council of Governments
30 3d Street NW, Old City Hall Building, Hickory 28601
R. Douglas Taylor, (704) 322-9191

Centralina Council of Governments—F
P.O. Box 4168, Charlotte 28204
Charles Page, (704) 372-2416

Piedmont Triad Council of Governments—6
2120 Pinecroft Road, Four Seasons Offices, Greensboro 27407
Roger Bell, (909) 294-4907

Pee Dee Council of Governments
P.O. Box 728, Troy 27371
Judith Crawford, (919) 576-6261

Triangle J Council of Governments
P.O. Box 12276, Research Triangle Park 27709
Dave Moser, (919) 549-0551

Region K Council of Governments
P.O. Box 709, Henderson 27536
Steven Norwood, (919) 492-8561

Region L Council of Governments
P.O. Drawer 2748, Rocky Mount 27801
Sandra R. Ray, (919) 446-0411

Region M Senior Services, Inc.
P.O. Box 53305, Fayetteville 28305
Cliff LeCornu, (919) 485-7111

Lumber River Council of Governments—N
P.O. Drawer 1528, Lumberton 28358
Betty Rising, (919) 738-8104

Neuse River Council of Governments—P
P.O. Box 1717, New Bern 28560
Gayle Thames, (919) 638-3185

Mid-East Economic Development Commission—Q
P.O. Box 1218, Washington 27889
Mary Long Tankard, (919) 946-8043

Albemarle Regional Planning Commission—R
P.O. Box 646, Hertford 27944
Annette Fairless, (919) 426-5756

North Dakota (*Federal Region VIII*)

Aging Services Unit, Community Services Board of North Dakota
State Capitol Building, Bismarck 58505
Gerald D. Shae, Administrator, (701) 224-2577

Ohio (*Federal Region V*)

Ohio Commission on Aging
50 West Broad Street, 9th floor, Columbus 43215
Martin Janis, Director, (614) 466-5500/5501

Council on Aging of the Cincinnati Area
601 Provident Bank Building, 7th and Vine Streets, Cincinnati 45202
William Bogart, (513) 721-1025

Area Agency on Aging, Miami Valley Council on Aging
184 Salem Avenue, Dayton 45406
Donald Trummel, (513) 225-3046

Area Agency on Aging PSA 3
311 East Market Street, 311 Building, Suite 201, Lima 45801
Roger J. Stauffer, (419) 227-7506

Area Agency on Aging
506 Madison, Suite 106, Toledo 43604
Billie Sewell, (419) 248-4234

District 5 Area Agency on Aging
50 Blymer Avenue, P.O. Box 966, Mansfield 44901
Caroline Ford, (419) 524-4178

Central Ohio Agency on Aging
272 South Gift Street, Columbus 43215
Ardath Lynch, (614) 222-7250

Area Agency on Aging District 7
Rio Grande College, Box 978, Rio Grande 45674
John Allen, (614) 245-5353

Buckeye Hille-Hocking Valley Development District
Suite 410, St. Clair Building, 216 Putnam Street, Marietta 45750
Molly Varner, (614) 374-9436

Area Agency on Aging Region 9
Box 429, 127 South 10th Street, Cambridge 43725
Boyer Simcox, (614) 439-4478

Western Reserve Area Agency on Aging
1276 West 3d Street, Marion Building, Room 512, Cleveland 44113
Paul Alandt, (216) 623-7560

Area Office on Aging
P.O. Box F351, Akron 44308
Barbara Love, (216) 376-9172

District 11 Area Agency on Aging
112 West Commerce Plaza, Suite 303, Youngstown 44503
Martha Murphy

Oklahoma (*Federal Region VI*)

Special Unit on Aging, Department of Institutions, Social and
    Rehabilitative Services
P.O. Box 25352, Oklahoma City 73125
Roy R. Keen, Director, (405) 521-2281

NECO Area Agency on Aging
P.O. Drawer E, Vinita 74301
Fred Gates, (918) 256-6478

EODD Area Agency on Aging
P.O. Box 1367, Muskogee 74401
Scott Moxom, (918) 682-7891

KEDDO Area Agency on Aging
P.O. Box 638, Wilburton 74578
Larry Duke, (918) 465-2367

SODA Area Agency on Aging Association
P.O. Box 848, 16 E Street SW, Ardmore 73401
Kenneth Hollingsworth, (405) 226-2250

COEDD Area Agency on Aging
16 East 9th Street, Shawnee 74801
Jan George Womack, (405) 521-3609/3944

Tulsa Area Agency on Aging
Room 214, 200 Civic Center, Tulsa 74103
Boyd Talley, (918) 518-5430-5439

NODA Area Agency on Aging
1800 South Van Buren, Enid 73701
Marcia Miller, (405) 237-4810

Areawide Aging Agency, Inc.
P.O. Box 1474, 125 NW 5th Street, Oklahoma City 73102
Charlotte Heard, (405) 236-2426

ASCOG Area Agency on Aging
802 Main Street, P.O. Box 17, Duncan 73533
Gene Werner, (405) 252-0595

SWODA Area Agency on Aging
P.O. Box 569, Burns Flat 73624
Dwayne King, (405) 562-4886

Oregon (*Federal Region X*)

Office of Elderly Affairs, Department of Human Resources
772 Commercial Street SE, Salem 97310
Marvin M. Janzen, Administrator, (503) 378-4728

District 1 Area Agency on Aging
Box 488, Cannon Deach 97110
Victor L. Stamm, (503) 436-1156

Clackamas County Area Agency on Aging
P.O. Box 32, Marylhurst 97036
Lyle Remington, (503) 655-8465

County Aging Programs, Washington County
Room 405, Administration Building, 150 North 1st Avenue,
   Hillsboro 97123
Robert J. Tepper, (503) 640-3489

Bureau of Human Resources, Aging Services Division
522 SW 5th Street, 8th floor, Portland 97204
Robert Holdridge, (503) 248-4752

District 3 Area Agency on Aging, Mid-Wilamette Valley Council of
   Governments
4th floor, Senator Building, 220 High Street NE, Salem 97301
Ed Sage, (503) 588-6177

Tri County Area Agency on Aging
No. 7 Wellsher Building, 460 SW Madison Street, Corvallis 97330
Betty Johnson, (503) 757-6851

District 5 Area Agency on Aging, Lane Council of Governments
Lane County Public Service Building, North Plaza Level, 125 8th Avenue,
    Eugene 97401
(503) 687–4283

Douglas County Program on Aging
Douglas County Courthouse, Room 309, 1034 SE Douglas Street,
    Roseburg 97490
John De Groot, (503) 672–3311

Coos-Curry Council of Governments
P.O. Box 647, North Bend 97459
Mark Bean, (503) 757–2563

District 8 Area Agency on Aging
33 North Central, Room 211, Medford 97501
Don Bruland, (503) 779–9134

Mid-Columbia Area Agency on Aging
Wasco County Courthouse, Annex B, 502 East 5th Street, The Dalles 97058
Keith Sutton, (503) 297–2266

Eastern Central Oregon Association of Counties
P.O. Box 339, Pendleton 97801
Rollin Reynolds, (503) 276–6734

Pennsylvania (*Federal Region III*)

Office for the Aging, Department of Public Welfare
Health and Welfare Building, Room 511, P.O. Box 2675, 7th and Forster
    Street, Harrisburg 17120
Robert T. Huber, Acting Commissioner, (717) 787–5350

Erie County Area Agency on Aging, Greater Erie Community Action
    Commission
18 West 9th Street, Erie 16501
Richard Browdie, (818) 454–4581

Crawford County Office of Aging
915 Liberty Street, Meadville 16335
Pauline Mooney, (814) 336–1580

North Central Pennsylvania Office of Human Services
208 Main Street, Ridgway 15853
Yolanda Jeselnick, (814) 776-2191

Beaver/Butler Area Agency on Aging
224 Beaver Street, Fallston 15066
R. Brandon James, (412) 728-2242

Indian County Area Agency on Aging
Indian Springs Road, Heatherbrae Square, Indiana 15701
Carole Ling, (412) 329-4500

Allegheny County Area Agency on Aging
1706 Allegheny Building, 429 Forbes Avenue, Pittsburgh 15219
Nancy Van Vuuren, (412) 355-4349

Westmoreland County Office of Aging
524 East Pittsburgh Street, Greensburg 15601
William Zalot, (412) 836-1111

Mon Valley Health and Welfare Council
Mon Valley Community Health Center, Eastgate 8, Monessen 15062
Bob Willison, (412) 684-9000

Somerset County Office for the Aging
147 East Union Street, P.O. Box 30, Somerset 15501
Martha Garman, (814) 443-2681

Cambria County Area Agency on Aging
R.D. 3, Box 429A, Ebensburg 15931
John W. Waterstream, (814) 472-5580

Blair County Office of Services for the Aging
1512 12th Avenue, Altoona 16601
Daniel Ainscough, (814) 946-1237

Bedford/Fulton/Huntingdon Area Agency on Aging
231 Juliana Street, Bedford 15522
Jeane McClure, (814) 623-8149

Centre County Area Agency on Aging
Centre Community Hospital, 2d floor, Willow Bank Unit, Bellafonte 16823
Cynthia Edvar, (814) 355-7861

Lycoming/Clinton Bi-County Office of Aging
P.O. Box 770, 352 East Water Street, Lock Haven 17745
Virginia Crosby, (717) 748–8665

Columbia/Montour Area Agency on Aging
243 West Main Street, Bloomsburg 17815
Robert LeVan, (717) 784–9272

Northumberland County Area Agency on Aging
235 West Sprice Street, Shamokin 17872
Michael Johnson, (717) 648–6828

Union/Snyder County Office of Aging
404 East Main Street, Middleburg 17842
Farida Zaid, (717) 837–0675

Mifflin/Juniata Area Agency on Aging
Buena Vista Circle, Lewistown 17044
Carlene Hack, (717) 242–0315

Franklin County Office for the Aging
Franklin Farm Lane, Chambersburg 17201
Robert Keith, (717) 263–2153

Adams County Area Agency on Aging
26 North Washington Street, Gettysburg 17325
Susan Yenchko, (717) 334–9577

Cumberland County Office on Aging
35 East High Street, Carlisle 17013
Jacqueline Nowak, (717) 243–8442

Perry County Office for the Aging
Court House Annex, South Carlisle Street, New Bloomfield 17068
Herbert Stewart, (717) 582–2131

Dauphin County Area Agency on Aging
17 South Second Street, Harrisburg 17101
Lewis L. Crippen, (717) 255–2877

Lebanon County Area Agency on Aging
710 Maple Street, Room 209, Senior Centers, Lebanon 17042
Michael Kristovensky, (717) 273–9262

York County Area Agency on Aging
125 East Market Street, York 17401
Kathleen Boas, (717) 846-4884

Lancaster County Office of Aging
50 North Duke Street, Lancaster 17602
Peter Dys, (717) 299-7979

Chester County Services for Senior Citizens
14 East Biddle Street, West Chester 19380
Wayne Stevenson, (215) 431-6350

Office on Older Adults
Montgomery County Court House,
One Montgomery Plaza, 4th floor, Norristown 19401
Edward Keenan, (215) 275-5000

Bucks County Adult Services
Neshaminy Manor Center, Doylestown 18901
Margaret O'Neill, (215) 343-2800

Delaware County Services for the Aging
322 West State Street, P.O. Box 166, Media 19063
John Bauer, (215) 565-4427

Philadelphia Corporation of Aging
1317 Filbert Street, Room 420, Philadelphia 19107
Rodney Williams, (215) 241-8200

Berks County Area Agency on Aging
124 South 5th Street, Reading 19602
Peter Archey, (215) 378-1635/1856

Lehigh County Area Agency on Aging
Court House Annex, 532 Hamilton Street, Allentown 18101
Peter Johnstone, (215) 434-9471

Northhampton County Area Agency on Aging
204 Northhampton Street, Easton 18042
Beverly Corkhill, (215) 253-9321

Wayne/Pike/Area Agency on Aging
314 10th Street, Honesdale 18431
Margaret Nuttycombe, (717) 253-5535

Area Agency on Aging, Northern Tier Regional Planning and Development
  Commission
507 Main Street, Honesdale 18431
Carole McLellan, (717) 265-9103

Luzerne/Wyoming Counties Office for Aging
85 East Union Street, Wilkes Barre 18701
Charles Adams, (717) 822-1158

Lackawanna County Area Agency on Aging
Lackawanna County Office Building, 200 Adans Avenue, Scranton 18503
Michael Rodgers, (717) 961-6707

Carbon County Area Agency on Aging
P.O. Box 251, Jim Thorpe 18229
Leonard Marzen, (717) 325-2726

Schuylkill County Area Agency on Aging
2d and Norwegian Streets, Pottsville 17901
Steve Schwalm, (717) 622-3103, (800) 832-3313

Clearfield County Office of Aging
P.O. Box 906, 121 South 2d Street, Clearfield 16830
Jack Frisch, (814) 765-2696

Jefferson County Office of Aging
R.D. No. 1 (Old Jefferson Manor), Brookville 15825
Shirley Sharp, (814) 849-3096

Area Agency on Aging, (Forest and Warren Counties) Experience, Inc.,
900 4th Avenue, P.O. Box 886, Warren 16365
W. Robert Walsh, (814) 726-1700

Clarion/Venango Area Agency on Aging, Venango County Bureau of
  Human Services
P.O. Box 231, Franklin 16323
Lois Daley, (814) 437-6821

Armstrong County Area Agency on Aging
200 Oak Avenue, Kittanning 16201
Wendell Davis, (412) 548-8205

Lawrence County Office on Aging
20 South Mercer Street, New Castle 10101
Myra Wolcott, (412) 658-5661

Mercer County Area Agency on Aging
Mercer County Court House, Mercer 16137
Ann Marie Spiardi, (412) 662-3800

Monroe County Area Agency on Aging
154 Washington Street, East Stroudsburg 18301
Dorothy Kaufman, (717) 424-5290

Rhode Island (*Federal Region I*)

Rhode Island Department of Elderly Affairs
79 Washington Street, Providence 02903
Anna M. Tucker, Director, (401) 277-2858

South Carolina (*Federal Region IV*)

Commission on Aging
915 Main Street, Columbia 29201
Harry Bryan, Director, (803) 758-2576

South Carolina Appalachian Council of Governments
211 Century Drive, P.O. Drawer 6668, Greenville 29606
Yvonne Simpson, (803) 242-9733

Upper Savannah Council of Governments
P.O. Box 1366, Greenwood 29646
Miriam Patterson, (803) 229-6627

Catawba Regional Aging Program
SCN Center Suite 300, 100 Dave Lyle Boulevard, Rock Hill 29730
Sandra Howie, (803) 327-9041

Council Aging Program, Central Midlands Regional Planning
Suite 155, Dutch Plaza, 800 Dutch Square Boulevard, Columbia 29210
George Dick, (803) 798-1243

Lower Savannah Council of Governments
P.O. Box 850, Highway 215, Aiken 29801
Connie L. Heider, (803) 649-7981

Santee-Lynches Council for Governments
36 East Calhoun Street, P.O. Box 1837, Sumter 29150
James A. Crawford, (803) 775-7382

Pee Dee Regional Planning and Development Program for the Aging
P.O. Box 5719, Darlington Highway, Florence 29502
Hampton MacIntyre, (803) 669–3138

Waccamaw Regional Planning and Development Council,
P.O. Drawer 419, 1001 Front Street, Georgetown 29440
Linda Coker, (803) 546–8502

Trident Area Program for the Aging
P.O. Box 2696, 106 King Street, Charleston 29403
Leslie Jamison, (803) 723–1676

Lowcountry Council of Governments,
P.O. Box 98, Point South, Yemassee 29945
Sue Scally, (803) 726–5536/5538

South Dakota (*Federal Region VIII*)

Office of Adult Services and Aging, Department of Social Services
Richard F. Kneip Building, Illinois Street, Pierre 57501
Sylvia Base, Administrator, (605) 773–3656

Texas (*Federal Region VI*)

The Governor's Committee on Aging, Office of the Governor
P.O. Box 12786, Capitol Station, Austin 78711
Vernon McDaniel, Director, (512) 475–2717

Panhandle Area Agency on Aging
P.O. Box 9257, Amarillo 79104
Mike McQueen, (806) 372–3381

South Plains Area Agency on Aging
1611 Avenue M, Lubbock 79401
Betty J. Shannon, (806) 762–8721

North Texas Area Agency on Aging
2101 Kemp Boulevard, Wichita Falls 76309
Yvonne Null, (817) 322–5281

North Central Texas Area Agency on Aging
P.O. Drawer COG, Arlington 76011
John Bruni, (817) 640–3300

Dallas County Area Agency on Aging
212 North Saint Paul, 1725 Corrigan Tower, Dallas 75201
Norman Moorehead, (214) 741-5851

Tarrant County Area Agency on Aging
210 East 9th Street, Fort Worth 76102
Wilton G. Jewell, (817) 335-3473

Arkansas–Texas Area Agency on Aging
P.O. Box 5307, Texarkana 75501
Beverly Cherney, (214) 794-3481

East Texas Area Agency on Aging
5th floor, Citizens Bank Building, Kilgore 75662
Claude Andrews, (214) 984-8641

West Central Texas Area Agency on Aging
P.O. Box 3195, 3349 North 12th Street, Abilene 79604
Chris Kyker, (915) 672-8544

West Texas Area Agency on Aging
The Mills Building, Suite 700, 303 North Oregon Street, El Paso 79901
Mario Griffin, (915) 532-2910

Permian Basin Area Agency on Aging
P.O. Box 6391, Midland 79701
W.E. Smith, (915) 563-1061

Concho Valley Area Agency on Aging
17 South Chadbourne, Suite 200, San Angelo 76903
Odene Crawford, (915) 653-1214

Heart of Texas Area Agency on Aging
110 South 12th Street Waco 76701
Cathy Terrell, (817) 756-6631

Capital Area Agency on Aging
611 South Congress, Suite 400, Austin 78704
Conley Kemper, (512) 443-7653

Brazos Valley Area Agency on Aging
P.O. Drawer 4128, 3006 East 29th Street, Bryan 77801
Roberta Lindquist, (713) 822-7421

Deep East Texas Area Agency on Aging
272 East Lamar Street, Jasper 75951
Martha Jones, (713) 384–5704

South East Texas Area Agency on Aging
P.O. Drawer 1387, Nederland 77627
James H. Robb, (713) 727–2384

Houston–Galveston Area Agency on Aging
P.O. Box 22777, Houston 77027
Paul Ulrich, (713) 627–3200

Harris County Area Agency on Aging
1010 Louisiana, Suite 910, Houston 77002
Raul De Los Santos, (713) 222–4445

Golden Crescent Area Agency on Aging
P.O. Box 2028, Victoria 77901
Betty Beck, (512) 578–1587

Alamo Area Council of Governments
Three Americas Building, Suite 400, San Antonio 78205
Frank Adamo, (512) 225–5201

Bexar County Area Agency on Aging
Three Americas Building, Suite 400, San Antonio 78205
Minnie Williams, (512) 225–5201

South Texas Area Agency on Aging
P.O. Box 2187, 600 South Sandman, Laredo International Airport,
    Laredo 78041
Lupita Rubio, (512) 722–3995

Coastal Bend Area Agency on Aging
P.O. Box 9909, Corpus Christi 78404
Bill Moore, (512) 883–5743

Lower Rio Grande Valley Area Agency on Aging
First National Bank Building, Suite 301/303, McAllen 78501
Gloria Saca, (512) 682–3481

Texoma Area Agency on Aging
10000 Grayson Drive, Denison 75020
Janis Gray, (214) 786–2955

Central Texas Area Agency on Aging
P.O. Box 729, Belton 76513
Dan Mizell, (817) 939-1801

Middle Rio Grande Area Agency on Aging
P.O. Box 1461, Del Rio 78840
Josefina Rowe, (512) 775-1581

Tennessee (*Federal Region IV*)

Commission on Aging
Room 102, S&P Building, 306 Gay Street, Nashville 37201
Tom Henry, Director, (615) 741-2056

First Tennessee-Virginia District Office on Aging
207 North Boone Street, Johnson City 37601
Tom Reece, (615) 928-0224

East Tennessee Human Resource Agency Office on Aging
4711 Old Kingston Pike, Knoxville 37919
Ann Elliott, (615) 584-0244

Southeast Tennessee Development District Office on Aging
James Building, 735 Broad Street, Chattanooga 37402
Viston Taylor, (615) 266-5781

Upper Cumberland Development District Office on Aging
300 Brugess Falls Road, Cookeville 38501
Nancy Peace, (615) 432-4111

Mid-Cumberland Development District Office on Aging
501 Union Building, 6th floor, 5th Avenue and Union Street,
    Nashville 37219
Rick Fowlkes, (615) 244-1212

South Central Tennessee Development District Office on Aging
805 Nashville Highway, Columbia 38401
Lowell Crawford, (615) 381-2040

Northwest Tennessee Development District Office on Aging
P.O. Box 63, Martin 38237
David Frizzell, (901) 587-4213

Southwest Tennessee Development District Office on Aging
P.O. Box 2385, Jackson 38310
Anne Lewis, (901) 668-1142

Memphis Delta Development District Office on Aging
1192 Vollintiae, Memphis 38107
Mary O. Coats, (901) 528-2600/2609

Utah (*Federal Region VIII*)

Division on Aging, Department of Social Services
150 West North Temple, Room 315, Box 2500, Salt Lake City 84102
Leon Povey, Director, (801) 533-6422

Bear River Area Agency on Aging, Cache County Aging Program,
236 North 100 E, Logan 84321
Robert Green, (801) 752-9456

Weber County Department on Aging
Human Services Building, 350 Healy Street, Ogden 84401
Ken Bradshaw, (801) 300-8318

Davis County Area Agency on Aging
Davis County Courthouse, Farmington 84025
Alice Johnson, (801) 295-2394

Salt Lake-Tooele Area Agency on Aging
Building No. 1 Basement, 2033 South State, Salt Lake City 84115
Shauna O'Neil, (801) 487-1344

Mountainland Area Agency on Aging
160 East Center Street, Provo 84601
Pat Bersie, (801) 377-2262

Center Utah Aging Programs,
Courthouse, Junction 84740
Robert Teichart, (801) 577-2834

District V Area Agency on Aging
P.O. Box O, St. George 84770
Gayla Foster, (801) 673-3548

Uintah Basin Area Agency on Aging
P.O. Box 1449, Roosevelt 84066
(801) 722-4518

Ute-Ouray Area Agency on Aging
P.O. Box 67, Fort Duchesne 84026
Robert Holmes, (801) 772-5141

Southeastern Utah Area Agency on Aging
P.O. Drawer A-1, Price 84501
William Howell, (801) 637-4268

Vermont (*Federal Region I*)

Office on Aging, Agency of Human Services
Waterbury Office Complex, State Office Building, Montpelier 05602
Pearl Somaini-Dayer, Director, (802) 241-2400

Southeastern Vermont Area Agency on Aging
139 Main Street, Brattleboro 05301
Geoffrey Gaddis, (802) 257-0569

Area Agency on Aging for Northeastern Vermont
44 Main Street, Box 640, St. Johnsbury 05819
Merry Brewer, (802) 748-5182

Champlain Valley Area Agency on Aging
179 South Winooski Avenue, Burlington 05401
Mary Ellen Spencer, (802) 862-3734

Bennington-Rutland Area Agency on Aging
135 North Main Street, Rutland 05701
Charles Sherman, (802) 775-0486

Central Vermont Area Agency on Aging
295 North Main Street, Barre 05641
Craig Hammond, (802) 479-0531

Virginia (*Federal Region III*)

Office on Aging
830 East Main Street, Suite 950, Richmond 23219
Edwin L. Wood, Director, (804) 786-7894

Mountain Empire Older Citizens
330 Norton, P.O. Box 1097, Wise 24293
Marilyn Pace, (703) 328-2303

Appalachian Agency for Senior Citizens
Box SVCC, Richlands 24641
Roger Sword, (703) 964-4915

Senior Citizens Services Division, District 3 Governmental Cooperative
110 Strother Street, Marion 24354
George Tulli, Jr., (703) 783-8158

New River Valley Agency on Aging
143 3d Street N.W., Pulaski 24301
Mary Elyn Lauth, (703) 980-8888

League of Older Americans
401 West Campbell Avenue, Roanoke 24016
Richard Young, (703) 345-0451

Valley Program for Aging Services, Inc.
P.O. Box 817, Waynesboro 22980
Ruth Perry, (703) 942-7141

Shenandoah Area Agency on Aging, Inc.
Route 1, Box 329 A, Winchester 22601
Michael Toht, (703) 869-4100

Alexandria Area Agency on Aging
115 North Patrick Street, Alexandria 22314
Susan Parry, (703) 750-6609

Arlington Area Agency on Aging
Arlington Court House, Room 204, Arlington 22201
Karen Evans, (703) 338-2401

Fairfax County Area Agency on Aging
4100 Chain Bridge Road, Fairfax 22314
Donna Foster, (703) 691-3384

Coordinator of Senior Services
18 North King Street, Leesburg 22075
Kathleen Bocek, (703) 777-0257

Coordinator of Senior Citizen Services
Office of Personnel, Prince William County, 9300 Peabody Street,
  Manassas 22110
Stephanie R. Egly, (703) 368-9171

City Hall Area Agency on Aging
300 Park Avenue, Falls Church 22046
Charlene Costello, (703) 241-5100

Rappahannock-Rapidan Area Agency on Aging
01 South Main Street, Culpepper 22701
Sallie Stemple, (703) 825-6494

Jefferson Area Board for Aging
415 8th Street N.E., Charlottesville 22901
Jim Elmore, (804) 977-3444

Central Virginia Commission on Aging
Forest Hill Center, Linkhorne Drive, Lynchburg 24503
Wallace Clair, (804) 384-0372

Piedmont Seniors of Virginia, Inc.
29 Broad Street, Martinsville 24112
June Gay, (703) 632-6442

Southside Office on Aging, Inc.
Brunswick County Courthouse Building, P.O. Box 726,
  Lawrenceville 23868
T.H.E. Jones, (804) 848-4433

Piedmont Senior Resources, Inc.
P.O. Box 398, Burkeville 23922
Ronald Dunn, (804) 767-5588

Capital Area Agency on Aging
6 North 6th Street, Richmond 23219
Louis Barretta, (804) 648-9391

Rappahannock Area Agency on Aging, Inc.
601 Caroline Street, 3d floor, Fredicksburg 22401
Frank Beddow, (703) 371-3375

Northern Neck-Middle Peninsula Area Agency on Aging Inc.
P.O. Box 387, Saluda 23149
Allyn Gemerek, (804) 758-2386

Crater District Area Agency on Aging
P.O. Box 1808, Petersburg 23803
Richard Bull, (804) 732–7020

SEVAMP
16 Koger Executive Center, Suite 145, Norfolk 23502
Kathleen Donoghue, (804) 461–9481

Peninsula Agency on Aging, Inc.
944 Denbigh Boulevard, Newport News 23602
Betty Reams, (804) 874–2495

Eastern Shore Community Development Group, Inc.
P.O. Box 316, Accomac 23301
William Davies, (804) 787–3532

Washington (*Federal Region X*)

Bureau of Aging, Department of Social and Health Services,
OB–43G, Olympia 98504
Charles Reed, Director, (206) 753–2502

Olympic Area Agency on Aging
P.O. Box 31, Montesano 98563
Terry Loughran, (206) 249–5736, SCAN 234–2632

Northwest Washington Area on Aging, Northwest Regional Council
Forest Street Annex of the Whatcom County Courthouse, 1000 Forest
    Street, Bellingham 98225
Dewey Desler, (206) 676–6749, SCAN 644–6749

Snohomish County Area Agency on Aging, Grants Administration Office
4th floor, County Administration Building, Everett 98201
Liz Roberts, (206) 259–9521, SCAN 649–9521

King County Area Agency on Aging
400 Yesler Building, Seattle 98104
Mark Stensager, (206) 625–4711, SCAN 861–4711

Area Agency on Aging No. 5
2401 South 35th Street, Pierce County Annex No. 15, Tacoma 98409
Bonnie McMahon, (206) 593–4828, SCAN 462–2494

Lewis/Mason/Thurston Area Agency on Aging
P.O. Box 1304, Chehelis 98532
Christine Spaulding, (206) 748-9121, (800) 562-6130

Southwest Washington Area Agency on Aging
P.O. Box 425, Vancouver 98666
Patricia Anderson, (206) 694-6577

North Central Washington Area Agency on Aging
1300 5th Street, Wenatchee 98801
Jack Charlton, (509) 662-1651, SCAN 241-2640

Yakima-Southeast Washington Area Agency on Aging
708 North 16th Avenue, Yakima 98901
Becky Martelli, (509) 575-4226/4331, SCAN 665-4226

Yakima Indian Nation Area Agency on Aging
P.O. Box 311, Toppenish 98948
Arlene Olney, (509) 865-4443

Spokane Co. Area Agency on Aging
West 1101 College Avenue, Suite 160, Public Health Building,
   Spokane 99201
Ted Stevens, (509) 327-3341

Colville Indian Area Agency on Aging
P.O. Box 150, Nespelem 99155
Margaret Rochelle, (509) 634-4203

West Virginia (*Federal Region III*)

West Virginia Commission on Aging
State Capitol, Charleston 25305
Louise B. Gerrard, Director, (304) 348-3317

Region 1 Area Agency on Aging, Region 1 Planning and Development
   Council
P.O. Box 1442, Princeton 24740
Sharon Hondos, (304) 425-9508

Southwestern Area Agency on Aging, Southwestern Community Action
   Council, Inc.
540 5th Avenue, Huntington 25701
Charles Karschnik, (304) 525-5151

Region 3 Area Agency on Aging, Community Council of Kanawha Valley,
  Inc.
702½ Lee Street, Charleston 25301
Gail Dreyer, (304) 342–5107

Eastern Highlands Area Agency on Aging, Nicholas County Community
  Action Association
909 Broad Street, Summerville 26651
Tim Bailes, (304) 872–1162

Region 5 Area Agency on Aging, Mid-Ohio Valley Regional Council
217 4th Street, Parkersburg 26101
Peggy Rush, (304) 422–0522, 485–3801

Region 6 Area Agency on Aging, Region 6 Planning and Development
  Council
201 Deveny Building, Fairmont 26554
Donald Spencer, (304) 366–5693

Region 7 Area Agency on Aging, Region 7 Planning and Development
  Council
64 West Main Street, Buckhannon 26201
Betty Burgess Betler, (304) 472–0395

Regions 8/9 Area Agency on Aging, Region 8 Planning and Development
  Council
P.O. Box 305, Petersburg 26847
Chris Franklin, (304) 257–4166

Northern Panhandle Area Agency on Aging, Bel-O-Mar Regional Council
2177 National Road, Wheeling 26003
A. Paul Holdren, (304) 242–1800

Wisconsin (*Federal Region V*)

Bureau of Aging, Department of Health and Social Services
One West Wilson Street, Room 700, Madison 53702
Douglas W. Nelson, Director, (608) 266–2536

Area Agency on Aging, District 1
1245 East Washington Avenue, Madison 53703
Arthur Hendrick, (608) 256–4460

Area Agency on Aging, District 2A
1442 North Farwell Avenue, Milwaukee 53202
Fred Lindner, (414) 278-4283

Area Agency on Aging, District 2B
500 Riverview Avenue, Room 204, Waukesha 53186
Charles F. Parthum, Jr., (414) 547-1573

Area Agency on Aging, District 3
314 West Wisconsin Avenue, Suite 8-9, Appleton 54911
Harry Collins, (414) 739-9531

Area Agency on Aging, District 4
1221 Bellevue Avenue, Green Bay 54302
James Kellerman, (414) 465-1662

Area Agency on Aging, District 5
Grandview Building, 1707 Main Street, La Crosse 54601
Larry White, (608) 784-4360

Area Agency on Aging, District 6
318 Eau Claire Street, Eau Claire 54701
Rosemary Howard, (715) 836-4105

North Central Area Agency on Aging
City Hall, 1004 East 1st Street, Merrill 54452
Barbara White, (715) 536-8323

Area Agency on Aging, District 8
Hayward Lakes Realty Building, 301 West 1st Street, P.O. Box 526,
   Hayward 54843
James Gratehouse, (715) 634-2464

Wyoming (*Federal Region VIII*)

Aging Services, Department of Health and Social Services
Hathaway Building, Room 372, Cheyenne 82002
Stan Torvik, Director, (307) 777-7561

Eastern Wyoming Area Agency on Aging
2125 Cy Avenue, Casper 82601
Carol Smith, (307) 265-1365

Western Wyoming Area Agency on Aging
205 Masonic Temple Building, Riverton 82501
Marjorie Woods, (307) 856-6378

Area Agency on Aging
Box 585, Arroyo 00615
Edna Rodriguez, (809) 839-3010

Area Agency on Aging
Box 178, Hunacao 00661

Area Agency on Aging
Box 447, Mayaguez 00708
Rogelio Casasus, (809) 833-4536

Area Agency on Aging
Box 5173, Ponce 00731
Luis A. Rolon, (809) 844-3195

Human Resources Department
Box 3632, Old San Juan Station, San Juan 00904
Eva Freyre, (809) 723-0077, 723-1129

Trust Territory of the Pacific (*Federal Region IX*)

Office of Aging, Community Development Division
Government of the Trust Territory of the Pacific Islands, Saipan, Mariana
    Islands 96950
Leona Peterson, Director, overseas operator 2134

Virgin Islands (*Federal Region II*)

Commission on Aging
P.O. Box 539, Charlotte Amalie, St. Thomas 00801
Gloria M. King, Director, (809) 774-5884

American Samoa (*Federal Region IX*)

Territorial Aging Program
Government of American Samoa, Office of the Governor,
    Pago Pago 96920
Tali Maae, Director, overseas operator Samoa 3-1254 or 3-4116

Guam (*Federal Region IX*)

Office of Aging, Department of Public Health and Social Service
P.O. Box 2816, Agana 96910
Joaquin Camucho, Director, (???) 749-9901

Puerto Rico (*Federal Region II*)

Gericulture Commission, Department of Social Services
Box 11398, Santurce 00910
Alicia Ramirez Suarez, Director, (809) 722-2429, 724-7400

Area Agency on Aging
Box 3997, Aguadilla 00603
Edgardo J. Rosa, (809) 891-1095

Area Agency on Aging
67 Cristobal Colon, Arecibo 00612
Olga Rodriguez, (809) 878-4095

Area Agency on Aging
Building C, Ruiz Soler Hospital, Road No. 2 Km. 8.6, Bayamon 00619
Gilbert Broco, Jr., (809) 781-5861

Area Agency on Aging
Box 6351, Caguas 00625
Fe Sotomayor, (809) 743-6867

Area Agency on Aging
100 East Ignacio Arzuago Street, Caeolina 00630
Maria D. Carrasquillo, (809) 752-4275

9

Education and Training Materials: Films, Booklets and Pamphlets, Educational Programs

Films

Aims Instructional Media Services, Inc.
626 Justin Avenue
Glendale, CA 91201
(213) 240–9300

> *Crime in the Streets* (18 minutes)
> Emphasizes prevalence of crime in the streets and need for care in avoiding dangerous places and circumstances. Many stereotypical situations featuring young people are depicted. Attack scenes are vivid and could tend to arouse considerable anxiety in an older population.

> *Rape Alert* (17 minutes)
> Advocates alertness and awareness of self-defense measures in the prevention of rape. Some myths regarding rape are discussed. Emphasizes importance of reporting all attempts and completed rapes to the police. Illustrated situations feature young women but film is applicable to all ages.

> *Rape—The Right to Resist* (17 minutes)
> Stresses the belief that women of all ages should be physically and mentally prepared to prevent physical attacks. Emphasizes the importance of self-defense and confidence to do anything necessary to thwart an attacker. Although the rape-defense class has a seventy-five-year old woman in it, advice is directed mainly toward younger women.

Aptos Film Productions, Inc.
792 Seward Street
Los Angeles, CA 90038
(213) 462–1241

> *Beware of Strangers* (20 minutes)
> Rape is a crime of opportunity. Film presents various ways of reducing the opportunity while outside, in cars, and at home. Presents practical

161

advice while confronting the rapist, although this is not directed specifically toward the elderly.

Invitation to Burglary (20 minutes)
Specific hardware presentations with personal tips applicable for use with community groups, apartment dwellers, and home residents.

Charles S. MacCrone Productions
8048 Soquel Drive, Suite H
Aptos, CA 95003
(408) 688-1040

> *Neighborhood Watch*
> Encourages neighborhood crime prevention programs, identification of valuables, and use of hardware and various alarm systems. Especially applicable for presentation to suburban residents but valuable for explicit presentations of hardware and alarm systems. Some elements of community organization.

> *Vulnerable to Attack*
> Stresses obtaining knowledge of protective procedures to obtain a meaningful margin of safety. Also stresses alertness to safety strategies in varied situations. Film is most appropriate for use with young women.

Dr. Mary Conroy
Department of Physical Education
California State University of Los Angeles
5151 State University Drive
Los Angeles, CA 90032
(213) 224-3216

> *Common Sense Self-Defense* (27 minutes)
> An educational and entertaining film that teaches the three strategies of self-defense: how to eliminate danger from daily living, how to recognize and avoid danger, and how to fight when necessary. Depicts older women confronting attackers.

Film Fair Communications
10900 Ventura Boulevard
Studio City, CA 91604
(213) 985-0244

> *Nobody's Victim* (20 minutes)
> Film covers basics of avoidance methods in varied situations and emphasizes escape as the main defense with easily learned physical self-

defense techniques. Geared for the young, suburban woman but has merit for all women viewers.

Motorola Teleprograms, Inc.
4825 North Scott Street, Suite 26
Schiller Park, IL 60176
(312) 671-1565

Crime, It's a Matter of Time—Residential (13 minutes)
Film makes several important statements: (1) There is a wide range of criminals; (2) burglary is the easiest crime to commit; (3) burglary is the most frequently committed crime in our society; (4) homeowners contribute greatly to its high incidence by making it easy for crime to occur. Humorous presentation of crimes has impact. Should be used with other films that stress prevention methods.

Rape: A Preventive Inquiry (18 minutes) (produced by the J. Gary Mitchell Film Company)
Film produced in cooperation with the Sex Crimes Detail of the San Francisco Police Department. Interviews with four rape/assault victims and four convicted rapists responsible for the rape/assault of over 125 victims. Gives practical advice; emphasizes awareness and avoidance techniques of not becoming a murder statistic. Film has considerable impact for all ages.

Pyramid Films
2801 Colorado Avenue
Santa Monica, CA 90404
(213) 828-7577

Lady Beware (16 minutes)
Promotes cultivating an awareness of danger in conjunction with many options for action for women of all ages. Should be used with another more age-specific film such as *Senior Power—And How to Use It!*

Sid Davis Productions
1144 South Robertson Boulevard
Los Angeles, CA 90035
(213) 278-5626

Beware the Rapist (20 minutes)
The avoidance of situations where rape might occur is suggested as the prevention measure. Many fundamental precautions are given for self-protection through avoidance behaviors. Does not encourage use of physical counterattack measures.

William Brose Productions, Inc.
10850 Riverside Drive
North Hollywood, CA 91602
(213) 760-0066

> *Senior Power—And How to Use It!* (19 minutes)
> Film advocates simple nonphysical lifestyle practices for older people.
> Positive approaches are made with humor. Recommended for use with
> groups of older women.

Booklets and Pamphlets

AARP–NRTA
1909 K Street NW
Washington, DC 20049

> *Your Retirement Anti-Crime Guide*

American Friends Service Committee
1501 Cherry Street
Philadelphia, PA 19102

> *Rape Resistance, Friendly Woman*

California Crime Prevention Unit
    Office of the California Attorney General
3580 Wilshire Boulevard, Suite 938
Los Angeles, CA 90010

> *On Guard: Nobody's Victim*
> *On Guard: Residential Security—And what to do about it*
> *On Guard: Safe Practices for Women at Night in Automobiles*
> *Crime Prevention Tips*

Center for Rape Concern
112 South 16th Street
Philadelphia, PA 19102

> *Rape*

Channing L. Bete Company, Inc.
45 Federal Street
Greenfield, MA 01301

What Every Woman Should Know about Rape
What Every Woman Should Know about Self-Protection

Cheltenham Township Police Department
8230 Old York Road
Elkins Park, PA 19117

Cheltenham Alert Neighbors Program

Chicago Illinois Department of Police
Public and Internal Information Division
1121 South State Street
Chicago, IL 60605

Out after Dark
Safety in the Streets for Senior Citizens
Protect Your High-Rise Apartment Office

Citizens Local Alliance for a Safer Philadelphia
1710 Spruce Street
Philadelphia, PA 19103

Hints for Human Safety
Holiday Shopping Safety Hints
Senior Citizen's Safety Hints
Freon Horns Make Your Neighborhood Safer—Safety Hints for Use of
*   Freon Horns*
Any Block Can . . .
For Block Safety, Senior Citizens Are Needed To:

Dallas, Texas
SER–MDTA Project
4332 Maple Avenue
Dallas, TX 75219

We Are Women: How to Defend Ourselves against Rape

Detroit Police Department
3165 Second Street
Detroit, MI 48201

Detroit Police Department Personal Safety Tips for Women at Home and
*   Protective Measures to Prevent Rape*
What You Should Know about Locks for Commercial Buildings
Burglary Prevention

Lane Inter-Agency Rape Team
125 East Eighth Street
Room 100
Eugene, OR 97401

Take Steps to Take Care

Mansfield Police Department
30 North Diamond Street
Mansfield, OH 44902

Rape

Maryland Center for Public Broadcasting
P.O. Box 1977
Owings Mills, MD 21117

Surelock Homes (Consumer Survival Kit)

Metro's Rape Awareness Public Education Program
1515 NW Seventh Street, Suite 215
Miami Beach, FL 33125

Rape Awareness—Precautions and Tactics to Avoid Rape

Miami Beach Police Department Community Relations Section
Crime Prevention Unit
120 Meridian Avenue
Miami Beach, FL 33139

Rape: Help Stop Crime
Operation CAP (Citizen Awareness Program)—How to Foil a Mugger

Mid-American Regional Council
20 West Ninth Street
Third Floor
Kansas City, MS 64105

Home Security
You Can Do Something to Protect Yourself from Robbery and Purse
*   Theft on the Street*
Burglary and Robbery in Your Home

Milwaukee County Neighborhood Security Aid Program
Courthouse, Room 1
901 North Ninth Street
Milwaukee, WI 53233

Home Protection Techniques
Tips for Women
Advice on Home Security

New York Police Department Crime Prevention Section
137 Centre Street
New York, NY 10013

Safety Tips for the Older Person

New York Police Department Sex Crimes Analysis Unit
1 Police Plaza, Room 1312
New York, NY 10038

Protective Measures to Prevent Rape
Rape: How To Keep It from Happening to You
Guide to Medical Services Following Sexual Assault

Pennsylvania Commission for Women
512 Finance Building
Harrisburg, PA 17128

Help for the Rape Victim: A Pennsylvania Commission for Women
    Resource Guide, 1975.

Pennsylvania State Police Troop K
2201 Belmont Avenue
Philadelphia, PA 19131

Lady Beware: Criminal Assaults on Women

Philadelphia Police Department
Eight and Race Streets
Philadelphia, PA 19106

Help Prevent Crimes against Women
How Do I Protect My Home?
Your Purse Is Their Target

Philadelphia Police Department
Eight and Race Streets
Philadelphia, PA 19106

Apartment Security
Security Suggestions for Senior Citizen
Burglary and What To Do About It

Rape Crisis Center of Syracuse, Inc.
709 Park Street
Syracuse, NY 13208

> *Precautions for the Elderly*
> *Rape Response for the Older Woman*

University of Pennsylvania, Security and Safety Department
3914 Locust Walk
Philadelphia, PA 19104

> *Take Care*
> *I Never Thought It Would Happen to Me*

Washington, D.C., Rape Crisis Center
P.O. Box 21005
Washington, DC 20009

> *Rape Prevention Tactics*
> *Why Women Need Self-Defense—Theoretical Discussion*
> *Effects of Self Defense*

Women Against Rape (Detroit)
2445 West 8 Mile Road
Detroit, MI 48203

> *Stop Rape*

Women Organized Against Rape
1220 Sansom Street
Philadelphia, PA 19107

> *Rape Prevention Tactics and Self-Defense Tips*

Wynnefield Resident Association
P.O. Box 4535
Philadelphia, PA 19131

> *Guidelines for Home and Neighborhood Security by SAW (Secure All*
> *Wynnefield)*

Educational Programs

AARP—NRTA
1909 K Street NW
Washington, DC 20049

Preventing Crime through Education
A four-part crime-prevention program featuring street crime, burglary, fraud bunco, and community police relations. Program includes planning instructions, a news release, scripts, films, and the use of a resource person in the community.

American Friends Service Commission
1501 Cherry Street
Philadelphia, PA 19102

Rape Resistance, Friendly Woman
The author of this article presents workshops on rape resistance. These workshops stress the use of vocal, nonviolent resistance in rape situations.

Baltimore City Commission on Aging and Retirement Education
Waxter Center
861 Park Avenue
Baltimore, MD 21201

Crime Prevention Programs for the Elderly
A program designed to educate the elderly about crime, including the crime of assault. Stresses the need for the elderly to "prevent their own victimization."

California Crime Prevention Unit
Office of the California Attorney General
3580 Wilshire Boulevard, Suite 938
Los Angeles, CA 90010

Crime Prevention for the Elderly
Aims at educating the elderly about crime and training staff members of agencies for the elderly in crime prevention. Hopes to reduce not only crime itself but fear of crime.

Wilmington Crime Resistance Program
P.O. Box 1872
Wilmington, DE 19899

Crime Resistance (FBI)
Describes crime-resistance programs to be used primarily in the community. Details steps for setting up other programs of a similar nature.

Cheltenham Township Police Department
8230 Old York Road
Elkins, Park, PA 19117

Cheltenham Alert Neighbors Program
A community-based program that organizes neighborhoods to prevent crime by educating people to be alert to and report suspicious situations.

Chicago Department of Police Public and Internal Information Division
1121 South State Street
Chicago, IL 60605

The Prevention Programs Division of the Chicago Police Department
Provides several crime-prevention services. Included are providing crime-prevention training sessions and security surveys, helping community organizations develop defenses against crime, and arranging presentations featuring speakers, movies, or slides and demonstrations dealing with crime-related subjects.

Citizens Local Alliance for a Safer Philadelphia (CLASP)
260 South 15th Street, 7th floor
Philadelphia, PA 19102

CLASP
Program for citizen participation to prevent crime and promote safety. This program focuses on block organization.

County of Cuyahoga Office of Aging
Marion Building, Room 512
1276 West Third Street
Cleveland, OH 44113

Senior Safety and Security Program
Consists of two slide presentations: "How to Avoid Street Attacks," which is based on the use of avoidance behaviors, and "How to Foil Burglars," which demonstrates hardware and its use and what to do if you're a victim of a burglary.

Denver Anti-Crime Council
1313 Tremont Place, Suite 5
Denver, CO 80204

Operation Rape Reduction
Proposed program to reduce rape in the City of Denver by improving public education, the capability of policing rape by the police department, prosecution, victim support, and offender evaluation and treatment.

Detroit Police Department
3165 Second Street
Detroit, MI 48201

Cass Corridor Safety for Seniors
This program, designed to promote safety and crime reduction, consists of five phases that operate simultaneously. These phases deal with education, transportation, identification of belongings (Operation Identification), banking (check cashing, savings account), and a telephone reassurance service for the elderly.

Department of Physical Education,
    California State University at Los Angeles
5151 State University Drive
Los Angeles, CA 90032

Teaching Self-Defense
Ten thirty-minute, color educational videotapes for television series.

Jamaica Service Program for Older Adults
92–47 165 Street
Jamaica, NY 11433

Jamaica Service Program for Older Adults
Deals with the educational, health, and social service needs of the elderly. A crime-prevention program has been developed around the use of block watchers and the Operation Identification programs.

Jersey City Department of Police Crime Prevention Unit
292 Central Avenue
Jersey City, NJ 07307

Pilot program designed specifically for the elderly. Deals with crime prevention and assisting elderly victims of crime.

Miami Beach Police Department Community Relations Section,
    Crime Prevention Unit
120 Meridian Avenue
Miami Beach, FL 33139

Safety Program
Designed by the police. Incorporated into this crime-prevention program are security surveys and Operation Identification.

Mid-America Regional Council (MARC)
20 West Ninth Street, 3d floor
Kansas City, MO 64105

Aid to Elderly Victims of Crime
A two-goal program seeking (1) to decrease crime against the elderly by the use of home security inspections, community block watchers, and crime-prevention training sessions and (2) to reduce the effects of this victimization by providing financial assistance, health and social services, and so forth to elderly crime victims.

Minnesota Governor's Commission on Crime Prevention and Control
444 Lafayette Road
St. Paul, MN 55101

Crime Watch
Educates citizens about crime and what they can do to reduce it. One part of this program deals with personal security.

Crime Prevention through Environmental Design
Shows how the design of buildings and surrounding areas affects crime and its prevention.

New York City Department for the Aging
155 West 72d Street
New York, NY 10023

Senior Citizens Crime Prevention Program
Helps elderly victims of crime through counseling, emergency, housing, transportation, and so forth. Also includes crime prevention training and an information outreach campaign.

Pennsylvania Commission for Women
512 Finance Building
Harrisburg, PA 17128

Help for the Rape Victim. A Pennsylvania Commission for Women Resource Guide, 1975.
Guildlines on how to start a rape crisis center program.

Rape Crisis Center of Syracuse, Inc.
709 Park Street
Syracuse, NY 13208

This program consists of precaution and education talks given at senior citizen housing projects and recreation centers. The talks center around the special considerations concerning rape and elderly women.

Sarasota Police Department
2050 Ringling Boulevard
P.O. Box 3528
Sarasota, FL 33578

Crime against the Elderly
Uses educational printed matter and films to increase the elderly's awareness of crime. Program also conducts security surveys.

St. Louis Mayor's Office for Senior Citizens
Senior Center
560 Delmar Boulevard
St. Louis, MO 63101

Senior Home Security Program
Seniors are employed to install security devices and to do minor home repairs for other elderly. Program goal is to make elderly more secure from and less fearful of crime.

University of Michigan–Wayne State University Institute of Gerontology
520 East Liberty Street
Ann Arbor, MI 48108

Age-Related Vision and Hearing Changes—An Empathic Approach
Audiovisual presentation of "empathic" slides and audiosimulation.

Wynnefield Residents Association
P.O. Box 4536
Philadelphia, PA 19131

Guidelines for Home and Neighborhood Security
Uses avoidance behaviors for crime prevention. This program was instituted by a neighborhood association.

10 Programs in Crime Prevention for Older Persons

California

Evaluation of AARP/NRTA Program
Attn: Sharon Y. Moriwaki
Ethel Perry Andrus Gerontology
University Park
University of Southern California
Los Angeles, CA 90007

Interagency Task Force on Crime against the Elderly
Attn: Leon Harper, Deputy Director
Los Angeles County Department of Senior Citizens Affairs
601 South Kingsley Drive
Los Angeles, CA 90005
(213) 385-4221

Prevention—Crimes against the Elderly
Attn: June Sherwood, Director
Office of the Attorney General
Crime Prevention Unit
3580 Wilshire Boulevard, Suite 938
Los Angeles, CA 90010
(213) 620-3286

Sacramento Police Department
Attn: Lieutenant Robert C. Benton
625 H Street
Sacramento, CA 95814
(916) 449-5731

Santa Cruz Research on Elderly as Victims of Crime
Attn: Thomas Nohrdan
Santa Cruz County Sheriff Office of Corrections
P.O. Box 623
Santa Cruz, CA 95016

Delaware

The Elderly as Victims of Street Crimes
Attn: Special Agent Mike Kirchenbauer
Wilmington Crime Resistance Task Force
Federal Bureau of Investigation
P.O. Box 1872
Wilmington, DE 19899

District of Columbia

Crime Prevention Program
Attn: George Sunderland, Senior Coordinator
NRTA/AARP
1909 K Street NW
Washington, DC 20049

Security Planning for HUD—Assisted Housing
Attn: Morton Leeds, Director
Special Concerns Staff, Office of Housing Management
U.S. Department of Housing and Urban Development
451 7th Street SW, Room 9108
Washington, DC 20410
(202) 755-6548

Florida

Pinellas County Junior Deputy League
Attn: Sargent Richard C. Mullen
Pinellas County Sheriff's Department Crime Prevention Unit
250 West Ulmerton Road
Largo, FL 33540
(813) 585-9911

Crimes against the Elderly
Attn: Captain F.G. Bowers, Jr.
Sarasota City Police Department
P.O. Box 3528
Sarasota, FL 33578
(813) 366-8000 x291

Locks for the Elderly
Attn: Caren Pemberton
Office of Crime Prevention
1510 First Avenue North
St. Petersburg, FL 33705
(813) 893-7623

Project: Concern
Attn: Jeffery Symons
City of St. Petersburg/Junior League of St. Petersburg, Incorporated
1510 First Avenue North
St. Petersburg, FL 33705
(813) 893-7623

Illinois

Chicago Police Department
Attn: Ira Harris, Director
1121 South State Street
Chicago, IL 60605
(312) 744-5490

Indiana

Symposium on Safety
Attn: Sargent Clarence Shepard
Evansville Police Department
15 NW 7th Street
Evansville, IN 47708
(812) 426-5542

Senior Citizen Lock Project
Attn: Sargent Joel H. Wolvos
South Bend Police
701 West Sample Street
South Bend, IN 46625
219-284-9265

Kentucky

Crime Prevention for Senior Citizens
Louisville Division of Police
633 West Jefferson Street
Louisville, KY 40202
(502) 581-2569, 581-3443

Maryland

Citizen Involvement Program
Attn: Catherine E. Pugh, Director
Council on Criminal Justice
26 South Calvert Street, Room 101
Baltimore, MD 21202

Crime Prevention Program for the Elderly
Attn: Bonnie Seiff de Olivares, Criminal Justice Planner
Mayor's Office of Baltimore City
Mayor's Coordinating Council on Criminal Justice
City Hall
26 South Calvert Street, Room 1101
Baltimore, MD 21202
(301) 396-4370

Crime, Safety, and the Senior Citizen
Attn: Philip J. Gross
International Association of Chiefs of Police
Technical Research Services Divisions
11 Firstfield Road
Gaithsburg, MD 20760
(301) 948-0922

Minnesota

Crime Cautions for Seniors
Attn: Captain Hartley
Minneapolis Police Department
Community Relations Division
Room 130, City Hall
Minneapolis, MN 55415
(612) 348-6870

Missouri

Aid to Elderly Victims of Crime
Attn: John Cyprus
Mid-America Regional Council
20 West 9th Street
Kansas City, MO 64105
(816) 474-4240

New York

Safety Committee of the JSPOA Senior Citizens Advisory Council
Attn: Alice Watson or Ellen Camerieri
Jamaica Service Program for Older Adults
92-47 165th Street
Jamaica, NY 11433
(212) 657-6500

Victimization of Elderly
Attn: Rita Schartz
New York City Department of the Aging
250 Broadway
New York, NY 10007
(212) 566-0154

Ohio

Cuyahoga County Commissioners Senior Safety and
    Security Program (SSSP)
Attn: Fred D. Middleton, Director
1276 West 3d Street, Suite 512
Cleveland, OH 44113
(216) 241-2700 x554, 696-1874

Oregon

Senior Citizens Volunteer Crime Prevention Program
Attn: Lieutenant Paul G. Smith
Cottage Grove Police Department
28 South 6th Street
Cottage Grove, OR 97424
(503) 942-2464

Older Americans' Crime Prevention Research
Attn: Marlene A. Young Rifai
Multnomah County Division of Public Safety
10525 SE Cherry Blossom Drive, Suite 101
Portland, OR 97216
(503) 255-1891

Texas

Houston Model Cities Victimization Project
AARP Funded Project on Victimization of Older Persons and
     Reporting Problems
Attn: Marvin Ernst, Director of Research
Dallas Geriatric Research Institute
2525 Centerville Road
Dallas, TX 75228

Improving the Reporting of Crimes
Attn: Marvin Ernst
Center for Studies in Aging
North Texas State University
Denton, TX 76203
(817) 788-2181

Utah

Senior Citizens Law Enforcement Involvement Program
Attn: Stephen M. Studdert
Brigham City Police Department
20 North Main Street
Brigham City, UT 84302
(801) 723-3421

West Virginia

Operations Lifeline
Attn: Linda G. Walton and Robert E. Harris
Huntington Police Department
Crime Prevention Unit
Huntington, WV 25717
(304) 696-5575

Wisconsin

Neighborhood Security Aide Program
Attn: William W. Chase, Director
Courthouse, Room 1
901 North 9th Street
Milwaukee, WI 53233
(414) 278-5021

11 Organizations

Academy for Educational Development
680 Fifth Avenue
New York, NY 10019

Action for Independent Maturity
1909 K Street NW
Washington, DC 20049

Administration on Aging
Office of Human Development
330 Independence Avenue SW
Washington, DC 20201

Adult Educational Association of the United States of America
810 18th Street NW
Washington, DC 20006

Advisory Council on Pension and Welfare Benefit Programs
3rd Street and Constitution Avenue NW
Washington, DC 20210

Aging Research Institute
342 Madison Avenue
New York, NY 10017

America Aging Association
c/o Denham Harman, Executive Director
University of Nebraska College of Medicine
Omaha, NE 68105

American Association of Community and Junior Colleges
Older Americans Programs
One Dupont Circle NW
Washington, DC 20036

American Association of Emeriti
P.O. Box 24451
Los Angeles, CA 90024

American Association of Homes for the Aging
1050 17th Street NW
Washington, DC 20036

American Association of Retired Persons
1909 K Street NW
Washington, DC 20049

American Association of Retired Persons (Long Beach)
215 Long Beach Boulevard
Long Beach, CA 90802

American Geriatrics Society, Inc.
10 Columbus Circle
New York, NY 10019

American Society for Geriatric Dentistry
Two North Riverside Plaza, Suite 1741
Chicago, IL 60606

American Society of Mature Catholics
110 West Wells Street
Milwaukee, WI 53233

American Society of Pension Actuaries
1023 Connecticut Avenue NW
Washington, DC 20006

Associacion Nacional pro Personas Mayores
3875 Wilshire Boulevard, Suite 401
Los Angeles, CA 90005

Association for Gerontology in Higher Education
1835 K Street NW, Suite 305
Washington, DC 20006

Association of Private Pension and Welfare Plans
1028 Connecticut Avenue NW
Washington, DC 20036

Boston Society of Gerontological Psychiatry, Inc.
International Universities Press, Inc.
315 Fifth Avenue
New York, NY 10003

Brookdale Center on Aging
Hunter College
129 East 70th Street
New York, NY 10021

Center on Arts and the Aging
National Council on the Aging
1828 L Street NW
Washington, DC 20036

Central Bureau for the Jewish Aged
225 Park Avenue South
New York, NY 10009

Church of the Brethren Homes and Hospitals Association
The Cedars
1111 East Kansas Street
McPherson, KS 67460

Citizens for Better Care in Nursing Homes, Homes for the Aged, and
      Other After-Care Facilities
960 East Jefferson Avenue
Detroit, MI 48207

Clearinghouse on Employment for the Aging
80 Reid Avenue
Port Washington, NY 11050

Club for Philately in Gerontology
2525 Centerville Road
Dallas, TX 75228

Coalition for Terminal Care
1101 University Avenue SE
Minneapolis, MN 55414

College Retirement Equities Fund
730 Third Avenue
New York, NY 10017

Colorado Gerontological Consortium
1020 15th Street, Room 25-M
Denver, CO 80202

Commission of Professors of Adult Education
Ritter Addition 217
College of Education
Temple University
Philadelphia, PA 19122

Community Services Administration
Office of Program Development
1200 19th Street NW
Washington, DC 20506

Concerned Seniors for Better Government
1346 Connecticut Avenue NW, Room 1213
Washington, DC 20036

Continuing Education Council
6 North Sixth Street
Richmond, VA 23219

Coordination Council for Senior Citizens
c/o Senior Citizen's Memorial Center
519 East Main Street
Durham, NC 27701

Diplomatic and Consular Officers, Retired
1718 H Street NW
Washington, DC 20006

Education Network for Older Adults
36 Wabash, Suite 714
Chicago, IL 60603

Elder Craftsmen, Inc.
850 Lexington Avenue
New York, NY 10021

Flying Senior Citizens of U.S.A.
96 Tamarack Street
Buffalo, NY 14220

Gerontological Society
One Dupont Circle
Washington, DC 20036

Golden Ring Council of Senior Citizens Clubs
22 West 38th Street
New York, NY 10018

Institute for Retired Professionals
New School for Social Research
66 West 12th Street
New York, NY 10011

Institute for Retirement Studies
7040 Crawford Hall
Case Western Reserve University
Cleveland, OH 44106

Institute for the Enrichment of Later Life
1600 South Minnesota Avenue
Sioux Falls, SD 57105

Institute of Industrial Gerontology
c/o National Council on Aging
1828 L Street NW
Washington, DC 20036

Institute of Lifetime Learning
1909 K Street NW
Washington, DC 20049

International Federation on Aging
1909 K Street NW
Washington, DC 20049

International Senior Citizens Association, Inc.
11753 Wilshire Boulevard
Los Angeles, CA 90025

International Social Security Association
Case Postale No. 1
CH–1211 Geneva 22
Switzerland

Jewish Association for Services for the Aged
222 Park Avenue South
New York, NY 10003

Jobs for Older Women Action Project
3103 Telegraph Avenue
Berkeley, CA 94705

Labor Department
Office of Pension Welfare Benefit Programs
3rd Street and Constitution Avenue NW
Washington, DC 20210

Legal Services for the Elderly
2095 Broadway
New York, NY 10023

Legislative Council for Older Americans, Inc.
110 Arlington Street
Boston, MA 02116

National Alliance of Senior Citizens
Box 40031
Washington, DC 20016

National Association for Human Development
1750 Pennsylvania Avenue NW
Washington, DC 20006

National Association for Public Continuing and Adult Education
1201 16th Street NW
Washington, DC 20036

National Association of Area Agencies on Aging, Inc.
1828 L Street NW
Washington, DC 20036

National Association of Counties Research Foundation Aging Program
1735 New York Avenue NW
Washington, DC 20006

National Association of Humanistic Gerontology
41 Tunnel Road
Berkeley, CA 94705

National Association of Jewish Homes for the Aged
2525 Centerville Road
Dallas, TX 75228

National Association of Mature People
Box 26792
Oklahoma City, OK 73118

National Association of Older Americans
12 Electric Street
West Alexandria, OH 45381

National Association of Retired and Veteran Railroad Employees
c/o Joseph J. Bredestage
1007 Regina
Cincinnati, OH 45205

National Association of Retired Federal Employees
1533 New Hampshire Avenue NW
Washington, DC 20036

National Association of State Retirement Administrators
302 Public Safety Building
Montgomery, AL 36130

National Association of State Units on Aging
West Virginia Commission on Aging
State Capitol
Charleston, WV 25305

National Center for Voluntary Action
National Information Center on Volunteerism
P.O. Box 1807
Boulder, CO 80306

National Center on the Black Aged
1424 K Street NW
Washington, DC 20005

National Clearinghouse on Aging
Administration on Aging
Department of Health and Human Services Building, Room 4146
330 Independence Avenue SW
Washington, DC 20201

National Committee on Art Education for the Elderly
Culver Stockton College
Canton, MO 63435

National Conference of State Social Security Administrators
Public Employees Social Security Bureau
Department of Employee Trust Funds
P.O. Box 7931
Madison, WI 53707

National Conference on Public Employee Retirement Systems
275 East Broad Street
Columbus, OH 43215

National Council of Senior Citizens
1511 K Street NW
Washington, DC 20005

National Council on Black Aging
Box 8522
Durham, NC 27707

National Council on Teacher Retirement
275 East Broad Street
Columbus, OH 43215

National Council on the Aging
1828 L Street NW
Washington, DC 20036

National Forum for Older Women
Center on Aging
University of Maryland
College Park, MD 20742

National Geriatrics Society
212 West Wisconsin Avenue, 3rd Floor
Milwaukee, WI 53203

National Health and Welfare Retirement Association
666 Fifth Avenue
New York, NY 10019

National Institute of Senior Centers
c/o National Council on Aging
1828 L Street NW
Washington, DC 20036

National Institute on Aging
National Institutes of Health
Bethesda, MD 20014

National Retired Teachers Association
1909 K Street NW
Washington, DC 20049

National Retirement Council
527 Madison Avenue
New York, NY 10022

National Voluntary Organization for Independent Living of the Aged
c/o National Council on Aging
1828 L Street NW
Washington, DC 20036

NOW Task Force on Older Women
6412 Telegraph Avenue
Oakland, CA 94609

Pension Benefit Guaranty Corporation
2020 K Street NW
Washington, DC 20006

Pension Rights Center
1346 Connecticut Avenue NW
Washington, DC 20036

President's Commission on Pension Policy
736 Jackson Place NW
Washington, DC 20006

Resource Center for Planned Change
One Dupont Circle
Washington, DC 20036

Retired and Pioneer Rural Carriers of United States
c/o George Rosebrooks
Gore Road
Webster, MA 05170

Retired Bankers Association
c/o Lucy Easterwood
6303 Prospect B
Dallas, TX 75214

The Retired Officers Association
201 North Washington Street
Alexandria, VA 22314

The Retired Professionals
1025 15th Street NW
Washington, DC 20005

Retirement Housing Foundation
555 East Ocean Boulevard
Long Beach, CA 90802

Salvation Army
503 East Street NW
Washington, DC 20001

Senior Employment Opportunities
c/o National Council of Jewish Women
15 East 26th Street
New York, NY 10010

Seniors for Adequate Social Security
136 West 91st Street
New York, NY 11024

Service Corps of Retired Executives
1441 L Street NW, Room 100
Washington, DC 20416

Urban Elderly Coalition
1828 L Street NW, Suite 505
Washington, DC 20036

Vacations for the Aging and Senior Centers Association
225 Park Avenue South
New York, NY 10003

Virginia Center on Aging
1617 Monument Avenue
Richmond, VA 23220

Western Gerontological Society
785 Market Street
San Francisco, CA 94103

12 Abstracts, Indexes, Periodicals, Journals

AAHA Washington Report (bimonthly)
American Association of Homes for the Aging
1050 17th Street NW
Washington, DC 20036

AARP News Bulletin (bimonthly)
American Association of Retired Persons
215 Long Beach Boulevard
Long Beach, CA 90820

Abstracts for Social Workers (quarterly)
National Association of Social Workers, Inc.
Box 504
New York, NY 10016

Added Years Newsletter (monthly)
New Jersey Division on Aging
Department of Community Affairs
P.O. Box 2768
Trenton, NJ 08625

Adult Education (quarterly)
Adult Education Association
810 18th Street NW
Washington, DC 20006

AFICS Bulletin (monthly)
Association of Former International Civil Servants
Palais des Nations
Geneva
Switzerland

Age (quarterly)
The American Aging Association
42nd Street and Dewey Avenue
Omaha, NE 68105

Age and Aging (quarterly)
British Geriatric Society and the British Society for Research in Ageing
Bailliere, Tindall and Cassell Ltd.
7 and 8 Henrietta Street
London WC2
England

Age Concern Information Circular (monthly)
Age Concern England
Bernard Sunley House
60 Pitcairn Road
Mitcham, Surrey CR4 3LL
England

Age in Action (bimonthly)
West Virginia Commission on Aging
State Capitol
Charleston, WV 25305

Age of Achievement (monthly)
Age of Achievement
337 Securities Building
Seattle, WA 98101

Aged Care and Services Review (bimonthly)
The Haworth Press
149 5th Avenue
New York, NY 10010

Aging International (quarterly)
International Federation on Ageing
1909 K Street NW
Washington, DC 20049

Aging Times (triannual)
British Society of Social and Behavioral Gerontology
c/o London Hospital Medical College
57, Turner Street
London El 2AD
England

Aging (bimonthly)
Administration on Aging
U.S. Department of Health and Human Services
Superintendent of Documents
U.S. Government Printing Office
Washington, DC 20402

Aging and Leisure Living (monthly)
Medical Life Systems
212 West Wisconsin Avenue
Milwaukee, WI 53203

Aging and Work (quarterly)
National Council on the Aging
1828 L Street NW
Washington, DC 20036

Aging Education News (monthly)
Center for Aging Education
Lansing Community College
419 North Capitol Street
P.O. Box 40010
Lansing, MI 48901

Aging in Pennsylvania (bimonthly)
Office for the Aging
Department of Public Welfare
P.O. Box 2675
Harrisburg, PA 17120

Aging in the News (quarterly)
Division on Aging
Department of Health and Social Services
1 West Wilson Street, Room 686
Madison, WI 53702

Aging News/Research and Training (monthly)
Care Reports, Inc.
1230 National Press Building
Washington, DC 20045

Aging Research and Training News (monthly)
Care Reports, Inc.
6529 Elgin Lane
Washington, DC 20034

Aging Services News
Care Reports, Inc.
1230 National Press Building
Washington, DC 20045

Aging Update (monthly)
Institute for the Study of Aging
University of Miami
P.O. Box 24816
Coral Gables, FL 33124

AHCA Journal (bimonthly)
American Health Care Association
1200 15th Street NW
Washington, DC 20005

AHCA Weekly Notes (41 per year)
American Health Care Association
1200 15th Street NW
Washington, DC 20005

AIM (Aging in Michigan) (bimonthly)
Office of Services to the Aging
300 East Michigan Avenue
P.O. Box 30026
Lansing, MI 48909

Aktuelle Gerontologie
Georg Thimen Verlag
P.O. Box 732
D–7000 Stuttgart
West Germany

American Geriatrics Society Journal (monthly)
American Geriatrics Society
10 Columbus Circle
New York, NY 10019

American Geriatrics Society Newsletter (monthly)
American Geriatrics Society, Inc.
10 Columbus Circle
New York, NY 10019

American Health Care Association Journal (monthly)
Modern Healthcare
P.O. Box 665
Highstown, NJ 08520

American Society for Geriatrics Dentistry Journal (monthly)
American Society for Geriatrics Dentistry
431 Oakdale Avenue
Chicago, IL 60657

Annual Statistical Supplement to the Social Security Bulletin
Superintendent of Documents
U.S. Government Printing Office
Washington, DC 20402

AOA Fact Sheet (monthly)
U.S. Administration on Aging
Superintendent of Documents
U.S. Government Printing Office
Washington, DC 20402

Aspects of Aging (bimonthly)
Central Bureau for the Jewish Aging
225 Park Avenue South
New York, NY 10003

BARP Newsletter (quarterly)
British Association of Retired Persons
14 Frederick Street
Edinburgh EH2 2HB
Scotland

Best Years (quarterly)
National Association of Mature People
Box 26792
Oklahoma City, OK 73125

Bioresearch Today: Human and Animal Aging (monthly)
Bio Sciences Information Services of Biological Abstracts
2100 Arch Street
Philadelphia, PA 19103

Black Aging (bimonthly)
National Council on Black Aging, Inc.
Box 8522
Durham, NC 27707

British Journal of Geriatrics and Psychogeriatrics (quarterly)
Stuart Phillips Publications
30 Ringstead Road
Sutton, Surrey
England

Bulletin on Aging (biannual)
Social Development Branch
Department of Economics and Social Affairs
United Nations
New York, NY 10017

The California Senior Citizen News (monthly)
McAnally and Associates
P.O. Box 765
La Canada, CA 92101

Canadian Association on Gerontology Newsletter (quarterly)
Minister of Community and Social Services
801 Bay Street
Toronto, Ontario
Canada

CARCH News (monthly)
California Association of Residential Care Homes
2530 J Street, Suite 302
Sacramento, CA 95816

Catching Up on Aging (bimonthly)
CASE Center for Gerontology Studies
The Graduate School and University Center
The City University of New York
33 West 42nd Street
New York, NY 10036

Center News (monthly)
Center for Studies in Aging
P.O. Box 13438
North Texas State University
Denton, TX 76203

The Center News (quarterly)
The Center for the Study of Aging and Human Development
Box 3003
Duke University Medical Center
Durham, NC 27710

Challenger (quarterly)
Virginia Office on Aging
830 East Main Street, Suite 95
Richmond, VA 23219

Chapter News (bimonthly)
American Association of Retired Persons
215 Long Beach, CA 90820

Choice (monthly)
Retirement Choice Magazine Company
100 Riverview Center
Middletown, CT 06457

Concern for Dying (quarterly)
Concern for Dying
250 West 57th Street
New York, NY 10019

Concern in Care of the Aging (bimonthly)
American Association Homes for the Aging
Medical Media Corporation
Box 852
31 Church Street
Flemington, NJ 08822

Concord (bimonthly)
British Association for Service to the Elderly (BASE)
Bernard Sunley House
60 Pitcairn Road
Mitcham, Surrey CR4 3LL
England

Contact for Aging (bimonthly)
Office on Aging
State of South Dakota
Department of Social Services
Illinois Street
Pierre, SD 57501

Current Literature on Aging (quarterly)
National Council on the Aging
1828 L Street NW
Washington, DC 20036

Dialogue (monthly)
American Association of Retired Persons–National Retired Teachers
    Association
1909 K Street NW
Washington, DC 20049

Dynamic Maturity (bimonthly)
Action for Independent Maturity
American Association of Retired Persons
1909 K Street NW
Washington, DC 20049

Dynamic Years (bimonthly)
AIM (Action for Independent Maturity)
American Association of Retired Persons
1909 K Street NW
Washington, DC 20049

Ebenezer (quarterly)
Ebenezer Society
2523 Portland Avenue South
Minneapolis, MN 54404

Education for Aging News (bimonthly)
Brookdale Center on Aging
Hunter College
129 East 79th Street
New York, NY 10021

Educational Gerontology (quarterly)
Hemisphere Publishing Corporation
1025 Vermonth Avenue NW
Washington, DC 20005

The Elder (monthly)
The Elder
P.O. Box 984
New Haven, CT 06504

The Elder Statesment (monthly)
Federated Legislative Council of Elderly Citizens Associations of British
    Columbia
946 West 7th Avenue
Vancouver 9, British Columbia
Canada

Emeritus College Newsletter (monthly)
Emeritus College of Marin
Kentfield, CA 94904

Employment Fellowship Review (quarterly)
Employment Fellowship
Allens Green
Sawbridgeworth, Hertfordshire
England

Era (monthly)
California Office on Aging
455 Capitol Mall
Sacramento, CA 95814

Especially for Seniors (quarterly)
Ontario Advisory Council on Senior Citizens
901 Bay Street, 3rd floor
Toronto, Ontario M5S 1Z1
Canada

Essence: Issues in the Study of Aging, Dying, and Death
Department of Psychology
Atkinson College
York College
4700 Keele Street
Downsview, Ontario M3J 2R7
Canada

European Demographic Information Bulletin (quarterly)
Martinus Nijhoff
The Hague
The Netherlands

Gerontology and Geriatrics (10 per year)
Excerpta Medica
Keizersgracht 305
Box 1126
Amsterdam
Netherlands

Experimental Aging Research (bimonthly)
EAR, Inc.
P.O. Box 29
Mt. Desert, ME 04609

Experimental Aging Research (bimonthly)
P.O. Box 85
Bar Harbor, ME 14609

Experimental Gerontology (quarterly)
Pergamon House, Inc.
Maxwell House
Fairview Park
Elmsford, NY 10523

Family Coordinator (quarterly)
National Council on Family Relations
1219 University Avenue SE
Minneapolis, MN 55414

Family Therapy (triannual)
Family Therapy Institute of Marin
1353 Lincoln Avenue
San Rafael, CA 94901

Generations (quarterly)
The Western Gerontological Society
785 Market Street, Suite 1114
San Francisco, CA 94103

Fifty Plus
150 East 58th Street
New York, NY 10022

Geriascope (quarterly)
Canadian Geriatrics Research Society
c/o Geriatric Study Center
350 Christie Street
Toronto, Ontario M6G 3CE
Canada

Geriatopics (quarterly)
Canadian Geriatrics Research Society
c/o Geriatrics Study Center
350 Christie Street
Toronto, Ontario M6G 3CE
Canada

Geriatric and Residential Care (monthly)
HRS Geriatrics Publishing Corp.
342 Pipe Stave Hollow Road
Mount Sinai, NY 11766

Geriatrics (monthly)
Lancet Publications
4015 West 65th Street
Minneapolis, MN 55435

Gerontologia
S. Karger AG
Arnold–Boecklinstrasse 25
4011 Basel
Switzerland

Gerontologia Clinica (bimonthly)
S. Karger AG
Arnold–Bocklinstrasse 25
4011 Basel
Switzerland

Gerontological Abstracts (11 per year)
University Information Services
P.O. Box 1948
Ann Arbor, MI 48103

The Gerontologist (bimonthly)
Gerontological Society
One Dupont Circle, Suite 520
Washington, DC 20036

Gerontophiles (bimonthly)
Center for Gerontological Studies and Programs
3352 General Purpose A
University of Florida
Gainesville, FL 32611

Geron Topics
A Forum for the Aging Network
15 Garrison Avenue
Durham, NH 03824

The Golden Page (bimonthly)
The National Center on the Black Aged, Inc.
1424 K Street NW, Suite 500
Washington, DC 20005

Gray Panther Network (irregular)
Gray Panthers
3700 Chestnut Street
Philadelphia, PA 19104

Higher Education in Retirement (bimonthly)
Institute for Retired Professionals
The New School for Social Research
66 West 12th Street
New York, NY 10011

Horizon (quarterly)
United Methodist Homes of New Jersey
71 Clark Avenue
Ocean Grove, NJ 07756

Home Health Care Services Quarterly (quarterly)
The Haworth Press
149 5th Avenue
New York, NY 10010

Human Development (quarterly)
S. Karger AG
Arnold–Boecklinstrasse 25
4011 Basel
Switzerland

Human Resources Abstracts (quarterly)
Sage Publications, Inc.
275 South Beverly Drive
Beverly Hills, CA 90212

Human Values and Aging (biannual)
David A. Van Tassel
History Department
Case Western Reserve University
Cleveland, OH 44106

Humanities Exchange (irregular)
National Council on Aging
1821 L Street NW
Washington, DC 20036

Index Medicus (monthly)
Superintendent of Documents
U.S. Government Printing Office
Washington, DC 20402

Indian Journal of Gerontology (quarterly)
Indian Gerontological Association
C–207 Arvind Marg
Tilaknagar, Jaipur
India

Industrial Gerontology (quarterly)
National Council on the Aging
1828 L Street NW, Room 504
Washington, DC 20036

International Journal of Aging and Human Development (quarterly)
Baywood Publishing Company
43 Central Drive
Farmingdale, NY 11735

International Journal of Aging and Human Development (quarterly)
National Council on the Aging
1828 L Street NW
Washington, DC 20036

International Labour Review (monthly)
Branch Office
1750 New York Avenue NW
Washington, DC 20006

International Senior Citizens News (quarterly)
International Senior Citizens Association, Inc.
11753 Wilshire Boulevard
Los Angeles, CA 90024

International Social Security Review (quarterly)
International Social Security Association
Case postale 1
CH–1211 Geneva 22
Switzerland

IRP Review (annual)
Institute for Retired Professionals
New School for Social Research
66 West 12th Street
New York, NY 10021

ITEMS (monthly)
Social Science Research Council
605 Third Avenue
New York, NY 10009

Journal of Geriatric Psychiatry (biannual)
Boston Society of Gerontological Psychiatry
90 Forest Avenue NW
Boston, MA 01021

Journal of Geriatric Psychiatry (biannual)
Boston Society of Gerontologic Psychiatry, Inc.
International Universities Press, Inc.
239 Park Avenue South
New York, NY 10003

Journal of Gerontological Nursing (bimonthly)
Charles B. Slack Publications
Thorafore, NY 08086

Journal of Gerontology (bimonthly)
Gerontological Society
1835 K Street NW
Washington, DC 20006

Journal of Housing (11 per year)
National Association of Housing and Redevelopment Officials
Watergate Building, Suite 404
2600 Virginia Avenue NW
Washington, DC 20037

Journal of Leisure Research (quarterly)
National Recreation and Parks Association
1601 North Kent Street
Arlington, VA 22209

Journal of Long-Term Care Administration (quarterly)
American College of Nursing Home Administrators
4650 East–West Highway
Washington, DC 20014

Journal of the American Geriatrics Society (monthly)
American Geriatrics Society, Inc.
10 Columbus Circle
New York, NY 10019

Journal of the Institute for Socieconomics Studies (quarterly)
Institute for Socioeconomic Studies
Airport Road
White Plains, NY

Keeping Informed about Senior Services (monthly)
Louisiana Health and Social and Rehabilitation Services Department
State Office Building, Suite 402
150 Riverside Mall
Baton Rouge, LA 70801

Legislative Update (quarterly)
Urban Elderly Coalition
1828 L Street NW, Suite 505
Washington, DC 20036

Lifelong Learning: The Adult Years (monthly)
Adult Education Association
810 18th Street NW
Washington, DC 20006

Life with Dignity (bimonthly)
Florida Division of Aging
1317 Winewood Boulevard
Tallahasse, FL 32301

Locke Report (bimonthly)
Edward M. Cooney
67 Pleasant Street
Marion, MA 02738

Long-Term Care Administrators (bimonthly)
4650 East–West Highway
Washington, DC 20014

Management Assistance Newsletter
Service Corps of Retired Executives
1441 L Street NW, Room 100
Washington, DC 20416

Mature Catholic (bimonthly)
American Society of Mature Catholics
1100 West Wells Street
Milwaukee, WI 53233

Mature Living (bimonthly)
Indiana State Commission on the Aging and the Aged
215 North Senate Avenue
Indianapolis, IN 46202

Mature Years (quarterly)
United Methodist Church
201 8th Avenue South
Nashville, TN 37202

Maturitas (quarterly)
Elsevier/North-Holland
52 Vanderbilt Avenue
New York, NY 10017

Mechanisms of Aging and Development (bimonthly)
Elsevier Seqouia S.A.
Box 851
1001 Lausanne
Switzerland

Medicare Report (bimonthly)
National Feature Syndicate, Inc.
1066 National Press Building
Washington, DC 20045

Metropolitan Pensioner (monthly)
Metropolitan Pensioners' Welfare Association
Box 2929
Vancouver 3, British Columbia
Canada

Minnesota Senior Spotlight (bimonthly)
Governor's Citizens Council on Aging
204 Metro Square
7th and Robert Streets
St. Paul, MN 55101

Modern Geriatrics (monthly)
Peter H. Barker
Empire House
414 High Road
Chiswick, London W4
England

Modern Maturity (bimonthly)
American Association of Retired Persons
215 Long Beach Boulevard
Long Beach, CA 90820

*Myth and Reality of Aging in America: Index to Available Data from
    National Council on the Aging/Harris Survey*
National Council on the Aging
1828 L Street NW
Washington, DC 20036

NARFE Newsletter (irregular)
National Association of Retired Federal Employees
1533 New Hampshire Avenue NW
Washington, DC 20036

National News (quarterly)
National Pensioners and Senior Citizens Federation
105 4th Street, 2d Floor
Toronto, Ontario MNBV 2Y4
Canada

New Age (quarterly)
Age Concern England
Bernard Sunley House
60 Pitcairn Road
Mitcham, Surrey
England

New Literature on Old Age (bimonthly)
The National Corporation for the Care of Old People
Nuffield Lodge, Regent's Park
London NW1 4RS
England

News (irregular)
Alabama Commission on Aging
740 Madison Avenue
Montgomery, AL 36104

News (monthly)
Alberta Council on Aging
8923 117th Street
Edmonton, Alberta
Canada

News (irregular)
Illinois Department on Aging
2401 West Jefferson Street
Springfield, IL 62706

News (bimonthly)
New York State Office for the Aging
855 Central Avenue
Albany, NY 12206

Newsletter (monthly)
American College of Nursing Home Administrators
8641 Colesville Road, Suite 409
Silver Springs, MD 20910

Newsletter
American Council on Consumer Interests
162 Stanley Hall
University of Missouri
Columbia, MO 065201

Newsletter (9 per year)
American Council on Consumer Interests
162 Stanley Hall
University of Missouri
Columbia, MO 65201

Newsletter (monthly)
Canadian Institute of Religion and Gerontology
296 Lawrence Avenue East
Toronto, Ontario M4N 1T7
Canada

Newsletter (monthly)
Office of the Secretary
Department of Elder Affairs
120 Boylston Street
Boston, MA 02116

Newsletter (bimonthly)
Flying Senior Citizens of U.S.A.
96 Tamarack Street
Buffalo, NY 14220

Newsletter (irregular)
Institute of Law and Aging
National Law Center
2000 H Street NW
The George Washington University
Washington, DC 20052

Newsletter (quarterly)
International Senior Citizens Association
11753 Wilshire Boulevard
Los Angeles, CA 90025

Newsletter (quarterly)
National Association of Humanistic Gerontology
41 Tunnel Road
Berkeley, CA 94705

Newsletter (quarterly)
Ontario Psychogeriatric Association
114 Starwood Road
Ottowa, Ontario K2G 3N5
Canada

Newsletter (monthly)
Senior Citizens of Canada
17 Ross Avenue
Agincourt, Ontario
Canada

News 'n' Views (monthly)
Center for Senior Citizens
National Council of Jewish Women
1 West 47th Street
New York, NY 10036

NHWRA Report (monthly)
National Health and Welfare Retirement Association
666 Fifth Avenue
New York, NY 10019

NoDak New Day (bimonthly)
Social Service Board of North Dakota
Aging Service
State Capitol Building
Bismarck, ND 58505

Normative Aging Study Newsletter
Boston Veterans Administration Outpatient Clinic
17 Court Street
Boston, MA 02107

NRTA-AARP Legislative Report (bimonthly)
National Retired Teachers Association–American Association of Retired
    Persons
1909 K Street NW
Washington, DC 20049

NRTA Journal (bimonthly)
National Retired Teachers Association
701 North Montgomery Street
Ojai, CA 93123

NRTA News Bulletin (bimonthly)
National Retired Teachers Association
701 North Montgomery Street
Ojai, CA 93123

Nursing Homes (bimonthly)
Nursing Homes
4000 Albermarle Street NW
Washington, DC 20016

Nursing Research (bimonthly)
American Nurses Association
National League for Nursing
10 Columbus Circle
New York, NY 10019

Onio's Heritage (bimonthly)
Ohio State Historical Society
1982 Velma Avenue
Columbus, OH 43211

Old Age: A Register of Social Research (irregular)
The National Corporation for the Care of Old People
Nuffield Lodge, Regent's Park,
London NW1 4RS
England

The Older Nebraskan's Voice (bimonthly)
State of Nebraska Commission on Aging
Box 94784, State Capitol
Lincoln, NE 68509

The Older Rhode Islander (quarterly)
Rhode Island Department of Community Affairs, Division on Aging
Providence, RI 02903

The Older Texan (bimonthly)
Governor's Committee on Aging
Box 12786
Capitol Station
Austin, TX 78711

Omega (quarterly)
Journal of Death and Dying
Baywood Publishing Company, Inc.
43 Central Drive
Farmindale, NY 11735

Options (monthly)
New York Office for the Aging
250 Broadway, 30th floor
New York, NY 10007

Oregon Pioneer (quarterly)
Oregon State Program on Aging
722 Commercial Street SE
Salem, OR 97310

The Outlook (monthly)
Maryland Office on Aging
1004 State Office Building
301 West Preston Street
Baltimore, MD 21201

Pension and Financial Planning News (quarterly)
Institute of Life Insurance
277 Park Avenue
New York, NY 10017

Pension and Welfare News (monthly)
Communication Channels, Inc.
461 8th Avenue
New York, NY 10001

Pensioners' Voice (bimonthly)
The National Federation of Old Age Pension Associations
91 Preston New Road
Blackburn
England

Pension World (monthly)
Pension World
461 Eighth Avenue
New York, NY 10001

Perspective on Aging (bimonthly)
National Council on the Aging
1828 L Street NW
Washington, DC 20036

Perspectives (quarterly)
Nursing Association
Taylor Place
Senior Adult Centre
1 Overland Drive
Don Mills, Ontario
Canada

Population Index (quarterly)
Population Association of America
Office of Population Research
21 Prospect Avenue
Princeton, NJ 08540

Population Studies (triannual)
Population Investigation Committee
London School of Economics
Haughton Street
Aldwyck, London
England

Prime Time (monthly)
Prime Time
420 West 46th Street
New York, NY 10036

Progress Report (quarterly)
National Association of Jewish Homes for the Aged
2525 Centerville Road
Dallas, TX 75228

Psychological Abstracts (monthly)
American Psychological Association, Inc.
1200 17th Street NW
Washington, DC 20036

Public Welfare (quarterly)
American Public Welfare Association
1155 16th Street NW
Washington, DC 20036

Report (bimonthly)
Mayor's Office for Senior Citizens and Handicapped
180 North LaSalle Street
Chicago, IL 60601

Research on Aging (quarterly)
Quarterly on Social Gerontology
Sage Publication, Inc.
275 South Beverly Drive
Beverly Hills, CA 90212

The Retired Officer (monthly)
The Retired Officers Association
201 North Washington Street
Alexandria, VA 22314

Retirement Life (monthly)
National Association of Retired Federal Employees
1533 New Hampshire Avenue NW
Washington, DC 20036

Retirement Living (monthly)
Harvest Years Publishing Co., Inc.
99 Garden Street
Marion, OH 43302

Second Spring (bimonthly)
121 Golden Gate Avenue
San Francisco, CA 94102

Senior Bulletin (quarterly)
Senior Services, Inc., Foundation
Box 189
Toms River, NJ 08753

Senior Center Report (monthly)
National Institute of Senior Centers
c/o National Council on Aging
1828 L Street NW
Washington, DC 20036

Senior Citizens (monthly)
Andrus Gerontology Center
University of Southern California
Los Angeles, CA 90007

Senior Citizens News (monthly)
National Council of Senior Citizens
1511 K Street NW
Washington, DC 20005

Senior Citizens News (monthly)
Senior Citizens News
10175 SW Barbur Boulevard
Room 109B
Portland, OR 97219

Senior Citizens' Post (monthly)
The Senior Citizen's Post
807 South Duke Street
Durham, NC 27707

Senior Citizens Today (monthly)
California Association of Residential Care Homes
2530 J Street, Suite 302
Sacramento, CA 95816

Senior Focus (irregular)
Arkansas Office on Aging Newsletter
Department of Human Services
1200 Westpark Building
Little Rock, AR 72204

Senior Guardian (monthly)
National Alliance of Senior Citizens
777 14th Street NW
Washington, DC 20005

Senior Newsletter (monthly)
Department of Social and Health Services
MS 433
Olympia, WA 98504

Senior Oklahomans (bimonthly)
Department of Institutions
Social and Rehabilitative Services
Oklahoma City, OK 73125

Senior Power (bimonthly)
Senior Power Publishing Co.
P.O. Box 62
500 North Murray Road
Lee's Summit, MO 64063

Senior World (monthly)
Senior World
4640 Jewell Street
San Diego, CA 92109

Seniority (monthly)
Social Devices Department
Amalgamated Clothing and Textile Workers Union, AFLO–CIO
15 Union Square
New York, NY 10003

Social Security Bulletin (monthly)
Social Security Administration
U.S. Department of Health and Human Services
Superintendent of Documents
U.S. Government Printing Office
Washington, DC 20402

Social Work Research and Abstracts (quarterly)
National Association of Social Workers, Inc.,
Box 504
New York, NY 10016

Sociological Abstracts (6 per year)
Sociological Abstracts, Inc.
Box 22206
San Diego, CA 92122

State Council of Older People Scoop (monthly)
State Council of Older People
P.O. Box 2507
Augusta, ME 04330

Statistical Notes (irregular)
Administration on Aging
U.S. Department of Health and Human Services
Superintendent of Documents
U.S. Government Printing Office
Washington, DC 20402

Supportive Services (biweekly)
Care Reports, Inc.
1230 National Press Building
Washington, DC 20045

Switchboard (irregular)
National Committee on Art Education for the Elderly
Culver Stockton College
Canton, MO 63435

Synagogue Aging
Synagogue Council of America
432 Park Avenue South
New York, NY 10016

Technical Information Exchange (bimonthly)
Urban Elderly Coalition
1828 L Street NW, Suite 505
Washington, DC 20036

The Tennessenior (monthly)
Tennessee Commission on Aging
306 Gay Street
Nashville, TN 37201

Update (monthly)
Center for Aging
University of Alabama
Birmingham, AL 35924

U.S. Administration on Aging, Index of Legislation
Superintendent of Documents
U.S. Government Printing Office
Washington, DC 20402

U.S. Social Security Administration, Journal Holdings of the Social Security Library
U.S. Social Security Administration Library
Social Security Building, Room 571
Baltimore, MD 21235

U.S. Social Security Administration, Library Notes (bimonthly)
Department of Health and Human Services
U.S. Social Security Administration Library
Social Security Building, Room 571
,Baltimore, MD 21235

U.S. Social Security Administration, Research and Statistics Notes
Office of Research and Statistics
1875 Connecticut Avenue NW
Washington, DC 20009

Van Steenberg, Carol, and Robin B. Karasik, Keyword Index to Training Resources in Aging
Duke University Medical Center Library
Durham, NC 27710

Vintage (bimonthly)
South Carolina Commission on Aging
915 Main Street
Columbia, SC 29201

Voice of United Senior Citizens of Ontario (monthly)
United Senior Citizens of Ontario
105 4th Street
Toronto, Ontario M8V 2Y4
Canada

Volunteer News (monthly)
Andrus Gerontology Center
University of Southern California
Los Angeles, CA 90007

Washington Report (biweekly)
American Association of Homes for the Aging
1050 17th Street NW
Washington, DC 20036

Washington Report on Long-Term Care (weekly)
Washington Report on Long-Term Care
475 National Press Building
Washington, DC 20045

Weekly Review (biweekly)
721 North LaSalle Street
Chicago, IL 60610

Word from Washington (irregular)
National Conference on Public Employees Retirement System
1390 Logan Street
Denver, CO 80203

Zantia (quarterly)
P.O. Box 149
Annapolis, MD 21404

Zeitschrift Fur Alternsforschung (6 per year)
Gesellschaft fur Gerontologie der DDR
Theodor Steinkopff Verlag
Loschwiterstrasse 32
DDR-8053 Dresden
East Germany

Zeitscrift Fur Gerontologie (bimonthly)
Dr. Dietrich Steinkopff Verlag
Saalbaustrasse 12
P.O. Box 1008
D-6100 Darmstadt
West Germany

Bibliography

The following coding scheme is intended to assist readers in searching the bibliography by subject:

A. Victimization: swindle, fraud, crime, pattern, violence, neglect

B. Physical abuse: murder, harrassment, rape, safety, security, drugs, alcohol

C. Mental abuse: psychological, attitudes

D. Fear: grief, depression

E. Prevention: roles, programs, networks, experiments, research, directories, bibliographies, materials

F. Reporting: generalizations, law, legislation, rights, reports, hearings

G. Background: history, facts

H. Rehabilitation

Abrahamson, D. *The Psychology of Crime*. New York: Columbia University Press, 1960   *A, B, C*
"Abstracts of the 34th Annual Scientific Meeting of the Gerontological Meeting of the Canadian Association on Gerontology." *Gerontologist* 21 (October 1981):67–315.   *E*

> Abstracts of papers presented at the annual meetings of two gerontological societies. Papers cover a wide spectrum of health and mental-health-related subjects: health-care services, informal support networks, hospitals, and so forth.

"Abuse of the Elderly by Informal Care Providers." *Aging* 299 (September 1979):10–15.   *A, B*
"Abusing the Aged: The Unreported Crime." *U.S. News* 90 (13 April 1981):10.   *E*
"Across the States." *Juvenile Justice Digest* 5 (4 March 1977):7.   *A*
———. *Juvenile Justice Digest* 4 (11 November 1976):7.   *A*
Adams, R., and T. Smith. *Fear of Neighborhood*. National Opinion Research Center Report No. 127C on the Social Change Project. Chicago: National Opinion Center, 1976.   *D*

"Additional LEAA Aid for Fearful Elderly." *Law Officer* 9 (2 January 1977):26–27.   E

Adkins, O. "Crimes against the Elderly." *Police Chief:* 42 (January 1975): 40–41.   A

"Afraid to Go Out at Night." *Crime Control Digest* 12 (10 April 1978):6–7.   D

"After-Effects of Crimes against Elderly Said Intense." *Crime Control Digest* 9 (8 December 1975):2–3.   H

———. *Police Chief* 42 (February 1976):12.   H

Ahart, S.V. "Criminal Victimization of the Elderly: Recent Experience of Center City America." *Dissertation Abstracts International* (1977):   A

Analyzed criminal victimization of the elderly; discusses proposals aimed at reducing the level of victimization of the elderly.

Albrecht, S., and M. Green. "Cognitive Barriers to Equal Justice before the Law." Paper presented at the 26th annual meeting of the Society for the Study of Social Problems.   F

Alexander, S. *Shana Alexander's State-by-State Guide to Women's Legal Rights.* Los Angeles: Wollstonecraft, 1975.   F

Altman, L.M. "Criminal Victimization of the Aged: Is It Really Unique?" *Gerontologist* 17 (1977):35.   A

"America's Seniors Seek Return to Toughness, A-G's Task Force Told." *Law Enforcement News* 7 (10 August 1981):5.   E

Amir, M. *Patterns in Forcible Rape.* Chicago: University of Chicago Press, 1971.   B

———. "Project Summary: Crime among the Aged in Israel." Malben (Home for the Aged), Jerusalem, July 1967.   E

———. "Victims Precipitate Forcible Rape." *Journal of Criminal Law, Criminology, and Political Science* 58 (1967):493–502.   B

Amir, M., and S. Bergman. "Patterns of Crime among Aged in Israel: A Second-Phase Report." *Israel Annals of Psychiatry and Related Disciplines* 14 (September 1976):280–288.   A

Examines crimes against the elderly; analyzes with respect to offender's sex and country of origin, ecological distribution, and immigration patterns.

Anderson, C.L. "Abuse and Neglect among the Elderly." *Journal Gerontological Nursing* (February 1981):77–85.   B, C

Andrews, F.M., and S.B. Withey. Assessing the Quality of Life as People Experience It. Paper presented at the annual meeting of the American Sociological Association, Montreal, August 1974.   A, B, C, D, E, F, G

———. *Developing Measures of Perceived Life Quality.* Paper presented at the annual meeting of the American Sociological Association, New York, August 1973.   E

"Anti-Crime Programs Assist Elderly Victims." *Enforcement Journal* 15 (12 October 1976):21.   E

Anttila, I. "Victimology: A New Territory in Criminology." *Scandinavian Studies in Criminology* 5 (1974).   A

Antunes, G.E., et al. "Patterns of Personal Crime against the Elderly: Findings from a National Survey." *Gerontologist* 17 (1977):321–327.
                                                                             F

Self-reported data on victimization collected over an eighteen-month period from a national survey of 370,000 persons; explores the social context in which crimes against the elderly occur.

Archbold, P. "Impact of Parent Caring on Middle-Aged Offspring." *Journal of Gerontological Nursing* 5 (February 1980):79–85.   E

Arnold, P. *Lady Beware*. Garden City, N.Y.: Doubleday, 1964.   A, B

Astor, G. *The Charge Is Rape*. New York: Playboy Press, 1974.   B

Atchley, R.C. *The Social Forces in Later Life: An Introduction to Social Gerontology*. Belmont, Calif.: Wadsworth, 1972.   A, E

Baggett, S., and M. Ernst. "Development of Police and Older Adult Training Modules." *Police Chief* (February 1977):51–54.   E

Bahn, C. "The Reassurance Factor in Police Patrol." *Criminology* 12 (1974):338–345.   E

Bahr, R.T. "The Battered Elderly: Physical and Psychological Abuse." *Family and Community Health* 4 (1981):61–69.   B, C

Considers the battered elderly in terms of the sources and reasons for physical and psychological abuse they suffer.

Baker, A.A. "Nursing Practices Which Do Harm to the Elderly: Granny Battering." *Nursing Mirror and Midwives Journal* 144 (1977):65–66.
                                                                          B, C, D

Discusses nursing practices that can be harmful to old people; notes the shock the elderly feel when taken from familiar surroundings and subjected to disorienting hospital routines.

Baldwin, L.A., ed. *PCR: Films and Video in the Behavioral Sciences*. University Park, Pa.: Pennsylvania State University; Audio Visual Services.   A, B, C

Bard, M., and K. Ellison. "Crisis Intervention and Investigation of Forcible Rape." *Police Chief* (May 1974):68–73.   B, E

Baroff, M. Los Angeles: University of California, Los Angeles School of Public Health, Data Bank of Program Evaluations (DOPE), 10833 Leconte Avenue.   E, G, H

Baron, R., and J. Rodin. "Personal Control as a Mediator of Crowding."
    In *Advances in Environmental Psychology,* vol. 1, edited by A. Baum.
    Hillsdale: CA. Lawrence Erlbaum, 1978.   *A, C*
Barrett, J.H. *Gerontological Psychology.* Springfield, Ill.: Charles C.
    Thomas, 1972.   *C*
Bauer, T.L. "The Dimensions of Fear: A Preliminary Investigation."
    Working paper M-3B. Northwestern University, Center for Urban
    Affairs, Reactions to Crime Project, 1977.   *D*
————. "Urban Crime and Protective Behaviors: A Comparative Analy-
    sis." Ph.D dissertation. Department of Sociology, Loyola University
    of Chicago, in preparation.   *E*
Baumer, T., and F.L. DuBow. "Fear of Crime in the Polls: What They Do
    and Do Not Tell Us." Paper presented at the annual meeting of the
    American Association of Public Opinion Researchers, Buck Hill Falls,
    Pa.,   May   1977.*A,*   *C*
Baumer, T., and A. Hunter. "Street Traffic, Social Integration, and the
    Fear of Crime." Mimeo. 1978.   *A, C, D*
Baurmann, M.C. "Alte Menschen Als (Kriminalitats) Opfer." *Z–Gerontol*
    14 (July/August 1981):245–258.   *A*

    Auto- and heterostereotypes of the elderly differ very much.

Beattie, W.M. "The Design of Supportive Environments for the Life
    Span." *Gerontologist* 10 (1970):190–193.   *E*
Beck, C.M., and D. Ferguson. "Aged Abuse." *Journal of Gerontological
    Nursing* 7 (January 1981):333–336.   *B, C*
Bell, D. *The End of Ideology.* New York: Free Press, 1960.   *A, G*
Bennett, R., and J. Eckman. "Attitudes toward Aging: A Critical Exam-
    ination of the Literature." In *The Psychology of Adult Development
    and Aging,* edited by C. Eisdorfer and M. Lawton. Washington, D.C.:
    American Psychological Association, 1973.   *G*
Bensinger, G.J. "As People Get Older, the Crime Gets Bolder." *Law
    Enforcement News* 7 (25 May 1981):6.   *A, B, C*
Benson, C.N. "Postal Service Helps Stamp Out Mail Fraud." *Enforcement
    Journal* 16 (6 April 1977):13.   *E*
Berardo, F., ed. "Decade Review: Family Research, 1970–1979." Minne-
    apolis, Minn.: National Council on Family Relations, 1219 University
    Avenue S.E.   *G*
Berghaus, G., et al. "Alkoholaffine Merkmalskonstellationen Bei Aggres-
    sionstatern." *Arch–Kriminol* 167 (March/April 1981):70–82.   *B*
Bergman, S., and M. Amir. "Crime and Delinquency among Aged in
    Israel." *Geriatrics* 28 (January 1973):149–158.   *A*
————. "Crime and Delinquency among Aged in Israel: An Experience

Survey." *Israel Annals of Psychiatry and Related Disciplines* 11 (1973): 33–48.   *A*

A survey of criminality and delinquency among the elderly in Israel.

Bernstein, J., and K. Nelson. "Medical Experimentation in the Elderly." *Journal of the American Geriatrics Society* 23 (1975):327–329.   *B, E*

Discusses participation in human experimental research as a major problem for the geriatric subject.

Beverley, E.V. "Shenanigans and Skulduggery in the Marketplace." *Geriatrics* 30 (September 1975):137.   *A, B, C*

Bickman, L., et al. "Toward Increasing Citizen Responsibility, Surveillance, and Reporting of Crimes." Paper prepared for the U.S. Department of Justice, Law Enforcement Assistance Administration, National Institute of Law Enforcement and Criminal Justice, Washington, D.C., 1975.   *F*

Biderman, A.D., et al. *Report on a Pilot Study in the District of Columbia on Victimization and Attitudes toward Law Enforcement.* Field Survey 1. Conducted for the President's Commission on Law Enforcement and Administration of Justice. Washington, D.C.: U.S. Government Printing Office, 1967.   *E*

Bild, B., and R. Havighurst. "Senior Citizens in Great Cities: The Case of Chicago." *Gerontologist* 16 (1975):1.   *E*

Binns, J.K., and K.G. Flack. "Section 54, Mental Health (Scotland) Act, 1960: Experience and Problems." *Health Bulletin* 30 (July 1972): 219–225.   *E, F*

Binstock, R.H. "Interest-Group Liberalism and the Politics of Aging." *Gerontologist* 12 (1972):265–280.   *E, G*

Birren, J.E. *The Psychology of Aging.* Englewood Cliffs, N.J.: Prentice Hall, 1964.   *G*

Bishop, G.F., and W.R. Klecka. *Victimization and Fear of Crime among the Elderly Living in High-Crime Urban Neighborhoods.* Paper prepared for the annual meeting of the Academy of Criminal Justice Sciences, 1978.   *A, D*

Bisio, B. "Rilievi sul Comportamento Antisociale degli Individui Anziani." *Ospedale Psichiatrico (Napoli)* 41 (1974):219–242.   *E*

Examines various aspects of antisocial and delinquent behavior in the elderly.

Blenkner, M. "The Normal Dependencies of Aging." In *The Dependencies of Old People,* edited by Richard Kalish, Ann Arbor, Mich.: University of Michigan, Institute of Gerontology, 1969.   *E*

————. "Social Work and Family Relationships in Later Life with Some Thoughts of Filial Maturity." In *Social Structure and the Family,* edited by E. Shana and G. Streib. Englewood Cliffs, N.J.: Prentice Hall, 1965.   E

Block, M.K., and G.J. Long. "Subjective Probability of Victimization and Crime Levels: An Econometric Approach." *Criminology* (May 1973): 87–93.   A

Block, M., and J.P. Sinnott, eds. *The Battered Elder Syndrome: An Exploratory Study.* College Park, Md.: University of Maryland, Center on Aging, 1979.   B, C

————. *Elder Abuse: The Hidden Problem: Hearing before the House Select Committee on Aging,* 96th Cong., Sess. 10–12 (23 June 1979). F

Block, R.L. "The Fear of Crime and Fear of Police." *Social Problems* 19 (1971):91–101.   D

Blubaum, P.E. "Maricopa County Sheriff's Department Volunteer Program." *Police Chief* (February 1976):34–36.   E

Boggs, S.L. "Formal and Informal Crime Control: An Exploratory Study of Urban, Suburban, and Rural Orientations." *Sociological Quarterly* 12 (1971):1–9.   E, F

Boland, B. "Patterns of Urban Crime." In *Sample Surveys of the Victims of Crime,* edited by W.G. Skogan. Cambridge, Mass.: Ballinger, 1976.   A

Bolte, J. "Bronx Police Unit Effectively Combats Robberies." *Enforcement Journal* 16 (9 July 1977):15.   E

Bonfiglio, G., et al. "L'Alcolismo Cronico: Una Demenza Arteriosclerotica? Verifica Sperimentale." *Lavord Neuropsichiatrico (Roma)* 58 (1976):23–40.   B

  Discusses an experimental study of the relationship between chronic alcoholism and arteriosclerotic dementia.

Bosarge, B.B. "Comprehensive Training Course on Crime and the Elderly Will be Available Next Spring." *Training Aids Digest* 4 (November 1979):1–3.   E

————. "With Shrinking Tax Bases, Older Volunteers Are Useful, But Police Must Train Them." *Training Aids Digest* 6 (July 1981):1–7.   E

Boszormenyi-Nagy, I., and G.M. Spark. "Invisible Loyalties Reciprocity in Intergenerational Family Therapy." Hagerstown, Md.: Harper & Row, 1973.   E

Botwinick, J. *Aging and Behavior: A Comprehensive Integration of Research Findings.* New York: Springer, 1973.   G

Bozzetti, L., and J. MacMurray. "Drug Misuse among the Elderly: A Hidden Menace." *Psychiatric Annals* 7 (1977):99–103.   B

  Examines the problem of misuse of drugs, including alcohol, among the elderly; notes implications for care providers.

Bradley, W.W. "Cass Corridor Safety for Seniors Project." *Police Chief* (February 1976):43–45.   E

Reviews prevalence of crimes against senior citizens; discusses a Detroit project that is attempting to promote government and community cooperation in crime prevention in this group.

Bragg, D.F., et al. "Abuse of the Elderly—The Hidden Agenda." *Journal of the American Geriatric Society* 29 (November 1981):503–507. *A, B, C*

Presents a scheme for future research and efforts to remediate abuse of the elderly.

Brandon, S. "The Violent Home: Violence in the Family." *Social Health Journal* 97 (October 1977):201–205.   *A*

Brehm, J.W. *A Theory of Psychological Reaction.* New York: Academic Press, 1966.   *C*

Brill, W. *Comprehensive Security Planning: A Program for Scott/Carver Homes.* Washington, D.C.: William Brill, 1974.   E

Brock, A.M. "Stop Abuse of the Elderly." *Journal of Gerontological Nursing* 6 (April 1980):191.   *A, B, C*

Broderick, K., and Z. Harel. "Reducing Victimization and Fear of Crime among Urban Aged." *Gerontologist* 17 (1977):43.   *A, D*

Summarizes findings from a preventive safety program aimed at reducing fear of crime and victimization among older persons in Cleveland, Ohio.

Brody, E.M. "Aging." *Encyclopedia of Social Work.* Vol. 1. Washington, D.C.: National Association of Social Workers, 1425 H Street NW, 1977.   *A, B, C, E, F, G*

———. "Aging and Family Personality: A Developmental View." *Family Process* 13 (March 1974):23–37.   *A, G*

———. "The Aging Family." *Gerontologist* 6 (1966):201–206.   *A, G*

———. "The Aging of the Family." *Annals AAPSS* 438 (July 1977):13–26.
                                                                        A, G

———. "Environmental Factors in Dependency." Paper prepared for the Anglo-American Conference on Care of the Elderly: Meeting the Challenge of Dependency, National Academy of Sciences, Washington, D.C., 17–19 May 1976.   E

———. "The Etiquette of Filial Behavior." *Aging and Human Development* 1 (1970):87–94.   E

———. "Women's Changing Roles, The Aging Family and Long-Term Care of Older People." *National Journal* 11 (October 1979):1828–1833.   E

———. "The Formal Support Network: Congregate Treatment Settings for

Residents with Senescent Brain Dysfunction." In *Clinical Aspects of Alzheimer's Disease* edited by N. Miller. New York: Raven Press, 1981.
                                                                                        E
Brodyaga, L., et al. *Rape and Its Victims: A Report for Citizens, Health Facilities, and Criminal Justice Agencies.* Washington, D.C.: U.S. Government Printing Office, 1975.   A, B
Brooks, J. "The Fear of Crime in the United States." *Crime and Delinquency* (July 1974):241–244.   D
Brostoff, P.M. *Metropolitan Police Contacts with the Elderly.* District of Columbia Report to the 1971 White House Conference on Aging, App. 2. Washington, D.C.: Washington School of Psychiatry, November 1971.   E
Brostoff, P.M., et al. "The Public Interest: Report No. 6—Beating Up on the Elderly. Police Social Work, Crime." *Aging and Human Development* (1972).   A, B
Brotman, H.B. "Income and Poverty in the Older Population in 1975." *Gerontologist* 17 (1977):23–26.
———. "The Older Population Revisited: First Results of the 1970 Census." *Facts and Figures on Older Americans, Number 2.* SRS–AOA Publication No. 182. Washington, D.C.: Administration on Aging, 1971, p. 1.   G
Brown, E.M. "Fear of Assault Among the Elderly." Paper presented at a meeting of the Gerontological Society, Louisville, Kentucky, 1975.   D
Brown, E.M., and S.J. Cutler. "Age and Other Correlates of the Fear of Crime: Further Evidence." Revised and expanded version of a paper presented at the annual meeting of the National Gerontological Society, Louisville, Kentucky, October 1975.   D
Brown, L.P., et al. "Crime Prevention for Older Americans: Multnomah County's Victimization Study." Police Chief 43 (February 1976): 38–40.   E
Brownmiller, S. *Against Our Will.* New York: Simon and Schuster, 1975.
                                                                                     A, B, C
Bundesgesetzblatt. "Gesetz uber Die Entschadigung fur Opfer von Gewalttaten." *Ausgegeben Zu Bon* (May 1976).   F
Burgess, A.W., and L. Holmstrom. "Rape Trauma Syndrome." *American Journal of Psychiatry* 131 (1974):981–986.   A, B
———. "Sexual Assault: Signs and Symptoms." *Journal of Emergency Nursing* (March/April 1975):11–15.   A, B
Burgess, A.W., and P.M. Johansen. "Assault: Patterns of Emergency Visits." *Journal Psychiatric Nursing* 14 (November 1976):32–36. A, B
Burston, G.R. "Do Your Elderly Parents Live in Fear of Being Battered"? *Modern Geriatrics* (16 November 1978).   D

———. "Granny Battering Letters." *British Medical Journal* (September 1976). A, F

———. "Letter: Granny Battering." *British Medical Journal* 3 (September 1975):592. A, F

Busse, E.W. "Theories of Aging." In *Behavior and Adaptation in Later Life,* edited by E.W. Busse, et al. Boston: Little, Brown, 1977. G

Butler, R.N. *Why Survive? Being Old in America.* New York: Harper & Row, 1975. G

Butler, R.N., and M.I. Lewis. *Aging and Mental Health: Positive Psychosocial Approaches.* St. Louis, Mo.: Mosby, 1973. G

Cairns, W.L. "Senior Citizens Turn Cop Spotters." *Police Chief* (February 1977):34–37. E

"Call for 24-Hour Watch on Battered Grannies." *Nursing Mirror (London)* 144 (1977):3. E

Incidences of cruelty to elderly people in their own homes cited by nurses.

"Campaign against Crime for Older Baltimoreans." *Crime Control Digest* 12 (15 May 1978):8–9. E

Campanini, T., et al. "Aspetti Medico Legali dell'Alcoolismo Cronico. Considerazioni sul Comportamento di 285 Etilisti Cronici." *Ateneo-Parmense (Acta Biomed)* 46 (July/August 1975):275–283. B

Campbell, D.T., and D.W. Fiske. "Convergent and Discriminant Validation by the Multitrait–Multimethod Matrix." *Psychological Bulletin* 56 (1959):81–105. C, G

Cann, A., et al. "Social Context Variables in the Social Perception of Rape." Paper presented at the convention of the American Psychological Association, Toronto, Canada. B

Cantor, M.H. "The Formal and Informal Social Support of Older New Yorkers." Paper presented at a symposium on The City—A Viable Environment for the Elderly, 10th International Congress of Gerontology, Jerusalem, Israel, 25 June 1975. G

———. "Older Women and Income Adequacy." Paper presented at a symposium on Problems of the Elderly in New York City—A Crisis for the Elderly Woman, New York, 25 February 1976. G

———. "The Urban Elderly Poor: An Overview with Particular Stress on Their Vulnerability and High Risk." Paper presented at a meeting of the American Orthopsychiatric Association in San Francisco, California, 1974. F

Capel, W.C., et al. "The Aging Narcotic Addict: An Increasing Problem for the Next Decades." *Journal of Gerontology* 27 (1972):102–106.   **B**

Examines older addicts in one city, New Orleans, in 1970.

Carlin, J.E. and J. Howard. "Legal Presentation and Class Justice." *U.C.L.A. Law Review* 12 (1965).   **F**
Carp, F.M. "The Mobility of Older Slum Dwellers." *Gerontologist* 12 (1972):57–65.   **G**
———. "Walking as a Means of Transportation in Retirement." *Gerontologist* 11 (1971):104–112.   **E**
Carrington, F.G. *The Victims*. New Rochelle, N.Y.: Arlington House, 1975.   **A**
Case, G.B., and G. Lesnoff-Caravaglia. "The Battered Child Grown Old." *Gerontological Society: 31st Annual Scientific Meeting* 18 (1978):58.   **B**

Tests the hypothesis that there exists a connection between elderly single-room occupants living in the inner city and the battered, abused child; indicates that a significant number of occupants were subjected to abuse in early childhood.

Center for Rape Concern. Unpublished data on 1974 rape cases. Philadelphia: Center for Rape Concern, 1977.   **B, E**
Center for Social and Community Development, School of Social Administration, Temple University, Philadelphia. "Turf Reclamation: A Model for the Development of Resident Security Systems in Multi-Family Housing." Mimeo, no date.   **E**
Chafetz, M.C. *Health Education: An Annotated Bibliography on Lifestyle, Behavior, and Health*. New York: Plenum Publishing Corporation.   **A, B, C**
"Challenge." *The Department* (September 1976):26–28.   **A**
Chappell, D., et al. "Forcible Rape: Bibliography." *Journal of Criminal Law and Criminology* 65 (1974):248–263.   **B**
———. *"Forcible Rape: A Comparative Study of Offenses Known to the Police in Boston and Los Angeles."* In *Studies in the Sociology of Sex*, edited by J.M. Henslein. New York: Appleton–Century–Crofts, 1971.   **B**
Cheah-Keong, C., and O.W. Beard. "Psychiatric Findings in a Geriatric Evaluation Unit Population and Implications." *Gerontological Society: 31st Annual Scientific Meeting* 18 (1978):59.   **E, F**

Summary of a paper read at the 31st annual meeting of the Gerontological Society, held in Dallas, November 1978; a breakdown of psychiatric findings presented also.

Cheah-Keong, C., et al. "Geriatric Evaluation Unit of a Medical Service: Role of a Geropsychiatrist." *Journal of Gerontology* 34 (1979):41-45.
                                                                         E

Analyzes psychiatric evaluations of 136 patients ranging from age 48 to 94; psychiatric evaluation included as part of the complete geriatric workup done on patients transferred to a medical geriatric evaluation unit after acute care in medical and surgical services.

"Chicago Aims New Program at Senior Citizens." *Crime Control Digest* 13 (September 1979):2-3.   E
"Chicago Police Combine Efforts of Robbery and Crime Prevention Units to Protect City's Elderly." *Security Systems Digest* 10 (12 September 1979):6-7.   E
Chicago Tribune. "City Takes Action to Cut CTA Crime." 26 June 1978.
                                                                         E
————. "CTA Holdups Cut 50%: Rochford." 24 October 1975.   F
————. "Despite Police Progress, Terror Still Rides the Subways." 7 March 1976.   F
————. "New Plan to Fight Crime on CTA." 23 June 1978.   E
————. "Rapid Transit Called 'Safe'." 25 September 1975.   F
————. "Veech Springs to Sox Neighborhood's Defense." 1 July 1977.   E
"Chiefs Outline Efforts Made in Crime Resistance Programs." *Crime Control Digest* 10 (1 March 1976):8-10.   E
Chien-Ching, P., et al. "Substance Use and Abuse among the Community Elderly: The Medical Aspect." *Addictive Diseases* 3 (1978):357-372. B

Studies prevalence and scope of use and abuse of substances by this age group through examination of 242 community-living elderly persons.

Chiricos, T.G., et al. "Inequality in the Imposition of a Criminal Label." *Social Problems* 19 (1972):553-572.   A

Studies inequality in the imposition of a criminal label.
Chmielenska, I. "Walka O Zdrowie Psychiczne." *Biuletyn Polskiego Towarzysta Higieny Psychieznej* 3 (1967):18-21.   B

Discusses community mental health and need for pleasantly and efficiently organized neighborhood backyards in which the aged relax and children play safely, developing their social consciousness and organizational abilities.

Cicirelli, V.G. *Helping Elderly Parents: The Role of Adult Children.* Code 080-4. Purdue University.   E
Cicourel, A. *Method and Measurement.* New York: Free Press, 1964.   E
Clark, M. "Cultural Values and Dependency in Later Life." In *The Depen-*

dencies of Old People, edited by R. Kalish. Ann Arbor: University of
Michigan, Institute of Gerontology, 1969.   *G*
Clark, R., and J. Spengler. "Population Aging in the Twenty-First Cen-
tury." *Aging* (January/February 1978):7–13.   *G*
Claster, D., and D.S. David. "The Resisting Victim: Extending the Concept
of Victim Responsibility." *Victimology* 2 (1977):56–57.   *A*

> Examines the concept of resistance within the theoretical framework of vic-
> timology.

Clemente, F., and M.B. Kleiman. "Fear of Crime among the Aged."
Gerontologist 16 no. 3 (1976):207–210.   *D*
Clinica delle Malattie Nervose e Mentali dell'Universita di Bari, Bari, Italy.
"In Tema di Reati Sessuali in Eta Senile." *Ospedale Psichiatrico
(Napoli)* 38 (1970):504–507.   *G*

> Considers the phenomenon of increasing incidence of sexual offenses with
> increasing age; briefly reviews possible causes.

Coakley, D., and W.E. Woodford. "Effects of Burglary and Vandalism on
the Health of Old People." *Lancet* 2 (17 November 1979):1066–1067.
                                                                       A

> Explains that the stress of burglary and vandalism can precipitate a major
> health crisis in old age that demands urgent admission to hospital.

Cocubinsky, N. "Elder Abuse." *Imprint* 29 (April 1982):24.   *A, B, C*
Cohen, M.L., et al. "The Psychology of Rapists." *Seminars in Psychiatry* 3
(1971):307–327.   *B*
Cohen, S. "Drug Abuse in the Aging Patient." *Lex e Scientia* 11 (1975):
217–221.   *B*
———. "Geriatric Drug Abuse." *Drug Abuse and Alcoholism Newsletter* 4
(March 1975):4.   *B*
Cohen, S.A., et al. *The Other Generation Gap: The Middle-Aged and Their
Aging Parents.* Chicago: Follett, 1978.   *G*
Cohn, E.S. "Fear of Crime and Feelings of Control: Reactions to Crime in
an Urban Community." Ph.D. dissertation. Temple University, Phila-
delphia, 1978.   *D*
Collins, A.H., and D.L. Pancoast. *Natural Helping Networks: A Strategy
for Prevention.* National Association of Social Workers, 1976.   *E*
"Commentary: The Age of Compassion." *Police Journal* 50 (9 July 1977):
207.   *A, G*
"Congressional Study Says Elderly Not Victimized More." *Crime Control
Digest* 11 (2 May 1977):6.   *A*
Conklin, J.E. "Dimensions of Community Response to the Crime Prob-
lem." *Social Problems* 18 (1971):373–385.   *E*

——. *The Impact of Crime.* New York: Macmillan, 1978. *A*

——. *Robbery and the Criminal Justice System.* Philadelphia: Lippincott, 1972. *A, F*

——. "Robbery, the Elderly and Fear: An Urban Problem in Search of a Solution." In *Crime and the Elderly,* edited by J. Goldsmith and S. Goldsmith. Lexington, Mass.: Lexington Books, 1976. *A*

Conrad, A.I., et al. *Automobile Accident Costs add Payments.* Ann Arbor: University of Michigan Press, 1964. *A*

Conroy, M. *The Rational Women's Guide to Self Defense.* New York: Grossett and Dunlap, 1975. *E*

Conroy, M., and E. Ritvo. *Common Sense Self-Defense.* St. Louis, Mo.: Mosby Times Mirror, 1977. *E*

"Consensus in Research on the Elderly." *Criminal Justice Newsletter* 8 (5 December 1977):3–4. *A, G*

Cook, F.L. "Criminal Victimization of the Elderly: A New National Problem." In *Victims and Society,* edited by E.C. Viano. Washington, D.C.: Visage, 1976. *A*

Discusses criminal victimization of the elderly in order to determine if it is a new national problem. Examines four types of evidence to establish whether a crisis exists: frequency of victimization; increase in the rate of victimization; relative severity of the consequences; and the relative fear of incidence and consequences.

Cook, F.L., and T.D. Cook. "Evaluating the Rhetoric of Crisis: A Case Study of Criminal Victimization of the Elderly." *Social Service Review* 50 (1976):633–646. *A*

Cormier, B.M., et al. "Behaviour and Ageing: Offenders Aged 50 and Over." Laval-Medical Journal 42 (1 January 1971):15–21. *A, G*

Corso, J.F. "Sensory Processes and Age Effects in Normal Adults." *Journal of Gerontology* 26 (1971):90–105. *G*

"County Anti-Crime Program for Elderly Citizens Receives National Attention." *Security Systems Digest* 8 (21 September 1977):10. *E*

"County Crime Program Gets National Attention." *Crime Control Digest* 11 (22 August 1977):4. *E*

"County Crime Program Gets National Attention." *Security Systems Digest* 8 (24 August 1977):2. *E*

Covert, A.B., et al. "The Use of Mechanical and Chemical Restraints in Nursing Homes." *Journal of the American Geriatrics Society* 25 (1977):85–89. *B, C*

Examines the use and potential for abuse of mechanical and chemical restraints in nursing homes; offers guidelines and alternatives to draw public and professional attention to the issues and difficulties involved.

Cox, F.M., et al., eds. *Strategies of Community Organization.* Itasca, Ill.: F.E. Peacock, 1970. *E*

"Crime against the Elderly Is Theme for Police Chief." *Systems, Technology & Science for Law Enforcement & Security* 8 (February 1977):7.

A, G

"Crime against Elderly Said to Hurt More Than Statistics Show." *Law Enforcement News* 8 (8 February 1982):2.   A, G

"Crime and the Elderly." *Geriatrics* 33 (August 1978):93–94.   A

Discusses the special problems of crime against the elderly; describes a self-help community crime-prevention program supported by the law-enforcement assistance administration.

"Crime and the Elderly." *I.A.C.P. Training Key* 12 (1979):1–6.   A

"Crime Control Briefs." *Crime Control Digest* 10 (8 March 1976):10. A, E

"Crime Fears Led to Suicides." *Crime Control Digest* 10 (11 October 1976):9.   A, D

"Crime Film to Aid Elderly Produced on Tiny Budget." *Crime Control Digest* 10 (25 October 1976):4–5.   A, E

"Crime Justice and the Elderly." *Training Aids Digest* 3 (November 1978): 5.   E, F

"Crime Prevention for Elderly." *Security Distributing and Marketing* 9 (April 1979):37.   E

"Crimes against Aged Said 'Easy'." *Juvenile Justice Digest* 4 (17 December 1976):2.   A, E

"Crimes against Elderly Cited in Senate Welfare Hearings." *Crime Control Digest* 9 (9 June 1975):8–9.   F

"Crimes against Elderly Study Set by Multnomah County Sheriff." *Crime Control Digest* 9 (7 July 1975):3.   E

"Criminal Justice Headlines." *Corrections Digest* 8 (11 May 1977):6–7.   E

"Criminal Victimization of Kansas City Elderly." *Enforcement Journal* 16 (9 July 1977):8–9.   A, E

Cromwell, P.E., ed. *Women and Mental Health.* Washington, D.C.: U.S. Department of Health, Education and Welfare, 1974.   G

Csida, J.B., and J. Csida. *Rape—How to Avoid It and What to Do about It If You Can't.* Chatsworth, Calif.: Better Books for Better Living, 21322 Lassen Street, 1974.   B

Cuber, J., et al. *Problems of American Society: Values in Conflict.* New York: Holt Rinehart and Winston, 1948.   A, G

Cunningham, C.L. "Crimes against Aging Americans—The Kansas City Study, 1975." Kansas City, MO.: Midwest Research Institute, 425 Vokker Boulevard, 1975.   A, B, C

———. "Pattern and Effect of Crime against the Aging: The Kansas City Study." In *Crime and the Elderly,* edited by J. Goldsmith and S. Goldsmith. Lexington, Mass.: D.C. Heath, 1976.   A

———. "The Scenario of Crimes against the Aged." In *Reducing Crimes*

against Aged Persons, edited by N.E. Tomas. Philadelphia: U.S. Department of Health Education and Welfare, 1974.   A
Curtis, L.A. *Criminal Violence.* Lexington, Mass.: D.C. Heath, 1974. *A, B*
———. "Victim Precipitation and Violent Crime." *Social Problems* 21 (1974):594–605.   A
Cushman, P. "Narcotic Addiction and Crime." *Rhode Island Medical Journal* 57 (May 1974):197–204.   B
Cutler, N.E. "Resources for Senior Advocacy: Political Behavior and Partisan Flexibility." In *Advocacy,* edited by Kerschner, p. 23.   *E, G*
Cutler, N.E., and R.A. Harootyan. "Demography of the Aged." In *Aging: Scientific Perspectives and Social Issues,* edited by D.S. Woodruff and J.E. Birren, p. 31. New York: Van Nostrand, 1975.   G
Cutler, N.E., and J.R. Schmidhauser. "Age and Political Behavior." In *Aging: Scientific Perspectives and Social Issues,* edited by D.S. Woodruff and J.E. Birren, p. 374. New York: Van Nostrand, 1975.   G
Cutler, S.J. "Safety on the Streets: Cohort Changes in Fear." *International Journal of Aging and Human Development* 10 (1979–1980):373–384.
A, D

Uses data from two national surveys; examines cohort changes in fear for one's safety on the streets over an eleven-year period; concludes that fear of walking alone at night has increased among all cohorts but the grestest increases have taken place among the older cohorts.

Dahl, E., and S. Modahl. "Personskader Forarsaket Av Vold. A 5-Ars Materiale Av Pasienter Innlagt I Sykehus." *Tidsskr Nor Laegeforen* 99 (20 June 1979):876–879.   *A, G*
Dandrilli, S.L. "Perspectives on Violent Crimes against the Elderly." *Law Enforcement News* 4 (2 May 1978):7, 9.   *A, G*
Daniel, R. "Psychiatric Drug Use and Abuse in the Aged." *Geriatrics* 25 (1979):144–145, 148–151, 154–155, 158.   *B, C*

It is still not fully appreciated by many physicians that mental symptoms of confusion in the elderly may result not only from a chronic brain syndrome but often are caused by an underlying physical illness, commonly cardiac and respiratory illness.

Davis, B.G. "Stress in Individuals Caring for Ill Elderly Relatives." Paper presented at the annual meeting of the Gerontological Society, Dallas, November 1978.   *E, G*
David, J.A. *National Data Program for the Social Sciences.* Chicago: University of Chicago Press, 1974.   E

Davies, C.T. "Body and Ego Concerns of Long- and Short-Term Incarcerates of Varying Ages." Ph.D. dissertation. University of Michigan, 1976.   G

Studies body and ego concerns in a prison population on the assumption that a prison environment approximates many of the deficits and deprivations of old age, such that prisoners and elderly people might be involved in similar kinds of crisis resolution in areas of the ego.

Davis, F.J. "Crime News in Colorado Newspapers." *American Journal of Sociology* 57 (1951):325-330.   A

Davis, L.J. "Rape and Older Women." In *Rape and Sexual Assault: Management and Intervention,* edited by C.G. Warner, p. 93. Germantown, Md.: Aspen Systems, 1980.   B

Discusses the prevalence and problem of victimization of older women: considers ways to reduce their vulnerability to sexual crime.

Davis, L.J., et al. "Rape and Older Women: Data Review with Implications for Program Intervention." *Gerontologist* 17 (1977):53.   B

Reviews data on rape and older women; draws implications for program intervention.

"Dealing with the Elderly." *Training Aids Digest* 3 (May 1978):5.   A, G

DeBeauvoir, S. *The Coming of Age.* New York: Putnam, 1972.   A, G

Denver Anti-Crime Council. *Denver High Impact Anti-Crime Program: Analysis of 1972 Denver Victimization Survey.* Denver, Colo.: Denver Anti-Crime Council, 1425 Kalamath Street, 1974.   E

———. "Operation Rape Reduction." Denver, Colo.: Denver Anti-Crime Council, 1425 Kalmath Street, 1973.   B, E

Depp, F.C. "Preventing Injuries Inflicted on Elderly Psychiatric Patients." *Mental Health Nursing* 3 (October/December 1981):353-363.   C, E

Derzon, R.A. "HEW's New Health Agency Explores Ways to Deliver Long-Term Care." *Geriatrics* 32 (1977):34-36.   E

"Descriptive Report on the Elderly as Victims of Fraud and Consumer Abuse: Flint and Seattle." Seattle, Wash.: Library Services, Battelle Seattle Research Center. P.O. 5395.   A, E

"Deukmejian and Congress of California. Seniors Join Forces against Crime." *Crime Control Digest* 14 (13 October 1980):10.   E

"Deukmejian Launches Victims Notification Program." *Crime Control Digest* 15 (20 April 1981):7-8.   E

Deutscher, I. *What We Say—What We Do.* Glenview, Ill.: Scott Foresman, 1973.   E

"Different Kind of Film Should Protect Elderly." *Law Officer* 9 (2 January 1977):28.   A, E

District of Columbia City Council. "Report of the Public Safety Committee Task Force on Rape." Memorandum. Washington, D.C.: City
Hall, 14th and E Streets NW, 9 July 1973.   E, F

Dobson, J.C. "30 Critical Problems Facing Today's Family." Waco, Tex.:
Word, Inc., P.O. Box 1790.   A, G

"Doesn't Have to Cost $2 Million." *Security Systems Digest* 7 19. (10
November 1976):6–7.   E

Dohrenwend, B.S., and B.P. Dohrenwend, eds. *Stressful Life Events: Their
Nature and Effects.* New York: John Wiley, 1974.   A, D

Dominick, J. "Crime and Law Enforcement on Prime-Time Television."
Public Opinion Quarterly (Summer 1973).   E

Douglass, H., and N.A. Douglas. *A Study of Maltreatment of the Elderly
and Other Vulnerable Adults.* Final report to the U.S. Administration
on Aging and the Michigan Department of Social Services, Ann Arbor,
Mich., November 1979.   E

Douglass, R. "A Study of Neglect and Abuse of the Elderly in Michigan."
Paper presented to the 32d annual meeting of the Gerontological Society, Washington, D.C., November 1979.   E

Dowd, J.J., et al. "Socialization to Violence among the Aged." *Journal of
Gerontology* 36 (1981):350–361.   A

Addresses the issue of the attitudinal consequences of fear and victimization by focusing on the degree to which people of different ages express
approval of violent behavior.

Drapkin, I., and E. Viano. *Victimology.* Lexington, Mass.: Lexington
Books, 1974.   A

DuBow, F., et al. "Reactions to Crime: A Critical Review of the Literature." Draft working paper, Reactions to Crime Project, Center for
Urban Affairs, Northwestern University, 1978.   G

DuBow, F., and D.E. Reed. "The Limits of Victim Surveys: A Community
Case Study." In *Sample Surveys of the Victims of Crime,* edited by
W.G. Skogan. Cambridge, Mass.: Ballinger, 1976.   E

Dunham, H.W. *Crucial Issues in the Treatment and Control of Sexual
Deviation in the Community.* Lansing, Mich.: Michigan State Department of Mental Health, 1951.   G

Dussich, J.P., and C.J. Eichman. "La Persona Anziana Come Vittima Del
Delitto: Sua Vulnerabilita." *Quad. Criminol Clinic* 20 (January/Febru-
ary 1978):49–62.   A, G

Edwards, J.N., and D.L. Klemmack. "Correlates of Life Satisfaction: A
Re-Examination." *Journal of Gerontology* 28 (1973):497–502.   C, G

Eisdorfer, C., and W.E. Fann. *Psychopharmacology and Aging.* New York: Plenum, 1973.   C, G

   Provides current information on the clinical uses and implications of psychoactive agents as they relate to the elderly patient's physical and mental well-being.

Eisdorfer, C., and M.P. Lawton. *The Psychology of Adult Development and Aging.* Washington, D.C.: American Psychological Association, 1973.   A, G
Elbow, M., ed. *Patterns in Family Violence.* New York: Family Service Association of America, 44 East 23rd Street.   A

   A collection of essays covering various areas of violence and abuse.

"Elder Abuse." *Aging* 315, 316 (January, February 1981):6–10.   A, B, C
Elder Abuse. Philadelphia: Franklin Institute, 1980.   A, B, C
"Elderly: A New Police Resource—An Interview with George Sunderland, National Director of the Crime Prevention Program of the NRTA/AARP." *Law Enforcement News* 5 (24 December 1979):7–10.   E
"Elderly Are Least Likely to Become Crime Victims." *Crime Control Digest* 13 (7 May 1979):8–9.   A
"Elderly Caught in Middle as Researchers Debate Older Americans' Victimization Statistics." *Law Enforcement News* 7 (7 September 1981):3, 5.   E, G
"Elderly Fear Crime, But Still Confident of Police." *Crime Control Digest* 15 (23 November 1981):8.   D
"Elderly Fear Crime Most, Study Says." *Criminal Justice Newsletter* 12 (23 November 1981):4.   D
"Elderly Get New Locks." *Security Distributing and Marketing* 9 (June 1979):84.   E
"Elderly: Newest Victims of Familial Abuse." *Journal of the American Medical Association* 243 (1980):1221–1225.   B, C, G

   Suggests that because older people tend to be less visible and more isolated from the public than others, abuse of the elderly may be more difficult to identify.

Ellenberger, H. "Relations psychologiques entre la criminel et la victime." *Revue internationale de criminologie et de police technique* 8 (January/March):103–121.   C, G
Ellis, A., and R. Rarncale. *The Psychology of Sex Offenders.* Chicago: Charles C. Thomas, 1956.   C
Ennis, P.H. "Criminal Victimization in the United States: A Report of a National Survey." Report of the President's Commission on Law

Enforcement and Administration of Justice. Washington, D.C.: U.S. Government Printing Office, 1967.   *A, G*

————. "Estimates of Crime from Victim Survey Research." *Criminal Behavior and Social Systems,* edited by A.L. Guenther. Chicago: Rand-McNally, 1970.   *A, E*

Epstein, L.J., et al. "Antisocial Behavior of the Elderly." *Comprehensive Psychiatry* 11 (January 1970):36–42.   *A, G*

> Discusses limited information that was obtained for every person age 60 or over and randomly selected sample of persons age 60 or older arrested for drunkenness and interviewed.

Ernst, M., et al. *Reporting and Nonreporting of Crime by Older Adults.* Denton, Tex.: North Texas State University, Center for Studies in Aging, 1976.   *F*

Erskine, H. "The Polls: Fear of Violence and Crime." *Public Opinion Quarterly* 38 (Spring 1974):131–145.   *A, D, F*

Ervard, J. "Rape: The Medical, Social and Legal Implications." *American Journal of Obstetrics and Gynecology* 11 (1971):197–199.   *A, F, G*

Etzler, F.L. "Crime and the Senior Citizen." *Police Chief* (February 1977): 58–59.   *A, D*

Farrar, M. "Mother-Daughter Conflicts Extended into Later Life." *Social Casework* 45 (May 1955):202, 207.   *B, C*

"Fear of Teenagers Greatly Affects Life for the Nation's Elderly." *Crime Control Digest* 14 (3 March 1980):9–10.   *D*

————. *Juvenile Justice Digest* 8 (22 February 1980):3.   *D*

————. *Security Systems Digest* 11 (27 February 1980):3.   *D*

Federal Register 38, no. 196 (Thursday, 11 October 1973):28039.   *F*

Feifel, H., and V.T. Nagy. "Death Orientation and Life-Threatening Behavior." *Journal of Abnormal Psychology* 89 (February 1980): 38–45.   *D*

Feinberg, N. "The Emotional and Behavioral Consequences of Violent Crime on Elderly Victims." *Dissertation Abstracts International* 38 (June 1978):7562.   *A, C*

> Studies the first fifty elderly victims of robbery, burglary, or sexual assault who received services from a recently innovated elderly victims assistance program in order to investigate the impact of violent crime on elderly persons.

Fishman, M. "Crime Waves as Ideology." Paper prepared for the annual meeting of the Society for the Study of Social Problems, Chicago, 1977.   *G*

Fleszar-Szumigajowa, J. "The Perpetrators of Arson in Forensic-Psychiatric Material." *Police Medical Journal* 8 (1969):212–219.   A, G

Fletcher, P. "Criminal Victimization of Elderly Women: A Look at Sexual Assault." Mimeo. Syracuse, N.Y.: Rape Crisis Center of Syracuse, 709 Park Street, 28 April 1977.   A, B

Florida State Department of Administration, Division of State Planning, Bureau of Criminal Justice Planning and Assistance. *The 1978 Plan to Reduce Crimes against Florida's Elderly.* Vol. 2: *Appendices of Supporting Data and Information,* 1978.   E

Flynn, L. "Women and Rape." *Medical Aspects of Human Sexuality* 8 (1974):183–197.   B

Ford, G. "President's Crime Message to Congress." Office of the White House Press Secretary, Washington, D.C., 19 June 1975. Also see "Remarks of the President to the California State Legislature," Office of the White House Press Secretary, Washington, D.C., 5 September 1975.   E

Forston, R.C. "Criminal Victimization of the Aged: The Houston Model Neighborhood Area." *Victimology* 1 (Summer 1976):316–318.   A, E

Forston, R.C., and L.G. Benson. "Differences in the Criminal Victimization of the Aged and Non-Aged and Their Fears of the Reactions to Crime." Denton, Tex.: North Denton State University, 1977.   A, D

> Uses data from a stratified sample of the Houston Model Neighborhood Area and a national sample to demonstrate the mythical nature of the popular belief that the aged in America are criminally overvictimized in proportion to their share of the population.

Forston, R., and J. Kitchens. *Criminal Victimization of the Aged: Houston Model Neighborhood Area.* Community Service Report No. 1. Denton, Tex.: North Texas State University, Center for Community Services, 1974.   A, E

Foulke, S.R. "Caring for the Parental Generation: An Analysis of Family Resources and Support." Masters thesis. University of Delaware, Newark, Del., May 1980.   E

Fowler, F.J., and T. Mangione. "The Nature of Fear." Mimeo. Survey Research Program, a facility of the University of Massachusetts-Boston and the Joint Center for Urban Studies of MIT and Harvard University.   D

Fowles, D.G. "U.S. 60+ Population May Rise 31% to 41 Million by Year 2000." *Aging* (June/July 1975):14–17.   A, G

Fox, H.G. "Grandpop: The Senior Citizen Decoy." *Law and Order* 26 (June 1978):20–22.   G

Fox, S.A., and D.J. Scherl. "Crisis Intervention with Victims of Rape." *Social Work* 17 (1972):37–42.   B, E

"Free Training Package to Help Publicize Plight of the Elders." *Law Enforcement News* 7 (9 March 1981):2.   E

Fry, M. *Arms of the Law.* London: Gollancz, 1951.   E, F

Furstenberg, F.F. "Fear of Crime and Its Effects on Citizen Behavior." Paper presented at a symposium on Studies of Public Experience, Knowledge, and Opinion of Crime and Justice, Bureau of Social Science Research, Washington, D.C., March 1972.   A, D

————. "Public Reaction to Crime in the Street." *American Scholar* 40 (Autumn 1971):601–610.   A, G

Gager, N., and C. Schurr. *Rape.* New York: Grosset and Dunlop, 1976.   B

————. *Sexual Assault: Confronting Rape in America.* New York: Grosset and Dunlop, 1976.   B

Gallup Poll. *Crime in America, Part Three: One Household in Four Hit by Crime in Last 12 Months.* Released 29 July 1975.   A, G

————. *Crime in America, Part Two: Fear of Crime Grows—45% Afraid to Walk in Neighborhood at Night.* Released 28 July 1975.   A, D

————. *Crime in America, Part One: Crime Named More Often Than Economic Problems as Top City Problem.* Released 27 July 1975.   A

Gallup Poll. *Special Report on Crime in the U.S.* Gallup Opinion Index, Report No. 91, 1973.   A, G

Galton, L. *Don't Give Up on an Aging Parent.* New York: Crown, 1975.   A, G

Garetz, F.K. "Common Psychiatric Syndromes of the Aged." *Minnesota Medicine* 57 (1974):618–620.   A, C

Outlines psychiatric syndromes of the elderly, their treatment, and points in differentiating the syndrome.

Garofalo, J. "Fear of Crime in Large American Cities." *The Application of Victimization Survey Results Project.* Analytic Report SD–VAD–19. Albany, N.Y.: National Criminal Justice Research Center, 1977.   A, D

————. *Public Opinion about Crime: The Attitudes of Victims and Nonvictims in Selected Cities.* Applications of the National Crime Survey Victimization and Attitude Data. SD–VAD–1. Washington, D.C.: U.S. Government Printing Office, 1977.   A, C

————. *Public Opinion about Crime: The Attitudes of Victims in Selected Cities.* Washington, D.C.: National Criminal Justice Research Center.   A, C

Geberth, V.J. "The Crews." *Law and Order* 28 (February 1980):38–44.   E

Geis, G., and D. Chappell. "Forcible Rape by Multiple Offenders." *Abstracts on Criminology and Penology* (July/August 1971).   B

Geis, D.M., et al. "Who Reports Shoplifters? A Field Experimental Study." *Journal of Personal and Social Psychology* 25 (February 1973):276–285.   E

Gentry, M. "Crime against the Elderly—A Growing Problem." *Criminal Justice Digest* 3 (December 1975):9.   A, G

Gibbens, T.C., et al. "Mental Health Aspects of Shoplifting." *British Medical Journal* 3 (11 September 1971):612–615.   A, C

Gibhard, P., et al. *Sex Offenders: An Analysis of Types.* New York: Harper & Row, 1965.   B

Gibson, R.W. "The President's Commission on Mental Health: Its Impact on the Future." *Journal of Continuing Education in Psychiatry* 38 (1978):23–32.   G

Glaser, B., and A. Strauss. *The Discovery of Grounded Theory.* Chicago: Aldine, 1967.   G

Glass, D., and J.E. Singer. *Urban Stress: Experiments on Noise and Social Stressors.* New York: Academic Press, 1972.   E

Glenn, N.D. "Aging, Disengagement, and Opinionation." *Public Opinion Quarterly* 33 (1969):17–33.   A, F

Glenn, N.D., and M. Grimes. "Aging, Voting, and Political Interest." *American Sociological Review* 33 (1968):563–575.   A, F

Goldberg, J.A., and W. Rosamond. *Girls on the City Streets: A Study of 1400 Cases of Rape.* New York: Arno Press, 1974.   B

Goldman, R. "Rest: Its Use and Abuse in the Aged." *Journal of the American Geriatrics Society* 25 (1977):433–438.   G

Discusses the therapeutic use and abuse of rest with consideration of the several functions that rest serves in immobilizing, relaxing, and diverting the elderly.

Goldner, N.S. "The Facts of Rape." *Human Behavior* 2 (1973):49–50.   B

Goldsmith, J. "Community Crime Prevention and the Elderly: A Segmental Approach." *Crime Prevention Review* 2 (July 1975):17–24.   A, E

———. "Police and the Older Victim—Keys to a Changing Perspective." *Police Chief* 43 (February 1976):18–20.   E

Discusses six keys to understanding the changing law enforcement perspective on crime and older persons.

———. "Why Are the Aged So Vulnerable to Crime—And What Is Being Done for Their Protection?" *Geriatrics* 31 (April 1976):40–42.   A

Goldsmith, J., and S. Goldsmith. *Crime and the Elderly: Challenge and Response.* Lexington, Mass.: D.C. Heath, 1976.   A, E

Goldsmith, J., and N.E. Tomas. "Crimes against the Elderly: A Continuing National Crisis." *Aging* (June/July 1974):10–16.   A

Goldsmith, S.S., and J. Goldsmith. "Crime, The Aging and Public Policy." *Perspective on Aging* 4 (May/June 1975):16–19.   A

Goldstone, R. "Crime Victims Strike Back." *Police Chief* 44 (June 1977):
26, 28.   *A, E*
"Government Reports on Security, Safety, Fire Control." *Security Letter*
10 (3 March 1980):1–4.   *F*
Gozali, J. "Improving Safety of Elderly Persons in High Crime Areas."
Gerontologist 15 (1975):82.   *E*

A paper presented at the 28th annual meeting of the Gerontological Society, Louisville, Kentucky, October 1975; an investigation of criminal activities against the elderly, designed to identify perpetrators and improve the
safety of the elderly.

"Gramslamming." *Society* 18 (January/February 1981):4.   *A, B*
"Granny Bashing." *Human Behavior* 8 (April 1979):48.   *A, B*
Greenstein, M. "Elderly Victimization and Crisis Intervention: A Pro-
posal." Paper presented at the National Bicentennial Conference on
Justice and Older Americans, Portland, Oregon, 28 September 1976.
                                                                                                           A, D
———. "Fear and Nonreporting by Elders." *Police Chief* (February 1977):
46–47.   *A, D*
Greenwood, P.W., and J. Petersilia. *The Criminal Investigation Process.*
Vol. 1: Summary and Policy Implications. R-1776-DOJ. Santa
Monica, Calif.: Rand, 1975.   *A, E*
Greer, S. *The Emerging City.* New York: Free Press, 1962.   *A, G*
Griffin, S. "Rape: The All-American Crime," In *Forcible Rape: The
Crime, The Victim, and the Offender,* edited by Duncan Chappell, et
al., p. New York: Columbia University Press, 1977.   *B*
———. "Rape: The All-American Crime." *Ramparts* (September 1971):
26–35.   *B*
Gross, D., and D. Capuzzi. "The Elderly Alcoholic: The Counselor's
Dilemma." *Counselor Education and Supervision* 20 (1981):183–192.
                                                                                                           B

Discusses the physiological, sociological, and psychological aspects of alcoholism with regard to the elderly in relation to counseling this type of client.

Gross, P. "Crime, Safety and the Senior Citizen." *Police Chief* (February
1977):18–26.   *A*
———. "Law Enforcement and the Senior Citizen." *Police Chief* 43 (Feb-
ruary 1976):24–27.   *E*

Discusses law enforcement in relation to the senior citizen in terms of utilizing retired persons as volunteers in local law-enforcement agencies and
developing crime prevention programs to reduce the vulnerability of the
older citizen to criminal victimization.

Gross, S. "Crime Prevention Education for the Elderly in Baltimore City." *Police Chief* 44 (October 1977):84–86.   A

Groth, A.N. "The Older Rape Victim and Her Assailant." *Journal of Geriatric Psychiatry* 11 (1978):203–215.   B

Gubrium, J.F. "Apprehensions of Coping Incompetence and Responses to Fear in Old Age." *International Journal of Aging and Human Development* 4 (Spring 1973):111–125.   D

————. *The Myth of the Golden Years.* Springfield, Ill.: Charles C. Thomas, 1973.   A, G

————. "Victimization and Three Hypotheses." *Crime and Delinquency* 20 (1974):245–250.   A

————. "Victimization in Old Age: Available Evidence and Three Hypotheses." *Crime and Delinquency* 20 (1974):245–250.   A

    Reviews available evidence on criminal victimization in old age; presents three hypotheses on the relationship of factors in old-age victimization.

Guttmacher, M.S. *Sex Offenses: The Problem, Causes and Prevention.* New York: W.W. Norton, 1951.   B

Haberman, P.W., and M.M. Baden. "Alcoholism and Violent Death." *Quarterly Journal of the Study of Alcoholism* 35 (March 1974): 221–231.   B

Hackler, J.C., et al. "The Willingness to Intervene Differing Community Characteristics." *Social Problems* 21 (1974):328–344.   A, G

Hallburg, J.C. "The Teaching of Aged Adults." *Journal of Gerontological Nursing* 2 (1976):13–19.   E

Halleck, S. "Emotional Effects of Victimization." In *Sexual Behavior and the Law,* edited by R. Slovenko. Springfield, Ill.: Charles C. Thomas, 1965.   A

Hallermann, W. "Uber Delikte Alter Menschen." *Beitr-Gerichtl-Med* 26 (1969):256–264.   A

Harbin, H.T., and D.J. Madden. "Battered Parents: A New Syndrome." *American Journal of Psychiatry* 136 (October 1979):1288–1291.   A

    Identifies a new syndrome of family violence—parent battering. Relevant dynamics include individual characteristics of the parent batterer, distortions in the generational authority hierarchy, the role of secrets and denial, and cultural influences.

Hareven, T. "Family Time and Historical Time." *Daedalus* 106 (Summer 1977):57–71.   G

Harris, L. *The Myth and Reality of Aging in America.* Washington, D.C.:
    National Council on the Aging 1973.   G
Hayman, C. "Rape in the District of Columbia." Paper presented at the
    99th annual meeting of the American Public Health Association, Min-
    neapolis, Minn., 12 October 1971.   B
*Hearings before the Subcommittee on Housing and Consumer Interests of
    the House Select Committee on Aging,* 94th Cong., 2d Sess. (28 April
    1976).   F
Hays, D.S., and M. Wisotsky. "The Aged Offender: A Review of the Liter-
    ature and Two Current Studies from the New York State Division of
    Parole." *Journal of the American Geriatrics Society* 17 (1969):
    1064–1073.   E

    The few studies reported have focused on offenses associated with the psy-
    chological or psychopathological aspects of aging.

Heber, R.B. "Effects of Elicited and Depicted Violence upon Measures of
    Hostility." *Dissertation Abstracts International* 40 (June 1980):5792.
                                                                    A
Hellmer, J. "Identitatstheorie und Gemeindekriminalitat: Bericht uber eine
    Felduntersuchung." *Arch–Kriminol* 16 (January/February 1978):1–19.
                                                                    A
"Helping the Elderly: Chesapeake (Va.) Sheriff Has Crime Victim Pro-
    gram." *National Sheriff* 32 (9 August 1980):24.   E
Herning, C.L. "The Sex Offender in Custody." In *Handbook of Correc-
    tional Psychology,* edited by R.M. Linder and R.V. Seliger, p. New
    York: Philosophical Library, 1974.   B
Hess, B. "Family Myths." *New York Times,* 9 January 1979, p. A19. A, G
Hickey, T. "Neglect and Abuse of the Elderly: Implications of a Develop-
    mental Model and Research and Intervention." Mimeo. Ann Arbor:
    University of Michigan, Institute of Gerontology, 19.   E
Hickey, T., and R.L. Douglas. "Mistreatment of the Elderly in the Domes-
    tic Setting: An Exploratory Study." *American Journal of Public
    Health* 71 (May 1981):500–507.   E

    Professionals and practitioners involved in providing services to the elderly
    were interviewed regarding their experiences with the mistreatment of older
    people by their families.

Hickey, T., and R.L. Douglas. "Neglect and Abuse of Older Family Mem-
    bers: Professionals' Perspectives and Case Experiences." *Gerontologist*
    21 (1981):171–176.   A, E

    Provides a data-base framework for understanding domestic mistreatment
    of elderly persons by family members.

Hicks, D.J. "Rape: Sexual Assault." *Obstetrics Gynecological Annual* 7 (1978):447–465.   *B*

Forcible rape is a violent crime, as are all cases of sexual assault; in more than one-third of the cases, the victims are children, and a significant number of victims are elderly women.

Hilberman, E. *The Rape Victim.* Baltimore, Md.: Garamound/Pridemark, 1976. Obtained and published by the American Psychiatric Association, 1700 Eighteenth Street NW, Washington, D.C. 20009.   *B*
Hindelang, M.J. *Criminal Victimization in Eight American Cities: A Descriptive Analysis of Common Theft and Assault.* Cambridge, Mass.: Ballinger, 1976.   *E*
————. "Public Opinion Regarding Crime, Criminal Justice, and Related Topics." *Journal of Research in Crime and Delinquency* 11 (July): 101–116.   *E*
Hindelang, M., and B.L. Davis. "Forcible Rape in the U.S.: A Statistical Profile." In *Forcible Rape: The Crime, the Victim, and the Offender,* edited by D. Chappell, et al., New York: Columbia University Press, 1977.   *B*
Hindelang, M., et al. *Victims of Personal Crime: An Empirical Foundation for the Theory of Personal Victimization.* Cambridge, Mass.: Ballinger, 1978.   *E*
Holstrom, L.L., and A.W. Burgess. "Assessing Trauma in the Rape Victim." *American Journal of Nursing* 75 (1975):1288–1291.   *B*
Holt, A.L. "Medicare/Medicaid Fraud and Abuse: Two Issues and Two Responsibilities." *NLN Publications* 41 (1980):1–8.   *A*
Hoover, E.P. "Incidents of Alcohol and Drug Related Arrests." *Maryland State Medical Journal* 20 (April 1971):99–101.   *B*
Hooker, S. *Caring for Elderly People: Understanding and Practical Help.* London: Routledge and Kegal Paul, 1976.   *A, G, E*
Horos, C. *Rape: The Private Crime, A Social Horror.* New Canaan, Conn.: Tobey, 1974.   *B*
"Hospital Detoxification Patient Attempted Rape on Female Geriatric Patient. *United States v. Bell,* 505 F.2d 539 (Illinois), U.S. Court of Appeals. Seventh Circuit. November 11, 1974." *Mental Health Court Digest* 19 (1975):4.   *B*

Affirmed the conviction of assault with intent to commit rape despite the fact that the female geriatric victim was suffering from a mental disease and was incapable of forming a reasonable apprehension of bodily harm.

"How to Design for Residential Crime Prevention." *Criminal Justice Newsletter* 7 (8 August 1976):6.   *E*
Hubbard, R.W., et al. "Alcohol and Older Adults: Overt and Covert Influences." *Social Casework* 60 (1970):166–170.   *B*

"IACP Publishes Training Keys on Use of Deadly Force." *Law Officer's Bulletin* 4 (31 January 1980):74.   *E*

Illing, M. "Granny Bashing. Comment on How We Can Identify Those at Risk." *Nursing Mirror* 145 (22 December 1977):34.   *A, B*

"Impact of Crime Much Heavier on the Elderly." *Crime Control Digest* 16 (25 January 1982):6–7.   *A, D*

"Impact of Fraud and Consumer Abuse on the Elderly." Seattle, Wash. 98105: Library Services, Battelle Seattle Research Center, P.O. 5395. *A*

"Interagency Federal Effort to Stop Public Housing Crime: It's Begun with $30 Million Grant." *Security Systems Digest* 10 (23 May 1979):4–5.
                                                                       E, F

"Interviewing Techniques for Senior Citizen Robbery Investigators." *Law and Order* 27 (June 1979):54–56.   *A, E*

Interview with victim, Multnomah County Victim Assistance Program, District Attorney's Office, Portland, Ore., 1976.   *A, E*

Jacobs, J. *The Death and Life of Great American Cities.* New York: Vintage Books, 1961.   *E*

Jamaica Service Program for Older Adults. *Seniors against Crime: A Crime Prevention Fair for Senior Citizens.* Jamaica, N.Y., 1973.   *E*

Jameson, R. "House Report Cites Elder Abuse as a Serious Problem." *Trial* 17 (July 1981):10.   *F*

———. "Study Finds Elderly Abused." *Trial* 16 (October 1980):15.   *E*

Jarosch, K. "Kollektive Aggressionsdelikte." *Beitr-Gerichtl-Med* 27 (1970): 151–156.   *A*

Jaycox, V.H. "The Elderly's Fear of Crime: Rational or Irrational?" *Victimology* 3 (Fall/Winter 1978):329–334.   *A, D*

Analyzes data related to the elderly's fear of crime.

Jenkins, R.L. "The Making of a Sex Offender." In *Criminology,* edited by C.B. Vedder, et al. New York: W.W. Norton, 1953.   *B*

Jensen, G.F. "Age and Rule Breaking in Prison: A Test of Sociocultural Interpretations." *Criminology* 14 (1977):555–568.   *A, G*

Examines age differences among women in prisons to determine sociocultural relationships between age and rule breaking.

Jewish Association for Services for the Aged. "Federation Safety Outreach Project in Washington Heights, East New York, The Lower Concourse." Mimeo. Summer 1975.   *E*

Johnson, D. "Abuse of the Elderly." *Practical Nursing* 6 (January/February 1981):29–34.   *A, B, C*

The phenomenon of elder abuse is beginning to be recognized by health professionals, but many cases are overlooked.

Johnson, E. "Good Relationships between Older Mothers and Their Daughters: A Causal Model." *Gerontologist* 18 (1978):301, 306.   *A, E*

Johnson, E.F. "Look at It This Way: Some Aspects of the Drug Mix-up Problem among Black, Poor, Aged, and Female Patients." *Journal of the National Medical Association* 70 (October 1978):745–747.   *B*

Discusses the current sale boom of over-the-counter pills, especially in populations that are susceptible (black, poor, aged, female) to loneliness and stress.

Johnson, E., and B. Brusk. "Relationship between the Elderly and Their Adult Children." *Gerontologist* 90 (June 1977):96.   *A, G*

Judge, M. "Increased Sensitivity Lowers Death Rate in Nursing Home Moves." *Social and Rehabilitation Record* (February 1977):21–23.   *E*

Kahana, B. "Different Generations View Each Other." *Geriatric Focus* 9 (1970):10.   *G*

Kahana, E. *Role of Home for the Aged in Meeting Community Needs: Final Report.* December, 1974.   *F*

Kahana, E., and R. Coe. "Alternatives in Long-Term Care." In *Long-Term Care: A Handbook for Researchers, Planners, and Providers,* edited by S. Sherwood, New York: Spectrum, 1975.   *E*

Kahana, E., et al. "Perspectives of Aged on Victimization, Agism, and Their Problems in Urban Society." *Gerontologist* 17 (April 1977): 121–129.   *A*

Despite widespread beliefs about the frequency of age discrimination, little systematic information exists about perceptions of agism; this study explores personal reports of problematic experiences with friends and family, agencies, and neighborhoods.

Kahana, R.J. "Grief and Depression." *Journal of Geriatric Psychiatry* 7 (1974):26–47.   *D*

Contrasts the influence of bereavement and depression on the psychological changes in young and older people.

Kahn, A.J., and S.B. Kamerman. *Social Services in International Perspective: The Emergence of the Sixth System.* New Brunswick, N.J.: Transaction Books.   *E*

Kaij, L., and J. Dock. "Grandsons of Alcoholics: A Test of Sex-Linked Transmission of Alcohol Abuse." *Archives of General Psychiatry* 32 (November 1975):1379–1381.   *A, G*

Tests the hypothesis of a sex-linked factor influencing the occurrence of alcoholism and alcohol abuse.

Kalish, R.A. *Late Adulthood*. 2d ed. Monterey, Calif.: Brooks/Cole. *A, G*

Updated and expanded demography of aging.

Kanouse, R., and A. Laricy. "A Study of the Interaction between a Group of Jewish Senior Citizens and a Group of Black Adolescent Girls Classified as Delinquent." *Dissertation Abstracts International.* *E*

Studies interactions between Jewish senior citizens in a low-income housing project and delinquent black adolescent girls in a neighboring children's shelter.

Kanowski, S. "Probleme der Begutachtung in der Alterspsychiatrie." *Medizinische Welt (Stuttgart)* 27 (1976):2213–2220. *C*

Reviews criteria for psychiatric certification of mental impairment in geriatric patients.

Kansas City Police Department. *Response Time Analysis: Executive Summary*. Kansas City, Mo.: Board of Police Commissions, 1977. *E*

Kaplan, H.B. "Age-Related Correlates of Self-Derogation: Contemporary Life Space Characteristics." *Aging and Human Development* 2 (1971): 305–313. *E*

Kaplan, O.J. *Psychopathology of Aging*. New York: Academic Press, 1979. *C*

Presents topics of interest to geriatric psychiatry.

Karpman, B. *The Sexual Offender and His Offense*. New York: Julian Press, 1954. *B*

"KC to Aid Elderly Victims." *Crime Control Digest* 9 (8 September 1975): 7. *E*

Kelling, G.L., et al. *The Kansas City Preventive Patrol Experiment: A Technical Report*. Washington, D.C.: Police Foundation, 1974. *E*

Kelly, J. "The Battered Parent." *Practical Psychology for Physicians* 2 (1975):65–67. *A, B*

Cites cases of physical abuse of the aged in a discussion of the battered parent syndrome; suggests that adult children tend to assume the role of parents to their elders.

"Kelly Says Crime Resistance Programs in Cities Making Progress." *Crime Control Digest* 10 (2 February 1976):8. *E*

Kent, D.P. "Aging—Fact and Fancy." *Gerontologist* 5 (June 1965):51–56. *G*

"Kentucky Hosts Statewide Discussion on Crime and the Elderly." *Crime Control Digest* 13 (12 November 1979):3. *E*

Kerschner, P.A. "Rape and the Elderly: An Initial Analysis." Paper presented at a meeting of the National Gerontological Society, New York, 17 October 1976.   B

Kidder, L. Personal communication. See also "Crime Prevention vs. Victimization Prevention: The Psychology of Two Different Reactions," by E. Cohn, L.H. Kidder, and J. Harvey, in *Victimology* 3 (1978):3-4.
                                                                          E

Kim, Y.J. "The Social Correlates of Perceptions of Neighborhood Crime Problems and Fear of Victimization." Working paper, Reactions to Crime Project, Center for Urban Affairs, Northwestern University, 1976.   A, C

Kimmel, D.C. *Adulthood and Aging: An Interdisciplinary Developmental View*. New York: John Wiley, 1974.   A, G

Kimsey, L.R., et al. "Abuse of the Elderly—The Hidden Agenda." *Journal of the American Geriatrics Society* 29 (1981):465–572.   A, B, C

Examines categories of abuse of the elderly in formal caretaking situations with a study of nursing homes; categories of abuse include physical, psychological, material, and fiscal.

Kirschner, C. "The Aging Family in Crisis: A Problem in Living." *Social Casework* 60 (April 1979:209–216.   A, G

Knopf, O. *Successful Aging: The Facts and Fallacies of Growing Old*. New York: Viking, 1975.   G

Knowles, M.S. *The Modern Practice of Adult Education: Andragogy versus Pedagogy*. New York: Association Press, 1970.   G

Krulewitz, J.E. "Sex Differences in the Perception of Victims of Sexual and Nonsexual Assault." Paper presented at the American Psychological Convention, Toronto, Canada, 1978.   B, C

Kruzas, A.T., ed. *Health Services Directory*. Detroit, Mich.: Gale Research.   E

Identifies clinics, treatment centers, rehabilitation facilities, care programs, and related services in areas of national health and social concern.

Kuntz, E. "Purchasing: Healthcare Kickbacks Widespread?" *Modern Health Care* 9 (June 1979):22.   B

Lamy, P.P. "Misuse and Abuse of Drugs by the Elderly—Another View." *American Pharmacy* 20 (1980):14–17.   B

Addresses problems of drug abuse of prescription drugs among the elderly, with implications for geriatric medicine practitioners and other health-care providers.

Lane Inter-Agency Rape Team. Unpublished data. Eugene, Ore.: Lane Inter-Agency Rape Team, 125 East Eighth Street, 1977.   *B, E*

Langer, E.J. "The Illusion of Control." *Journal of Personality and Social Psychology* 32 (1975):311–328.   *C, G*

Langer, E.J., and J. Rodin. "The Effects of Choice and Enhanced Personal Responsibility for the Aged: A Field Experiment in an Institutionalized Setting." *Journal of Personality and Social Psychology* 34 (1976):191–198.   *E*

Largen, M.A. "Keynote Address." Mimeo. Special Populations Conference, Arlington, Va., 13–15 April 1977. Funded by National Center for the Prevention and Control of Rape, National Institute of Mental Health.   *F*

Larson, R.C. *Urban Police Patrol Analysis.* Cambridge, Mass.: MIT Press, 1972.   *E*

Last, G. "Sleep Disorders in an Asylum: Lack of Sleep in Elderly Prisoners." *Zeitschrift fur Gerontologie* 12 (May/June 1979):235–247.   *A*

Latzen, M.A. "Setting-up a Senior Citizens Robbery Unit." *Law and Order* 26 (June 1978):60–63.   *E*

Lau, E., and J.I. Kosberg. "Abuse of the Aged by Informal Care Providers: Practice and Research Issues." *Gerontological Society: 31st Annual Scientific Meeting* 18 (1978):92.   *A, C, F*

> Summary of a paper read at the 31st annual meeting of the Gerontological Society, held in Dallas, November 1978. Examines abuse of the aged by informal care providers.

Lavrakas, P.J., et al. *CPTED Commercial Demonstration Evaluation Report.* Evanston, Ill.: Westinghouse Electric, February 1978.   *F*

Lawder, L.E. "Book Reviews." *Law and Order* 26 (March 1978):67–93.   *E*

"Law to Crack Down on Juveniles Who Assault the Elderly Will Be Introduced Next Month." *Juvenile Justice Digest* 4 (17 December 1976):2.   *F*

Lawton, M., and M.H. Kleban. "The Aged Resident of the Inner City." *Gerontologist* 11 (1971):277–283.   *A, G*

Lawton, M.P. "The Dimensions of Morale." In *Research, Planning and Action for the Elderly,* edited by D. Kent, et al. New York: Behavioral Publications, 1972.   *A, C*

————. *Planning and Managing Housing for the Elderly.* New York: John Wiley, 1975.   *A, G*

Lawton, M.P., et al. "The Aged Jewish Person and the Slum Environment." *Journal of Gerontology* 26 (1971):231, 239.   *A, G*

————. "The Ecology of Social Relationships in Housing for the Elderly." *Journal of Gerontology* 8 (1968):108–115.   *A*

————. "The Inner-City Resident: To Move or Not to Move." *Gerontologist* 13 (1973):443–448.   *A, G*
————. "Neighborhood Environment and the Well-Being of Older Tenants in Planned Housing." *International Journal of the Aging and Human Development* 11 (1980):211–227.   *A, G*

Studies the relationship between neighborhood characteristics and the well-being of elderly tenants through a national area probability sample of 153 planned housing environments and over 3,000 tenants.

————. "Psychological Aspects of Crime and Fear of Crime." In *Crime and the Elderly,* edited by J. Goldsmith and S. Goldsmith, p. 21. Lexington, Mass.: Lexington Books, 1976.   *A, C, D*
Lawton, M.P., and S. Yaffe. "Victimization and Fear of Crime in Elderly Public Housing Tenants." *Journal of Gerontology* 35 (September 1980):768–769.   *A, D*

Studies crime rate, personal victimization, and fear of crime in relation to a variety of measures of well-being of 662 older people in 53 public housing sites.

Lazarus, R.S. *Psychological Stress and Coping.* New York: McGraw–Hill, 1966.   *C*
"LEAA Anticrime Program Assists Elderly Victims." *Police Chief* 42 (February 1976):12.   *E*
"LEAA Pamphlet Describes How Elderly Are a Plus to Policing." *Law Enforcement News* 5 (10 September 1979):13.   *E*
Lebowitz, B.D. "Age and Fearfulness: Personal and Situational Factors." *Journal of Gerontology* 30 (November 1975):696–700.   *D, G*
Lee, B. "Precautions against Rape." *Sexual Behavior* 2 (1972):33.   *B*
Leeds, M., and K. Evans. "The Older Person as Victim." *Police Chief* 43 (1976):27–28.   *A*
————. "Residential Crime—The Older Person as Victim." *Police Chief* (February 1976):46–51.   *A*

Discusses the special vulnerability of the elderly to residential crime; examines programs aimed at reducing the incidence of crime directed toward this group.

Lefcourt, H.F. "The Function of the Illusions of Control and Freedom." *American Psychologist* 28 (1973):417–425.   *C, D*
LeJune, R., and N. Alex. "On Being Mugged: The Event and Its Aftermath." *Urban Life and Culture* (October 1973):259–287.   *A*
Levinson, R.M., and G. Ramsay. "Dangerousness, Stress, and Mental Health Evaluations." *Journal of Health and Social Behavior* 20 (June 1979):178–187.   *A, C*

Levitan, S. *Programs in Aid of the Poor.* Baltimore: Johns Hopkins University Press, 1976.   *E*

Lewis, D.A., and M.G. Maxfield. "Fear in the Neighborhoods: A Preliminary Investigation of the Impact of Crime in Chicago." Draft paper, Northwestern University, Center for Urban Affairs, Reactions to Crime Project, 1978.   *D, E*

Ley, D., and R. Cybriwsky. "The Spatial Ecology of Stripped Cars." *Environment and Behavior* 6 (March 1974).   *A*

Liang, J., and M.C. Sengstock. "The Risk of Personal Victimization among the Aged." *Journal of Gerontology* 36 (1981):463–471.   *A*

Investigates the likelihood that personal victimization among the aged is a function of a multitude of factors (such as characteristics of the victim and emotional conditions).

Lion, J.R., et al. "A Violence Clinic." *Maryland State Medical Journal* 23 (January 1974):45–48.   *A*

Lipstein, D., et al. *Baltimore City Crime Prevention Program for the Elderly.* March 1977. Available from City of Baltimore, Commission on Aging and Retirement Education, Waxter Center, 861 Park Avenue, Baltimore, Md. 21201.   *E*

Logan, M.M. "Crime against the Elderly: Cruel and Unusual Punishment." *Victimology* 4 (Spring 1979):129–131.   *A*

Briefly discusses problems experienced by the elderly victims of violent crimes in older inner-city neighborhoods.

"Long Island: Fighting Abuse by Elderly." *Narcotics Control Digest* 10 (8 August 1980):6.   *A, E*

Long, N. "Information and Referral Services: A Short History and Some Recommendations." *Social Service Review* 47 (March 1973):49.   *E*

Lovell, B. "Informaton and Referral Service: Insights and Affirmations." *Public Welfare* 33 (Winter 1975):41.   *E*

Lynch, W.W. *Rape! One Victim's Story.* Chicago: Follett, 1974.   *B*

Lynn, J. "Abuse of the Elderly." *Journal of the American Medical Association* 246 (16 October 1981):1772.   *A, B, C*

Lyons, H.A. "Terrorists' Bombing and the Psychological Sequel." *Journal of Ireland Medical Association* 67 (12 January 1974):15–19.   *A, C, D*

———. "Violence in Belfast—A Review of the Psychological Effects." *Public Health* 87 (September 1973):231–238.   *A, F*

MacAloon, F.G. "Senior Citizens." *Law and Order* 29 (April 1981):8.
A, G

Maccoby, E., and C. Jacklin. *The Psychology of Sex Differences.* Stanford, Calif.: Stanford University, 1974.   C

MacKellar, J.S., and M. Amir. *Rape: The Bait and the Trap.* New York: Crown, 1975.   B

MacMillan, P. "Stop the World . . . I Want to Get Off." *Nursing Times* 76 (9 October 1980):1780.   A, G

Magidson, E. "Transportation Problems of the Elderly." Chicago, Ill.: City of Chicago, Mayor's Office for Senior Citizens, 330 South Wells Street, December 1972.   A, B

Malinchak, A.A. "Book Reviews." *Victimology* 3 (Fall/Winter 1978): 358-360.   E

Mancini, M. "Adult Abuse Laws." *American Journal of Nursing* 80 (April 1980):739-740.   F

Mandell, M. *Being Safe.* New York: Saturday Review Press, 1972.   A, F

Mangione, T.W., and F.J. Fowler. "Correlates of Fear: A Prelude to a Field Experiment." *Personality and Social Psychology Bulletin* 1 (1974):371-373.   D

Markham, G.R. "A Community Service for Elderly Offenders." *Police Journal* 54 (9 July 1981):235-238.   E

Martin, C.A., and A.S. Reban. *Criminal Victimization of the Aged in Texas.* Community Service Report No. 5. Denton, Tex.: North Texas State University, University Center for Community Services, 1976.
A, E

Maultsby, M.C., and L. Carpenter. "Emotional Self-Defense for the Elderly." *Journal of Psychedelic Drugs* 10 (1978):157-160.   A, C, E

An overview of research into drug abuse as a coping strategy for elderly emotionally distressed individuals. Presents use of rational behavior therapy and self-counseling in replacing drug use as a coping strategy followed by a summary of drug-use patterns in an elderly population.

Mayer, M.J. "Alcohol and the Elderly: A Review." *Health and Social Work* 4 (November 1979):128-143.   B

The abuse of alcohol by the elderly is currently poorly documented.

Mayrl, R.B., and V.L. Witzel. *Program Needs of Milwaukee County's Older Adults.* Milwaukee, Wis.: Milwaukee County Commission on Aging, April 1975, p. 51.   E

McCreary, C.P., and I.N. Mensh. "Personality Differences Associated with Age in Law Offenders." *Journal of Gerontology* 32 (1977): 164-167.   A, C

Compares the Minnesota multiphasic personality inventory profiles of law offenders at different ages in order to examine personality changes associated with aging and to assess certain clinically derived impressions about patterns of personality disturbance in older and younger offenders.

McDonald, J.M. *Rape: Offenders and Their Victims.* Springfield, Ill.: Charles C. Thomas, 1971.   B
McFarland, M.C. "The Emergence of a New Concept—Congregate Housing for the Elderly." *Aging* (February/March 1976):7–9.   A
McGowan, R.H. "The Implementation of a Victim Assistance Team Program for the Elderly. Our Senior Citizens: Now a Way to Help." *Police Chief* 44 (1977):54–55.   E

Describes the implementation of a Pasadena, California, victim-assistance team program that helps elderly citizens cope with problems relating to crime.

McIntyre, J. "Public Attitudes toward Crime and Law Enforcement." *Annals of the American Academy of Political and Social Science* 374 (1967):34–46.   C
Medlicott, R.W. "Fifty Thieves." *New Zealand Medical Journal* 67 (February 1968):183–188.   A
Mellina, S. "Il Significato della Violenza nella Condizione del' Anziano: Considerzioni di Terapia Sociale." *Lavoro Neuropsichiatrico (Roma)* 62 (1978):309–315.   A

Discusses the problem of violence among the elderly as a reaction against the marginal role forced on them by society. Suggests that the elderly no longer possess such social values as youth, work productivity, and ideological conformity and find themselves pushed out of the collective whole.

Mental Health Association. Various publications. Arlington, Va.: Mental Health Association, National Headquarters, 1800 Kent Street.   E

Devoted to the fight against mental illness and the advancement of mental health. Offers materials on mental-health issues such as aging, childhood, depression, drug abuse, family life, legislation.

Merlis, S., and H.H. Koepke. "The Use of Oxazepam in Elderly Patients." *Diseases of the Nervous System* 36 (1975):27–29.   E

Discusses the use of oxazepam in geriatric patients with reference to metabolic and physiological properties that differentiate oxazepam from other benzodiazepines.

Merry, S.E. "The Management of Danger in High-Crime Urban Neighborhood." Paper presented at the meeting of the American Anthropological Association, November 1976.   A, G

"Message from the Director." *Federal Bureau of Investigation Law Enforcement Bulletin* 45 (January 1976):1-2.   F

Metro's Rape Awareness Public Education Program. *Precautions and Tactics to Avoid Rape.* Miami, Florida.   B, E

Metzger, D. "It Is Always the Woman Who Is Raped." *American Journal of Psychiatry* 113 (1976):405-508.   B

Midwest Research Institute. *Crimes against the Aging: Patterns and Prevention.* 1977.   A

Milgram, S. "The Experience of Living in Cities." *Science* 167 (1970): 1461-1468.   A, G

Missouri Research Institute. *Interim Report: Crimes against Aging Americans—The Kansas City Report.* Kansas City, Mo.: Missouri Research Institute, 1975.   A, G

Moore, B. *Reflections on the Causes of Human Misery.* Boston: Beacon Press, 1972.   F, G

Moos, R.H., and P.M. Insel, eds. *Issues in Human Ecology. Vol. 1: Human Milieus.* Palo Alto, Calif.: National Press Books, 1973.   A, G

Moran, R., and S. Schafer. "Criminal Victimization of the Elderly in the City of Boston." *Victimology* 2 (1977):75.   A

Paper presented at the 2d International Symposium on Victimology, held in Boston, September 1976. Examines characteristics of crimes against 418 victims above age 62.

Morris, N., and G. Hawkins. *The Honest Politician's Guide to Crime Control.* Chicago: University of Chicago Press, 1970.   E

Morrison, D.E., and R.E. Henkel. *The Significance Test Controversy.* Chicago: Aldine Press, 1970.   E

Moss, T.E. "Senior Citizen Escort Project." *Crime Control Digest* 13 (8 October 1979):4-5.   E

Morrant, J.C. "Medicines and Mental Illness in Old Age." *Canadian Psychiatric Association Journal (Ottawa)* 20 (1975):309-312.   A, E

Discusses the use of drugs in treating mental illness in the elderly; reviews psychiatric side-effects of drugs commonly used with elderly patients.

"More Security for the Elderly a Paramount National Concern, Washington Attorney General Says." *Security Systems Digest* 7 (17 March 1976):1, 8.   E, G

Morgan, M. "The Middle Life and the Aging Family." *The Family Coordinator* 29 (1969):37-46.   A, G

Mourad, F.A., and H. El-Saati. "L'Applicazione del Diritti Penale Islamico e i Suoi Effetti sulla Prevenzione del Delitto (Una Ricerca sul Campo)." *Quad. Criminol, Clinic* 18 (October/December 1976): 495-536.   *A, G*

Maintains that modern countries, despite their economic and social development, have not been able to find an efficient way to combat crime and that the improvement of the material conditions of human and social life is accompanied by a regression in moral conditions and an increase in crime.

Mowrer, O., and P. Viek. "An Experimental Analogue of Fear from a Sense of Helplessness." *Journal of Abnormal and Social Psychology* 43 (1948):193-200.   *D, E*
"MRI Releases Study of Criminal Victimization of Elderly." *Crime Control Digest* 11 (16 May 1977):7-8.   *D*

Nahum, L.H. "Some Advances in Biomedical Science with Social and Moral Implications." *Connecticut Medicine* 36 (1972):29-31.   *C, E*
National Academy of Sciences. *Surveying Crime.* Washington, D.C.: National Academy of Sciences, Committee on National Statistics, 1976.   *E*
"National Bicentennial Conference on Justice and Older Americans." *Victimology* 1 (Winter 1976):4.   *A*
National Center for the Prevention and Control of Rape. "Rape and Older Women: A Guide to Prevention and Protection." Department of Health Education and Welfare Publication No. 78-734. Washington, D.C.: U.S. Government Printing Office, 1979.   *A, B*

Special vulnerabilities of older women to rape or other physical assaults, prevention strategies and educational programs and training aids.

National Commission on the Causes and Prevention of Violence. *Crimes of Violence.* Vol. 11 Washington, D.C.: U.S. Government Printing Office, 1969.   *A*
————. *Violent Crime.* New York: George Braziller, 1969.   *A*
National Council on Aging. *Facts and Myths about Aging.* Washington, D.C.: National Council on Aging, 1976.   *A, G*
————. *The Myth and Reality of Aging in America.* Washington, D.C.: National Council on Aging, 1975.   *A, G*
National Crime Panel Survey Report. 1976.   *F*
National Institute of Mental Helath. "Rape and Older Women: A Guide to Prevention." Rockville, Md.: National Institute of Mental Health, 5600 Fishers Lane.   *B, E*

Recommends prevention and protection activities for the special needs of older women and for those interested in their welfare.

National Institute on Drug Abuse. "The Aging Process and Psychoactive Drug Use." Services Research Monograph No. 79–813. Rockville, Md.: National Institute on Drug Abuse.   *A, B, C, G*

> Three reports representing the three phases of the study: Part 1 examines the literature on the physiological and psychological changes accompanying the aging process and the relationship of these changes to drug use; Part 2 examines the pattern of psychoactive drug use by the elderly; part 3 identifies operating programs for prevention or treatment of drug misuse or abuse by the elderly.

———. "Elder Education: Wise Use of Drugs for Older Americans." Rockville, Md.: National Institute on Drug Abuse, Office of Communication and Public Affairs, 5600 Fishers Lane.   *A, B, G*

> This 16 mm film or videocassette presents a training program on prevention of drug abuse among older Americans. Topics include the importance of giving complete information to the doctor and getting complete information about drugs being taken, the wise purchase of drugs, typical problems of drug use at home, and some alternates to their use.

National League of Cities and U.S. Conference of Mayors. *Proceedings.* Washington, D.C.: National Conference on Women and Crime, February 1976, pp. 26–27.   *A, F*

——— *Rape.* Washington, D.C.: National League of Cities and the U.S. Conference of Mayors, November 1974.   *A, B*

National Victim/Witness Resource Center. Various publications. Alexandria, Va.: National Victim/Witness Resource Center, 108A South Columbus Street.   *E*

> Publishes concern newsletter; sponsors a national hotline and an information center. Useful for current information concerning sexual abuse, spouse abuse, child abuse, victimization of parents, grandparents, and so forth.

"Neglect—Parent's Criminal History Is Relevant to Custody—Custody to Aged, Employed Grandfather Not to Be Considered—Montana." *Juvenile Law Digest* 12 (November 1980):334–335.   *A, G*

Neugarten, B.L. "The Future and the Young–Old." *Gerontologist* 15 (February 1975):4–9.   *G*

Neugarten, B.L., et al. "The Measurement of Life Satisfaction." *Journal of Gerontology* 16 (1961):134–143.   *A, G*

Nevada. "From the State Capitals: Judicial Administration Modernization Progress." 18 June 1979.   *F*

Newman, O. *Defensible Space: Crime Prevention through Urban Design.* New York: Macmillan, 1972.   *A, E*

———. *Design Guidelines for Creating Defensible Space.* Washington, D.C.: U.S. Department of Justice.   *A, E*

"New Publication from the NCJRS." *Crime Control Digest* 13 (23 July 1979):10   *E*

"New Training Course to Increase Police Effectiveness in Dealing with the Elderly." *Crime Control Digest* 12 (6 February 1978):8   *E, G*

New York. "From the State Capitals: Judicial Administration Modernization Progress." 24 March 1980.   *A, G*

————. "From the State Capitals: Judicial Administration Modernization Progress." 12 September 1977.   *A, G*

————. "From the State Capitals: Judicial Administration Modernization Progress." 28 March 1977.   *A, G*

————. "From the State Capitals: Juvenile Delinquency and Family Relations." 1 April 1980.   *A, G*

————. "From the State Capitals: Juvenile Delinquency and Family Relations." 1 April 1977.   *A, G*

New York State Office for the Aging. "Criminal Victimization of the Elderly: Unique Causes—Distinctive Effects." Albany, N.Y.: New York State Office for the Aging, 855 Central Avenue, August 1976.
                                                                     A, E

"New York Teenage Patrol to Protect the Elderly." *Systems, Technology and Science for Law Enforcement and Security* 11 (August 1979):7   *E*

"New York to Furnish CB Radios to Elderly in Rochester Project." *Crime Control Digest* 11 (30 May 1977):4–5.   *E*

New York Times. "Aged Couple Beaten in a Street of Strangers." 16 March 1977.   *B*

————. "Editorial." 5 April 1977.   *A, G*

————. "Gerontology Is Still a Very Young Science." 19 June 1977.   *A, G*

————. "Many Elderly in the Bronx Spend Their Lives in Terror of Crime." 12 November 1976, p. B1.   *A, C*

————. "Two Boys Face Trial in Fatal Beating of a Brooklyn Woman." 18 March 1977   *A, B*

"NIJ Study Debunks Need for Police/Elderly Program." *Law Enforcement News* 7 (23 November 1981):6.   *E*

Norman, E. *Rape.* Los Angeles: Wollstonecraft, 1973.   *B*

"Northern Virginia Overdose Deaths Up 50 Percent—Mostly Elderly." *Narcotics Control Digest* 7 (16 February 1977):10.   *B, C*

North-Walker, N., and S. Borkowski. "Toward Increasing Citizen Responsibility, Surveillance, and Reporting of Crimes." Prepared for U.S. Department of Justice, NILECJ, Law Enforcement Assistance Administration, 1975.   *E, G*

O'Brien, J.E. "Components of Quality of Life among Severely Impaired Urban Elderly." Paper presented at the annual meeting of Gerontological Society, Miami Beach, November 1973. Abstract in *Gerontologist* 13 (1973):85   *G*

Ochtill, H.N., and M. Krieger. "Violent Behavior among Hospitalized Medical and Surgical Patients." *Southern Medical Journal* 75 (February 1982):151–155.   *A, B, C*

Ohio. From the State Capitals: Judicial Administration Modernization Progress." 3 July 1978, p. 3.   *A, G*

———. "From the State Capitals: Judicial Administration Modernization Progress." 22 May 1978, p. 4.   *A, G*

———. "From the State Capitals: Juvenile Delinquency and Family Relations." 1 July 1978, p. 4.   *A, G*

———. "From the State Capitals: Police Administration Trends in the States." 1 June 1978, p. 4.   *A, G*

"Older Persons Main Targets as Thousands Are Swindled of Billions." *Crime Control Digest* 14 (21 January 1980):6.   *A*

———. *Security Systems Digest* 11 (30 January 1980):3–4.   *A*

Ollenburger, J.C. "Criminal Victimization and Fear of Crime." *Research on Aging* 3 (1981):101–118.   *A, D*

> The relationship between criminal victimization and age-related characteristics; investigates the extent and reasons for high rates of fear of crime among the elderly.

O'Malley, H. *Hearings before the House Select Committee on Aging,* 96th Congress., 12–16 (23 June 1979).   *F*

O'Malley, H. et al. *Elder Abuse in Massachusetts: A Survey of Professionals and Paraprofessionals.* Boston: Legal Research and Services for the Elderly, 1979.   *E*

O'Malley, P.P. "Attempted Suicide, Suicide and Communal Violence." *IR. Medical Journal* 8 (March 1975):102–109.   *A, C*

"One-Hundred-and-Three-Year-Old Is Mugging Victim." *Crime Control Digest* 10 (15 November 1976):4.   *B*

Otten, J., and F.C. Shelley. *When Your Parents Grow Old.* New York: Crowell, 1977.   *A, G*

———. *When Your Parents Grow Old.* New York: Funk and Wagnalls, 1976.   *A, G*

"Ounce of Prevention: We Can Prevent Crime." *Security Management* 24 (September 1980):118–119.   *A, E*

Oyer, H.J., and E.J. Oyer, eds. *Aging and Communication.* Baltimore: University Park Press: 1976.   *A, G*

Palmore, E. "Variables Related to Needs among the Aged Poor." *Journal of Gerontology* 26 (1971):524–531.   *G*

Parks, R.B. "Police Response to Victimization: Effects on Citizen Attitudes and Perceptions." In *Sample Surveys of the Victims of Crime,* edited by Skogan. Cambridge, Mass.: Ballinger, 1976.   *E*

"Pasadena Police Banking New Crime Fight Will Help Senior Citizens."
Crime Control Digest 12 (14 August 1978):4–6.   E
Pascarelli, E.F. "Drug Dependence in the Elderly." *Gerontologist* 13
(1973):56.   B

Investigates characteristics of older drug addicts, stressing the increasing
numbers of such persons and the need for special treatment approaches for
them.

———. "Drug Dependence in the Elderly." *International Journal of Aging
and Human Development* 5 (1974):347–356.   B

A study of drug dependence in the elderly refutes the assumption that long-
term addicts die before they reach old age while survivors have generally
given up the use of drugs.

Patterson, A. "Territorial Behavior and Fear of Crime in the Elderly."
Police Chief (February 1977):42–45.   A, C

Studies territorial behavior and fear of crime in the elderly in 156 male and
female homeowners age 65 or older.

Paulus, I., and R. Halliday. "Rehabilitation and the Narcotic Addict:
Results of a Comparative Methadone Withdrawal Program." *Canadian Medical Association Journal* 96 (1967):655–659.   B, H

Compares effectiveness of regular methadone withdrawal treatment with
prolonged treatment; interviews with 153 of an original 176 patients one to
five years following first clinical treatment.

Peck, R.E. "Gantlet." In *The City 2000 A.D.: Urban Life through Science
Fiction,* edited by R. Clem, et al. Greenwich, Conn.: Fawcett Crest,
1976.   G
Persson, G. "Five-Year Mortality in a 70-Year-Old Urban Population in
Relation to Psychiatric Diagnosis, Personality, Sexuality and Early
Parental Death." *Acta Psychiatrica Scandinavica* 64 (1981):244–253.
                                                                C, B
Peters, J.J., et al. "The Philadelphia Assault Victim Study." RO1
MH12304. Philadelphia: Center for Rape Concern, 112 South 16th
Street, 30 June 1976.   E
Peterson, D.M., and C.W. Thomas. "Acute Drug Reactions among the
Elderly." *Journal of Gerontology* 30 (September 1975):552–556.   B

Notes that research in the field of social gerontology has not examined drug
use and abuse among the aged.

Peterson, D.M. and F.J. Whittington. "Drug Use among the Elderly: A
Review." *Journal of Psychedelic Drugs* 9 (1977):25–37.   B

Presents a review and summation of the relevant literature and available research evidence on drug use and misuse among the elderly.

Petit, A.G., and G. Petit. "Accidents, decheances polyviscerales, violences et suicides: leur relation medico–legale avec le taux d'alcoolemie." *Med–Leg–Domm–Corpor (Paris)* 3 (July/September 1970):251–257. *A*

Philadelphia Inquirer. "Crime Worries Aged More Than Poverty, Sickness." 16 November 1976, p. D1. *A, E*

———. "Easy Prey: A Story of Terror and Old Age." 20 March 1977, p. A1. *A, E*

———. "Fearing for Their Lives, They Chose to Die." 25 October 1976, p. A1. *F*

Phillips, L., and R. Fraelich. "Family Relationships between Two Samples of Frail Elderly Individuals." *Dissertation Abstracts International* 41 (1981):3741B. *A, G*

Uses a staged causal model to examine the nature of the family relationships between two groups of frail elderly subjects who reside at home and are cared for by a related caregiver.

Pies, H.E. "Control of Fraud and Abuse in Medicare and Medicaid." *American Journal of Law and Medicine* 3 (Fall 1977):323–332. *A*

Explores issues concerning the control of fraud and abuse in health programs financed with public funds, specifically the Medicare and Medicaid programs.

Plzak, M. "Vyskyt Depresivnich Stavu ve Stari." *Prakticky Lekar (Praha)* 48 (1968):612–613. *A, G*

Pollack, L.M., and A.H. Patterson. "Territoriality and Fear of Crime in Elderly and Non-Elderly Homeowners." *Journal of Social Psychology* 111 (June 1980):119–129. *A, C*

Pope, C.E., and W. Feyerheim. "The Effects of Crime on the Elderly: A Review of Recent Trends." *Police Chief* 43 (1976):29–32. *A, C, D*

———. "A Review of Recent Trends: The Effects of Crime on the Elderly." *Police Chief* (February 1976):48–51. *A, C, D*

Reviews opinion polls and victimization surveys focusing on crime against the elderly; suggests that the crime problem is of paramount concern to those age 65 and over.

Pope, W., and F. Hentschel. "Alcoholismus bei Burgern im Hoheren Lebensalter: Eigenarten des Alkoholismus beim Alten Menschen." *Deutsches Gesundheitswesen* 33 (1978):56–59. *B*

Discusses alcohol-related illness in old age.

Pottieger, A.E., and J.A. Inciardi. "Aging on the Street: Drug Abuse and
    Crime among Older Men." *Journal of Psychoactive Drugs* 13 (April/
    June 1981):199–211.   *A, B*
Poveda, T. "The Fear of Crime in a Small Town." *Crime and Delinquency*
    18 (1972):147–153.   *C*
Powell, D.E. "The Crimes against the Elderly." *Journal of Gerontological
    Social Work* 3 (1980):27–39.   *A*
Pratt, H.J. *The Gray Lobby.* Chicago: University of Chicago Press, 1976.
                                                                           E, F
President's Commission on Law Enforcement and Administration of Jus-
    tice. *The Challenge of Crime in a Free Society.* Washington, D.C.:
    U.S. Government Printing Office, 1967, p. 99.   *A*
———. *Report on a Pilot Study in the District of Columbia on Victimiza-
    tion and Attitudes toward Law Enforcement.* Field Survey I. Washing-
    ton, D.C.: U.S. Government Printing Office, 1967.   *F*
President's Council on Aging. *The Older American.* Washington, D.C.:
    U.S. Government Printing Office, 1963.   *A, G*
"Professional Literature and Films." *Jail Administration Digest* 2 (June
    1979):5–6.   *E*
"Project Concern: Cooperative Program Focuses on Youth and Elderly
    Victims." *Police Chief* 44 (April 1977):58–59.   *E*
"Publications and Audiovisual Aids List, 1980–1981." New York: Na-
    tional Homecaring Council, 67 Irving Place.   *E*

    Books and monographs, papers and reprints, pamphlets, policy state-
    ments, interpretive materials, legislative statements, audiovisual materials
    on a wide variety of subjects.

Queen's Bench Foundation. *Rape—Prevention and Resistance.* San Fran-
    cisco: Bench Foundation, 244 California Street.   *B*
Quinney, R. "Crime, Delinquency, and Social Areas." *Journal of Research
    Crime Delinquency* 1 (July 1964):2.   *A*

Raab, E. *Major Social Problems.* New York: Harper & Row, 1959.   *A*
Rafoul, P.R., et al. "Drug Misuse in Older People." *Gerontologist* 21
    (1981):146–150.   *B*

    Studies drug misuse of prescription and over the counter drugs among
    sixty-seven age 60-persons and over to determine the frequency of abuse
    and its relationship to psychosocial, medical, and pharmacological factors.

Ragan, P.K. "Crime against the Elderly: Findings from Interviews with
    Blacks, Mexican Americans and Whites." in *Justice and Older Ameri-*

cans, edited by M.A. Young-Rifai. Lexington, Mass.: Lexington Books, 1977. *A, F*

Ragan, P.K., and J.J. Dowd. "The Emerging Political Consciousness of the Aged: A Generalization Interpretation." *Journal of Social Issues* 30 (1974):137–158. *A, F*

Rainwater, L. "Fear and the House-as-Haven in the Lower Class." *Journal of the American Institute of Planners* 32 (1966):23–31. *D, E*

Rathbone-McCuan, E. "Elderly Victims of Family Violence and Neglect." *Social Casework* 61 (1980):296–304. *A*

———. "Intergeneral Family Violence and Neglect: The Aged as Victims of Reactivated and Reverse Neglect Paper." Presented at the 11th International Congress of Gerontology, Tokyo, August 1978. *A*

Rathbone-McCuan, E., and J. Bland. "A Treatment Typology for the Elderly Alcohol Abuser." *Journal of the American Geriatrics Society* 23 (December 1975):553–557. *B, E*

Notes that alcohol abuse is a serious although often unrecognized problem among the elderly.

Rathbone-McCuan, E., and B. Voyles. "Case Detection of Abused Elderly Parents." *American Journal of Psychiatry* 139 (February 1982): 189–192. *E*

Reckless, W.C. *The Crime Problem.* New York: Appleton-Century-Crofts, 1973. *A, G*

Reed, M.B., and F.D. Glamser. "Aging in a Total Institution: The Case of Older Prisoners." *Gerontologist* 19 (1979):354–360. *A, G*

Studies the impact of social arrangements on the aging process; interviews with older prisoners at a major state penitentiary.

Regnier, V. "The Effect of Environmental Incentives and Delimiters on Use and Cognition of Local Neighborhood Areas by the Elderly." Paper presented at the 27th annual meeting of the Gerontological Society. *A, G*

Regnier, V., and J. Hamburger. "Comparison of Perceived and Objective Crime against the Elderly in an Urban Neighborhood." *Gerontological Society: 31st Annual Scientific Meeting* 18 (1978):115. *A, G*

Summary of a paper read at the 31st annual meeting of the Gerontological Society held in Dallas, November 1978. Studies the relationship between older people's perception of dangerous areas in their neighborhood and the actual location of reported crime involving elderly victims.

"Regulations and Legislators: HR-3—The Medicare-Medicaid Anti-Fraud and Abuse Amendments." *American Pharmacy* 18 (January 1978): 46–47. *F*

Reiss, A. "Public Perceptions and Recollections about Crime, Law Enforcement, and Criminal Justice." In *Studies in Crime and Law Enforcement in Major Metropolitan Areas. vol. 1: President's Commission on Law Enforcement and Administration of Justice, Field Survey III,* edited by A. Reiss. Washington, D.C.: U.S. Government Printing Office, 1967.   A

————., ed. *Studies on Crime and Law Enforcement in Major Metropolitan Areas, vol. 1: President's Commission on Law Enforcement and Administration of Justice, Field Survey III,* Washington, D.C.: U.S. Government Printing Office, 1967.   E

"Released." *Security Systems Digest* 8 (18 May 1977):2-3.   E

"Report of the Discussion Sections of the 2d International Symposium on Victimology." *Victimology* 2 (Spring 1977):32-48   F

Reppetto, T.A. "Crime Presentation and the Displacement Phenomenon." *Crime and Delinquency* 22 (1976):166-177.   E

————. *Residential Crime.* Cambridge, Mass.: Ballinger, 1974.   A, G

"Research on Fear of Crime in the United States." *Victimology* 3 (Fall/ Winter 1978):3-4.   E

"Residential Crime: The Older Person as Victim." *Police Chief* 43 (February 1976):46-47.   A, G

"Resisting Victim: Extending the Concept of Victim Responsibility." *Victimology* 2 (Spring 1977):109-117.   A

"Review of Recent Trends: The Effects of Crime on the Elderly." *Police Chief* 43 (February 1976):48-51.   E

Rifai-Young, M.A. "Criminal Victimization of the Older Adult." *Victimology* 2 (1977):79.   A

Paper presented at the 2d International Symposium on Victimology, held in Boston, September 1976; presents results of a study of victimization and fear of victimization of older adults.

————. "Implications for Crime Prevention: The Response of the Older Adult to Criminal Victimization." *Police Chief* 44 (1977):48-50.
                                                                   A, E, F

————. *Older Americans' Crime Prevention Research (Final Report).* Project funded through a state bloc grant under the LEAA in conjunction with Multnomah County Division of Public Safety, 10525 SE Cherry Blossom Drive, Portland, Ore., December 1976.   E

————. "The Older Crime Victim and the Criminal Justice System." *Victimology* 2 (1977):79.   A, F

————."The Response of the Older Adult to Criminal Victimization." *Police Chief* (February 1977):48-50.   A, E

Richey, L.W. "Crime—Can the Older Adult Do Anything about It?" *Police Chief* (February 1977):56-57.   A, F

Ritzel, G. "Zur Kriminalitat Alter Menschen." *Beitr*-Gerichtl Med. 31 (1973):87–91.   A

"Rochester Police Give Elderly Two-Way Radios to Report Crimes." *Security Systems Digest* 10 (5 December 1979):8–9.   E

Rodin, J., and E.J. Langer. "Long-Term Effects of a Control-Relevant Intervention with the Institutionalized Aged." *Journal of Personality and Social Psychology* 35 (1977):897–902.   E

Rodstein, M. "Crime and the Aged: 1. The Victims." *Journal of the American Medical Association* 234 (1975):533–534.   A

———. "Crime and the Aged: 2. The Criminals." *Journal of the American Medical Association,* 234 (10 November 1975):639.   A

———. "Crime and the Aged: The Victims and the Criminals." *Journal of the American Medical Association* 2 (May 1976):65–67.   A

Rosow, I. *Social Integration of the Aged. Glencoe, Ill.: Free Press, 1967.*   A, G

Roshier, R. "The Selection of Crime News by the Press." In *The Manufacture of News,* edited by S. Cohen and J. Young, p. 28. Beverly Hills, Calif.: Sage, 1973.   A, E

Rose, A. "The Subculture of the Aging: A Framework for Research in Social Gerontology." In *Older People and Their Social World,* edited by A.M. Rose and W.A. Peterson. Philadelphia: Davis, 1965.   E

Rosenberg, M. *The Logic of Survey Analysis.* New York: Basic Books, 1968.   A

Rosenthal, J. "The Cage of Fear in Cities Beset by Crime." *Life* 67 (11 July 1969).   D

Roslund, B., and C.A. Larson. "Crimes of Violence and Alcohol Abuse in Sweden." *International Journal of Addiction* 14 (1979):1103–1115.   A, B

Rosow, I. "Retirement Housing and Social Integration." In *Social and Psychological Aspects of Aging,* edited by C. Tibbits and W. Donahue. New York: Columbia University Press 1962.   A, B

Rothman, J. "An Analysis of Goals in Roles in Community Organization Practice." In *Readings in Community Organization Practice,* edited by R.M. Kramer and H. Specht. Englewood Cliffs, N.J.: Prentice Hall, 1969.   E, F

———. "Three Models of Community Organization Practice." In *Strategies of Community Organization,* edited by F.M. Cox, et al. Itasca, Ill.: FE. Peacock, 1970.   E

Rotthaus, K.P. "Der Alternde Gefangene." *Monatsschrift fur Kriminology und Strafrechtsreform (Koln)* 54 (1971):338–344.   A

Roucek, J.S. "Sexual Attack and Crime of Rape." *Topics of Our Time.* No. 13. Charlottesville, N.Y.: Sam Har Press, 1975.   A, B

"Roundtable: Rape and Its Consequences." *Medical Aspects of Human Sexuality* 6 (1979):12–31.   B

Rowe, A.R., and C.R. Tittle. "Life Cycle Changes and Criminal Propensity." *Sociological Quarterly* 18 (1977):223–236.   A, G

Samuel, D.T. *Safe Passage on City Streets.* Nashville, Tenn.: Abigdon Press, 1975.   A, E

Samuelson, R.J. "Aging America—Who Will Shoulder the Growing Burden?" *National Journal* 43 (28 November 1978):1712–1717.   A, E

San Francisco Chronicle. "Brutal San Francisco Murder of a Brave Old Lady." 6 January 1977, p. 3.   B

Savitz, L. *Intergenerational Patterns of the Fear of Crime.* Paper presented at the Inter-American Congress on Criminology, Caracas, 19–25 November 1972.   D

Schafer, C.H. "Analysis of Victimization." Mimeo. Washington, D.C.: National Retired Teachers Association/American Association of Retired Persons, 1909 K Street, NW, 20 September 1974.   A

———. "Misplaced Fears." Mimeo. Washington, D.C.: National Retired Teachers Association/American Association of Retired Persons, 1909 K Street NW, no date.   D

Schafer, H. "Alter und Kriminalitat: Zum Problem des Abbruchs Krimineller Karrieren." *Kriminologisches Journal (Munchen)* 6 (1974): 209–216.   A

Uses data gleaned from official crime statistics and case studies of offender careers to indicate that habitual offenders tend to withdraw from active criminality when growing older.

Scher, J.M. "The Collapsing Perimeter: A Commentary on Life, Death and Death-in-Life." 30 (1976):641–657.   A, G

Schichor, D., and S. Kobrain. "Note: Criminal Behavior among the Elderly." *Gerontologist* 18 (April 1978):213–218.   A, G

Schneider, A.L. *The Portland Forward Records Check of Crime Victims.* Eugene, Ore.: Oregon Research Institute, 1977.   E

Schreiber, L.H. "Mistreatment of Children and Old People." Hamburg, Germany: Kriminalistik Verlag, 1971.   A, B, C

Presents criminological aspects of violence directed against children and old people with reference to West German prosecutions dating mainly from the period 1960–1968.

Schuckit, M.A. "Geriatric Alcoholism and Drug Abuse." *Gerontologist* 17 (April 1977):168–174.   B

Reviews the literature and presents some new data on alcohol and drug problems in older individuals.

Schultz, G. *How Many Victims?* Philadelphia: Lippincott, 1965.   *A*

Schultz, L., ed. *Rape Victimology.* Springfield, Ill.: Charles C. Thomas, 1975.   *B*

Schulz, R. "Effects of Control and Predictability on the Physical and Psychological Well-Being of the Institutionalized Aged." *Journal of Personality and Social Psychology* 33 (1976):563-573.   *A, B, C*

"Second International Symposium on Victimology." *Victimology* (Spring 1977):51-86.   *E*

————. *Victimology* 1 (Winter 1976):573-579.   *E*

Seligman, M.E.P. *Helplessness.* San Francisco: Freeman, 1975.   *A, E*

Seligman, M.E.P., and S.F. Maier. "Failure to Escape Traumatic Shock." *Journal of Experimental Psychology* 74 (1967):1-9.   *D*

Sellin, T. "The Significance of Records of Crime." *Law Quarterly Review* 47 (1951):489-504.   *E*

Selltiz, D., et al. *Research Methods in Social Relations.* 3d ed. New York: Holt, Rinehart, 1976.   *E*

Senior Californian. June 1975.   *A*

"Senior Citizens Aided in Chicago." *Enforcement Journal* 19 (12 October 1980):45.   *A*

"Senior Citizens' Attitudes toward Crime." *Police and Security Bulletin* 13 (November 1981):5-6.   *A, C*

"Seniors Take Comic Approach toward Crime." *Law Enforcement News* 5 (24 September 1979):8.   *A*

SER-MDTA Project. *How to Defend Ourselves against Rape.* Dallas, Tex.: SER-MDTA, 1973.   *E*

Shanahan, P.M. "The Elderly Alcoholic." *Issues in Mental Health Nursing* 1 (Spring 1978):13-24.   *B*

Discusses alcoholism as a major problem among elderly individuals; suggests that health professionals can play a role in enlightening community reactions to elderly alcoholics.

Sherman, E., et al. *Crimes against the Elderly in Public Housing.* Albany, N.Y.: State University of New York, School of Social Welfare, Policy Alternatives Institute of Gerontology, June 1975.   *A*

Shichor, D., and S. Kobrain. "Criminal Behavior among the Elderly." *Gerontologist* 18 (April 1978):213-218.   *A*

Indicates that the share of the elderly among the arrestees is relatively minor but has increased over time for index offenses.

Shimizu, M. "A Study on the Crimes of the Aged in Japan." *Acta Criminologiae et Medicinae Legalis Japonica* 39 (1973):202-213.   *E*

Investigates crimes committed by the elderly in Japan, where the criminal activity of the aged is very low.

Sicker, M. "The Elderly and the Criminal Justice System." *Police Chief* (February 1977):38–41. E, F

Silfen, P., et al. "The Adaptation of the Older Prisoner in Israel." *International Journal of Offender Therapy (London)* 21 (1977):57–65. A

An investigation designed to determine whether the physical and mental conditions of the older individual deteriorate rapidly while in prison.

Silverstone, B., and H.K. Hyman. *You and Your Aging Parent.* New York: Pantheon Books 1976. A

Silveira, M.H., and S.L. Gotlieb. "Acidentes, Envenenamentos e Violencias Como Causa de Morte dos Residentes no Municipio de Sao Paulo, Brazil." *Rev–Saude–Publica* 10 (March 1976):45–55. A

Simon, A., and L.J. Epstein. "The Elderly Offender." *Gerontologist* 8 (1968):23. A, B, C

Discusses arrests of persons age 60 or older.

Simpson, A.E. "The Literature of Criminal Justice: Victimology." *Law Enforcement* 5 (7 May 1979):523–524. A, E, F

Singer, S.I. "The Seriousness of Crime and the Elderly Victim." *Victimology* 2 (1977):83. A

Examines research on crimes against the elderly and age-specific rates of victimization.

———. "The Concept of Vulnerability and the Elderly Victim in an Urban Environment." In *Criminal Justice Planning,* edited by J.E. Scott and S. Dinitz, p. 75. New York: Praeger, 1977.

Skodol, A.E., and T.B. Karasu. "Emergency Psychiatry and the Assaultive Patient." *American Journal of Psychiatry* 135 (February 1978): 202–205. C

Studies sixty-three emergency-room patients with violent ideation or action to assess the feasibility of predicting assaultive behavior.

Skogan, W.G. "Crime in Contemporary America." In *The History of Violence in America.* 2d ed., edited by H.D. Graham and T.R. Gurr. Beverly Hills, Calif.: Sage, 1979. G

———. "The Fear of Crime among the Elderly." *Research into Crimes against the Elderly (Part II): Joint Hearings before the House Select Committee on Aging and the House Committee on Science and Technology,* 95th Cong., 2d Sess. Washington, D.C.: U.S. Government Printing Office, 1978. D, E

————. "Measurement Problems in Official and Survey Crime Rates." *Journal of Criminal Justice* 3 (1975):17–31.   E

————. "Public Policy and the Fear of Crime in Large American Cities." In *Public Law and Public Policy,* edited by J.A. Gardiner, p.   . New York: Praeger, 1977.   D, F

————. *Sample Surveys of the Victims of Crime.* Cambridge, Mass.: Ballinger, 1976.   E

Skogan, W.G. and W.R. Klecka. *The Fear of Crime.* Washington, D.C.: American Political Science Association, 1976.   A, D

Slayton, A. "Fraud Control Units Gear Up to Detect Illegal Billings and Prosecute Offenders." *Forum* 2 (1978):2–5.   A

Smith, L.C., and L.D. Nelson. "Predictors of Rape Victimization Reportage." Mimeo. Revised version of paper presented at the annual meeting of the American Sociological Association, 30 August–3 September 1976.   A, B

Smith, R.J. "Crime against the Elderly: Implications for Policy-Makers and Practitioners." *Journal of Police Science and Administration* 8 (June 1980):245.   A, E, F

————. "Crime against the Elderly: Implications for Policy-Makers and Practitioners." *Police Journal* 53 (12 October 1980):397.   A, E, F

————. "Crime against the Elderly: Implications for Policy-Makers and Practitioners." *Security Management* 25 (February 1981):50.   A, E, F

————. "Crime against the Elderly: Implications for Policy-Makers and Practitioners." *Security Systems Digest* 10 (7 November 1979):5.   A, E, F

Social Practice Resource Center at the Franklin Research Center. *Elder Abuse.* Washington, D.C.: U.S. Department of Health and Human Services, Office of Human Development Services, Administration on Aging, National Clearinghouse on Aging, Service Center for Aging Information. Washington, D.C.   A, B, C

> Defines abuse; study methodology and incidence of abuse; incidence of various forms of abuse; charactertistics of the abused elderly; characteristics of abusers; characteristics of the professional and paraprofessional respondents; intervention efforts. Discusses violence in American and the American family; potential causes of abuse; intervention: legal, social, and preventive; public policy formulation.

Sosowsky, L. "Crime and Violence among Mental Patients Reconsidered in View of the New Legal Relationship between the State and the Mentally Ill." *American Journal of Psychiatry* 135 (January 1978):33–42.   A, B, C

Spector, H. "Team Effort Plays Off in Curbing Fraud and Abuse." *Forum* 1 (September/October 1977):15–17.   E

Springer, L. "Crime, Feelings of Safety, and Street Surveillance." Mimeo. Blacksburg, Va.: Department of Geography, Virginia Polytechnic and State University.   *A*

Stannard, C.I. "Old Folks and Dirty Work: The Social Conditions for Patient Abuse in a Nursing Home." *Social Problems* 20 (1973): 329–342.   *B, C*

Examines patient abuse in a nursing home using data gathered by participant observation.

"Statutes and Ordinances—Battery—Elderly Victim." *Criminal Law Reporter: Court Decisions and Proceedings* 27 (16 April 1980):2067.
                                                                        F

"Statutes and Ordinances—Juveniles—Mandatory Placement." *Criminal Law Reporter: Court Decisions and Proceedings* 27 (16 April 1980): 2068.   *F*

Stein, J.H., ed. "The Senior Citizen Anti-Crime Network." *Criminal Justice and the Elderly Newsletter.* Washington, D.C.: National Council of Senior Citizens, Summer 1978.   *E*

Steinmetz, S.K. "Battered Parents." *Society* 15 (1978):54–55.   *A, B, C*

Discusses parallel between the battered child and the battered elderly parent; observes that both are in a dependent position and rely on their caretakers for basic survival needs.

———. *The Cycle of Violence.* New York: Praeger, 1977.   *A*

———. "The Politics of Aging, Battered Parents." *Society* (July/August 1978):54–55.   *A*

———. "Prepared Statement on Elder Abuse: The Hidden Problem." *Hearing before the House Select Committee on Aging,* 96th Cong. (23 June 1979).   *E, F*

Stephens, J. "Making It in the SRO: Survival Strategies of the Elderly Tenants in a Slum Hotel." *Australian and New Zealand Journal of Sociology* 10 (October 1974):215–218.   *A, G*

Stern, S.S. "Victims—A Closer Look." *Police Chief* 44 (June 1977):18–19.
                                                                        A

Steuer, J., and E. Austin. "The Abused Elderly." *Gerontological Society: 31st Annual Scientific Meeting* 18 (1978):129.   *A, B, C*

Examines family abuse of the elderly via a series of cases of abused, physically disabled elderly.

———. "Family Abuse of the Elderly." *Journal of the American Geriatrics Society* 28 (1980):372–376.   *A, B, C*

In twelve cases of family abuse of disabled elderly persons, the majority of
the abused were women.

Stiles, S.R. "The Future Is Now: Planning, Training Needed to Deal with
    Social Change." *Crime Control Digest* 14 (12 May 1980):6–12.   G
Stinchcombe, A., et al. *Crime and Punishment in Public Opinion:
    1948–1974.* National Opinion Research Center. A report of the Na-
    tional supported project, *Social Change since 1948,* December 1977.
                                                                       E
"Stockton Police Department's Senior Citizens Assistance Program."
    Crime Prevention Review 6 (April 1979):16–20.   E
Stollak, G. "Little Rapes and Big Ones." *Barrister* 3 (1976).   B
Stone, K. and R.A. Kalish. "Of Poker, Roles, and Aging: Description,
    Discussion, and Data." *International Journal of Aging and Human
    Development* 4 (1973):1–13.   E

    Studies participants in legally organized poker palaces in California with
    particular attention to the role of the elderly.

Storaska, F. *How to Say No to a Rapist—and Survive.* New York: Ran-
    dome House, 1975.   B, E
Straus, M.A. "Social Stress and Marital Violence in a National Sample of
    American Families." *Annual of the New York Academy of Science* 347
    (1980):229–250.   A, C
Strieb, G. "Are the Aged a Minority Group?" In *Applied Sociology,* edited
    by A.W. Gouldner and S. Miller. Glencoe: Free Press, 1965.   G
Stromberg, R.E., and A.D. Jergesen. "Medicare and Medicaid Anti-Fraud
    and Abuse Amendments Explained." *Hospitals* 54 (August 1980):
    64–65.   A
"Strong Citizen/Police Relations Credited for Crime Drop." *Crime Con-
    trol Digest* 12 (22 May 1978):1–2.   E
"Study Finds Most Burglars Walk Right into Victims' Homes." *Law En-
    forcement News* 6 (24 March 1980):3.   E, F
Sullivan, J.C. "Crime: Designs for Defensible Space." *Trial* 12 (October
    1976):10   E
———. "Crime: F.B.I. Assists Elderly at Neighborhood Level." *Trial* 12
    (December 1976):19.   E
Sundeen, R.A. "Differences in Attitudes toward Criminal Justice Agencies
    and Practices: A Comparative Study among Elderly." *Justice System
    Journal* 5 (Fall 1979):97–106.   C, E
———. "The Fear of Crime and Its Consequences among Elderly in Three
    Urban Communities." *Gerontologist* 16 (June 1976):211–219.
                                                                       A, D, E

Studies fear of crime among 104 elderly in three southern California communities through collection of data concerning physical and social environments, perception of safety, and fear of crime and precautions taken.

————. "The Fear of Crime and Urban Elderly." Paper presented at the National Bicentennial Conference on Justice and Older Americans, Portland, Ore., 27 September 1976.   *A, D*

Sundeen, R.A., and J.T. Mathieu. "The Fear of Crime and Its Consequences among Elderly in Three Urban Communities." *Gerontologist* 16 (1976):211-219.   *A, E, E*

————. "The Urban Elderly: Environments of Fear." In *Crime and the Elderly*, edited by J. Goldsmith and S.S. Goldsmith, p. 51. Lexington, Mass.: Lexington Books, 1976.   *A, D*

Sunderland, G. "The Older American—Police Problem or Police Asset?" *F.B.I. Law Enforcement Bulletin* 45 (August 1976):3-8.   *A, G*

"Survey of Elderly about Crime in Cincinnati—Hamilton County Shows Many Needs Must Be Met." *Crime Control Digest* 14 (23 June 1980): 4-6.   *E*

Sussman, M. "Relationship of Adult Children with Their Parents in the U.S." In *Social Structure and the Family Generational Relationship*, edited by E. Shanas and G. Streib. Englewood Cliffs, N.J.: Prentice Hall, 1965.   *A, G*

Sutherland, S., and D.T. Scherl. "Patterns of Response among Victims of Rape." *American Journal of Orthopsychiatry* 40 (1970):503-511.   *B*

Sykes, G.M. "Legal Needs of the Poor in the City of Denver." *Law and Society Review* (1969).   *F*

"Symposium on Crime and the Elderly." *Police Chief* (February 1976). Report and papers from the National Conference on Crime against the Elderly, College of Public Affairs, The American University, Washington, D.C., 1975.   *A, E, F*

Szobor, A. "Intellectualis Hanyatlas es Affectivitas Szerepe Idoskori Buncselekmenyekben." *Morphol-Igazsagugyi-Orv-Sz* 12 (July 1972): 202-208.   *A, G*

"Tackling the Crime Problems of the Elderly." *Criminal Justice Newsletter* 8 (25 April 1977):2.   *A, B, C*

Tardiff, K. "Assault in Hospitals and Placement in the Community." *Bulletin of the American Academy of Psychiatry and Law* 9 (1981): 33-39.   *B*

Tardiff, K., and A. Sweillam. "Characteristics of Violent Patients Admitted to Public Hospitals." *Bulletin of the American Academy of Psychiatry and Law* 7 (1979):11–17.   C

———. "The Relation of Age to Assaultive Behavior in Mental Patients." *Hospital and Community Psychiatry* 30 (October 1979):709–711.   C

"TCPI Hosts Crimes against Elderly School." *Security Systems Digest* 7 (10 November 1976):10.   E, F

Technical Committee on Creating an Age-Integrated Society. *Implications for the Family.* Washington, D.C.: White House Conference on Aging, 330 Independence Avenue SW.   E, F

> Policy recommendations made for the 1981 White House Conference on Aging to foster referral assistance of socially isolated aged individuals.

Technical Committee on Physical and Social Environment and the Quality of Life. *Full Report.* Washington, D.C.: White House Conference on Aging, 330 Independence Avenue SW.   E, F

> Investigates present quality of American life as particularly relating to elderly Americans with respect to their housing problems, transportation needs, criminal victimization, legal service, employment opportunities, and so forth.

Tedrick, R.E. "Fear of Crime in Older Persons: An Identification of Predictor Variables." *Dissertation Abstracts International* 41 (1980): 2790–A.   A, D, F

> Investigates the utility of forty-six selected independent variables in explaining fear of crime in the elderly.

Tedrow, J.L. "The Law and the Elderly." *Current Practices in Gerontological Nursing* 1 (1979):207–220.   F

Teller, F.E. "Criminal and Psychological Characteristics of the Older Prisoner." *Dissertation Abstracts International* 40 (1980):5423–B.
                                                                        B, C

> Examines criminal and psychological characteristics of incarcerated offenders over age fifty.

Teller, F.E., and R. J. Howell. "The Older Prisoner: Criminal and Psychological Characteristics." *Criminology* 18 (1981):549–555.   B, C

Tegnor, B., and A. McGrath. *Self-Defense for Women: A Simple Method.* Ventura, Calif.: Thor, 1974.   E

Temple University. "Local Residents Should Be Involved in Crime Prevention." *Temple University Alumni Review* 27 (1977):4.   E

"Ten-Year-Old-Muggers." *Security Gazette* 24 (April 1981):45.   B

"There's No Security for Elderly, Welfare Hearings Disclose." *Security Systems Digest* 6 (18 June 1975):7.   B, F

Thompson, K., and A. Medea. *Against Rape*. New York: Farrar, Straus and Giroux, 1974.   B

"Three Elderly Florida Women Beaten, Robbed by Young Thugs: One Woman Cruelly Killed." *Juvenile Justice Digest* 4 (17 December 1976):7.   B

Thurman, D. "Psychological Impact of Crime and Physical Insecurity on the Older Person." Paper presented at the Mid-Atlantic Federal Regional Council (HEW) Workshop on Reducing Crimes against the Elderly, Wilmington, Del., 25 October 1973.   C

Time. "The Elderly: Prisoners of Fear." 29 November 1976.   *A, B, C, D*

Tissue, T. "Old Age, Poverty, and the Central City." *Aging and Human Development* 2 (1971):235-249.   *A, E*

Tobin, S.S. "The Future Elderly: Needs and Services." *Aging* (January/February):23, 26.   *A, E*

———. "The Mystique of Deinstitutionalization." *Society* 15 (1978): 73-75.   *A*

Discusses the problems posed by deinstitutionalization of the very old who now live mostly in proprietary nursing homes.

Tomas, N.E., et al. "Crimes against the Urban Aged: Redefining Statistical Priorities." Paper prepared for the 27th annual meeting of the Gerontological Society, 1974. Abstract in *Gerontologist* 14 (1974):100.   *A, F*

Tomorug, M.E., and T. Pirozynski. "Victimological Relations in Psycho-Involutive Maladjustment." *Victimology* 2 (1977):84.   *A, C*

Integrates victimology into the concept of relational psychopathology of elderly people. Paper presented at the 2d International Symposium on Victimology, Boston, September 1976.

Topp, D.O. "Fire as a Symbol and as a Weapon of Death." *Medical Science and Law* 13 (April 1973):79-86.   B

Torres-Gil, "Political Behavior: A Study of Political Attitudes and Political Participation among Older Mexican-Americans." Ph.D. dissertation, Brandeis University, 1976.   F

Torres-Gil, F. and R. Verdugo. "The Politics of Aging among the Mexican American Elderly." Paper presented at the 29th annual scientific meeting of the Gerontological Society, New York, (13-17 October 1976.   *E, F*

Toward a National Policy on Aging. Final Report of the White House Conference on Aging, (Vol. 2). Washington, D.C., 1973, p. 235.   F

Townsend, C. "Unloving Care." *Trial* 10 (1974):16-17.   A

Some of the most obvious abuses of the nursing homes in the United States are discussed.

Townsend, P. "The Emergence of the Four-Generation Family in Industrial Society." In *Middle Age and Aging,* edited by B.I. Neugarten. Chicago: University of Chicago, 1968.   *A, G*

"Training Elderly Volunteers: Help Needed." *Training Aids Digest* 6 (January 1981):8–9.   *E*

"Training Materials for Elderly Audiences." *Training Aids Digest* 4 (January 1979):5.   *E*

Treas, J. "Family Support Systems for the Aged: Some Social and Demographic Considerations." *Gerontologist* 17 (1977):486–491.   *E*

Trela, J.E. "Some Political Consequences of Senior Center and Other Old Age Group Memberships." *Gerontologist* 11 (1971):118–123.   *F*

Trube, B.E. "Die Kriminalitat der Frau." *Beitr*-Gerichtl-Med 29 (1972): 42–54.   *A*

Tuason, V.B. "The Psychiatrist and the Violent Patient." *Dieseases of the Nervous System* 32 (November 1971):765–768.   *C*

Tucker, L. "Psychotherapeutic Drugs and the Elderly." *American Pharmacy* 19 (1979):22–24.   *B, C*

"Types of Housing and Mix of Residents Affect Crime Rates." *Juvenile Justice Digest* 4 (23 July 1976):4–5.   *A*

United Way of America, *National Standards: Information and Referral Services. Arlington, Va., February 1973.*   *E, F*

University of Michigan, Wayne State University, The Institute of Gerontology. *Age-Related Vision and Hearing Changes—An Empathic Approach.* 1975.   *E*

Unsinger, P.C. "Book Review: Older Americans' Crime Prevention Research Project." *Crime Prevention Review* 4 (July 1977):44–45.   *E*

————. "Book Reviews." *Crime Prevention Review* 6 (January 1979): 38–39.   *E*

U.S. Bureau of the Census. *Current Population Reports.* P-25, No. 643. Washington, D.C.: U.S. Government Printing Office, 1977, tables 1, 5.   *F*

U.S. Congress, House Select Committee on Aging. *Elderly Crime Victimization (Crime Prevention Programs): Hearings before the Subcommittee on Housing and Consumer Interests of the House Select Committee on Aging,* 94th Cong., 2d Sess. (29 March 1976).   *E, F*

————. *Elderly Crime Victimization (Local Police Department Crime Prevention Programs): Hearings before the Subcommittee on Housing and Consumer Interests of the House Select Committee on Aging,* 94th Cong., 2d Sess. (28 April 1976).   *A, E, F*

————. *Elderly Crime Victimization (Federal Law Enforcement Agencies— LEAA and FBI): Hearings before the Subcommittee on Housing and*

Consumer Interests of the House Select Committee on Aging, 94th Cong., 2d Sess. (12 and 13 April 1976).   A, E, F

―――. *Elderly Crime Victimization (Personal Accounts of Fears and Attacks): Hearings before the Subcommittee on Housing and Consumer Interests of the House Select Committee on Aging,* 94th Cong., 2d Sess. (18 September 1976).   E, F

―――. *Elderly Crime Victimization (Residential Security): Hearings before the Subcommittee on Housing and Consumer Interests of the House Select Committee on Aging,* 94th Cong., 2d Sess. (15 March 1976).   A, F

―――. *Elderly Crime Victimization (Wilmington, Delaware, Crime Resistance Task Force): Hearings before the Subcommittee on Housing and Consumer Interests of the House Select Committee on Aging,* 94th Cong., 2d Sess. (6 May 1976).   A, E, F

―――. *In Search of Security: A National Perspective on Elder's Crime Victimization.* Washington, D.C.: U.S. Government Printing Office, 1977.   B, F

U.S. Congress, Senate Special Committee on Aging. *Hearings before the Subcommittee on Housing for the Elderly of the Senate Special Committee on Aging,* 92d Cong., 1st Sess. (October 1972).   F

―――. *Mental Health and the Elderly.* Washington, D.C.: U.S. Government Printing Office, 1976.   A, G

U.S. Department of Commerce, Bureau of the Census. *Social and Economic Characteristics of the Older Population, 1974.* Special Studies, Series P-23-3457. Washington, D.C.: Government Printing Office, 1974).   F

―――. *Statistical Abstracts of the U.S. 1976.* 97th ed. Washington, D.C.: Bureau of the Census, 1976.   E, F

―――. *A Statistical Portrait of Women.* Washington, D.C.: Bureau of the Census, April 1976, pp. 57-59.   E, F

―――. *Status: A Monthly Chartbook of Social and Economic Trends.* Prepared for the Office of Management and Budget, compiled by the Federal Statistical System. Washington, D.C.: Bureau of the Census, September 1976.   E, F

―――. *U.S. Census of Population, 1970. Vol. 1: Characteristics of the Population—Part 1. U.S. Summary.* Washington, D.C.: Bureau of the Census, May 1972.   F

U.S. Department of Commerce, Executive Office of the President, Office of Management and Budget. *Social Indicators, 1973.* Washington, D.C.: U.S. Government Printing Office, 1973.   A, F, G

U.S. Department of Health, Education, and Welfare. "Slums and Social Insecurity." Social Administration Report No. 1, by A. Schorr. Washington, D.C.: U.S. Government Printing Office, 1966.   C, F

―――. *Transportation for the Elderly: The State of the Art.* DHEW Pub-

lication No. (OHD)75–20081. Washington, D.C.: U.S. Government
Printing Office, 1975.   F
U.S. Department of Health, Education, and Welfare, National Center for
Health Statistics. *Health: United States, 1975.* Rockville, Md.: Na-
tional Center for Health Statistics, 1976.   E, F
U.S. Department of Health, Education, and Welfare, Office of Human
Development, Administration on Aging. *Indicators of the Status of the
Elderly in the United States.* DHEW Publication No. (OHD)74–20080.
Washington, D.C.: U.S. Government Printing Office, 1974.   E, F
———. "NCOA Releases Findings of Harris Poll on Older People." *Aging*
247 (May 1975):6.   E, F
U.S. Department of Health, Education, and Welfare, Social and Rehabili-
tation Service. "Public Transit and Retired People." Transportation
No. 32, by F.M. Carp. Washington, D.C.: U.S. Government Printing
Office.   F
———. *A Trainer's Guide to Andragogy.* Rev. ed. DHEW Publication No.
(SRS)73–05301, by J.D. Ingalls. Washington, D.C.: U.S. Government
Printing Office, May 1973.   E, F, H
U.S. Department of Housing and Urban Development. "Defensible
Space," by O. Newman. In *HUD Challenge,* pp. 6–11 Washington,
D.C.: Department of Housing and Urban Development, September
1973.   B, F
———. *A Design Guide for Improving Residential Security.* Washington,
D.C.: U.S. Government Printing Office, 1973.   E
———. "The Drama of Southwork Plaza," by M.P. Lawton. In *HUD
Challenge,* pp. 9–12. Washington, D.C.: Department of Housing and
Urban Development, February 1975.   E
———. *Housing Management Block Captain Training.* Washington, D.C.:
Department of Housing and Urban Development, March 1976. Avail-
able from National Technical Information Service, U.S. Department of
Commerce, 5285 Port Royal Road, Springfield, Va. 22161.   E
———. *Housing Management Guidelines for Organizing Residents.* Wash-
ington, D.C.: Department of Housing and Urban Development, March
1976. Available from National Technical Information Service, U.S.
Department of Commerce, 5285 Port Royal Road, Springfield, Va.
22161.   E, F
———. Housing Management Technical Memorandum No. 3. Washing-
ton, D.C.: Department of Housing and Urban Development, November 1976.   F
———. *HUD Challenge—Residential Security 1.* Washington, D.C.:
Department of Housing and Urban Development, September 1973.
                                                                B, F

————. *HUD Challenge—Residential Security 2.* Washington, D.C.: Department of Housing and Urban Development, May 1975.   *B, F*

————. "An Innovative Approach to Public Housing Security," by E.T. Ostrowski. In *HUD Challenge,* pp. 22–23. Washington, D.C.: Department of Housing and Urban Development, November 1975.

B, E

————. "Living Arrangements and Security among the Elderly: A Study," by E. Sherman, et al. In *HUD Challenge,* pp. 12–13. Washington, D.C.: Department of Housing and Urban Development, June 1976.

B, F

————. *Manual of Acceptable Practices—1973.* Addition to *HUD—Minimum Property Standards,* No. 4930.1. Washington, D.C.: U.S. Government Printing Office, 1973.   *E, F*

————. *Minimum Property Standards for Multi-Family Housing.* Revision No. 2—No. 4910-1. Washington, D.C.: U.S. Government Printing Office, January 1975.   *E, F*

————. "New York's Experiment in Tenant Safety," by S. Granville. In *HUD Challenge,* pp. 22–25. Washington, D.C.: Department of Housing and Urban Development, September 1974.   *E, F*

————. "Safety and Security." Housing Management Technical Memoranda No. 1. Washington, D.C.: Department of Housing and Urban Development, 1975.   *B, F*

————. *Security Planning for HUD-Assisted Multi-Family Housing.* No. 7460.4. Washington, D.C.: Department of Housing and Urban Development, April 1974.   *B, F*

————. "Turf Reclamation Revisited," by S.J. Rosenthal and A. Allan. In *HUD Challenge,* pp. 26–28. Washington, D.C.: Department of Housing and Urban Development, September 1976.   *E, F*

U.S. Department of Justice. *Criminal Victimization in the United States.* Washington, D.C.: U.S. Government Printing Office, 1974.   *A, G*

U.S. Department of Justice, National Criminal Justice Information and Statistics Service, Law Enforcement Assistance Administration. *Criminal Victimization in the United States: A Comparison of 1973 and 1974 Findings.* Washington, D.C.: U.S. Government Printing Office, 1976.

A, E

————. *Criminal Victimization in the United States, 1973.* Washington, D.C.: U.S. Government Printing Office, 1976.   *A, E*

U.S. Department of Justice, Federal Bureau of Investigation. *Crime in America, 1976. Washington, D.C.: U.S. Government Printing Office, 1977.*   *A, G*

————. *Uniform Crime Reporting Handbook.* Washington, D.C.: U.S. Government Printing Office, 1976.   *E, F*

————. *Uniform Crime Reports for the U.S.—1975.* Washington, D.C.: U. S. Government Printing Office, 1976.   *E, F*

————. *Uniform Crime Reports for the U.S.—1974.* Washington, D.C.: U. S. Government Printing Office, 1975.   *E, F*

————. *Uniform Crime Reports for the U.S.—1973.* Washington, D.C.: U. S. Government Printing Office, 1974.   *E, F*

————. *Uniform Crime Reports for the U.S.—1972.* Washington, D.C.: U. S. Government Printing Office, 1973.   *E, F*

————. *Uniform Crime Reports for the U.S.—1971.* Washington, D.C.: U. S. Government Printing Office, 1972.   *E, F*

————. *Uniform Crime Reports for the U.S.—1970.* Washington, D.C.: U. S. Government Printing Office, 1971.   *E, F*

————. *Uniform Crime Reports for the U.S.—1960.* Washington, D.C.: U. S. Government Printing Office, 1961.   *E, F*

————. Police Foundation; and Police Departments of Birmingham, Alabama; Wilmington, Delaware; DeKalb County, Georgia; Norfolk, Virginia. *Crime Resistance.* 1976. May be obtained from Wilmington Crime Resistance Program, P.O. Box 1872, Wilmington, Del. 19899. *F*

U.S. Department of Justice, Law Enforcement Assistance Administration, National Criminal Justice Information and Statistics Service. *Crime in Eight American Cities.* Washington, D.C.: U.S. Government Printing Office, 1975.   *E, F*

————. *Criminal Victimization Surveys in the Nation's Five Largest Cities.* Washington, D.C.: U.S. Government Printing Office, 1975.   *E, F*

————. *Criminal Victimizations in the U.S.* Washington, D.C.: U.S. Government Printing Office, 1977.   *A, E, F*

————. *Criminal Victimization Surveys in Thirteen American Cities.* Washington, D.C.: U.S. Government Printing Office, June 1975.   *E, F*

————. *Local Victim Surveys: A Review of the Issues.* Washington, D.C.: U.S. Government Printing Office, 1977.   *A, E, F*

————. *The Patterns and Distribution of Assault Incidents Characteristics among Social Areas (Utilization of Criminal Justice Statistics Project— Analytic Report 14).* Washington, D.C.: U.S. Government Printing Office, 1976.   *E, F*

————. *Patterns of Robbery Characteristics and Their Occurrence among Social Areas.* Washington, D.C.: U.S. Government Printing Office, 1976.   *E, F*

————. *Sourcebook of Criminal Justice Statistics—1976.* Washington, D.C.: U.S. Government Printing Office, February 1977.   *E, F*

————. *Sourcebook of Criminal Justice Statistics—1975.* Washington, D.C.: U.S. Government Printing Office, 1976.   *E, F*

U.S. Department of Justice, Law Enforcement Assistance Administration, National Institute of Law Enforcement and Criminal Justice. *Design*

Guidelines for Creating Defensible Space, by O. Newman. Washington, D.C.: U.S. Government Printing Office, April 1976.   *C, E, F*
————. *Forcible Rape: A National Survey of the Response by Prosecutors.* Vol. 1. Washington, D.C.: U.S. Government Printing Office, March 1977.   *B, E, F*
U.S. Department of Labor, Bureau of Labor Statistics. *The Employment Problems of Older Workers.* Washington, D.C.: U.S. Government Printing Office, 1971.   *A*

Van Matre, P. "Elderly Cognition of Crime Areas in the Neighborhood: Findings and Policy Implications." *Gerontologist* 15 (1975):81.   *A, E*

Paper presented at the 28th annual meeting of the Gerontological Society, Louisville, Kentucky, October 1975. Discusses the relationship between actual crime areas and crime areas perceived by the elderly; discusses the effect such perception has on employment of the elderly and on employment of defense mechanisms and usage of the neighborhood by elderly respondents.

Vasquez, F.H. "Crime Resistance for the Elderly." *Law and Order* 26 (June 1978):64–65.   *A*
Verba, S., and N.H. Nie. *Participation in America.* New York: Harper & Row, 1972, ch. 6.   *A, G*
"Victimization and Fear of Crime among the Urban Aged." *Police Chief* 47 (March 1980):34–36.   *A, D*
Victimology: A New Focus. 5 vols. Lexington, Mass.: Lexington Books, 1974.   *A*
Victims: A Report for Citizens, Health Facilities, and Criminal Justice Agencies. Washington, D.C.: The Administration, November 1975.   *A, E*
Village Voice. "I Am 77. Last Night I Was Raped." 18 October 1976, p. 44.   *B*
Vincent, R.H., and R.N. Berg. "Medicare–Medicaid Anti-Fraud and Abuse Amendments." *Journal of the Medical Association of Georgia* 66 (December 1977):973–974.   *A*
"Visiting Elderly Is Paying Off, Sheriff W.D. Nichols Says." *National Sheriff* 30 (5 April 1978):31.   *A*
Vladeck, B.C. *Unloving Care: The Nursing Home Tragedy.* New York: Basic Books, 1980.   *A, B, C*

Walker, E.T. *Family Trouble Clinic: A Police*-Social Work Approach to Family Violence. Detroit: Family Service of Detroit and Wayne County, 51 West Warren Street.   *E*

Describes the Family Trouble Clinic (FTC), which provides counseling to families and individuals involved in domestic violence situations.

Walshe, B.K. "Granny Bashing." *Nursing Mirror* 145 (22 December 1977): 32–34.   *A, B*
Walter, B.L. "A Description of the Elderly Offender in Pennsylvania." *Dissertation Abstracts International* 41 (1980):813–A.   *A, G*

Describes entire elderly offender population in Pennsylvania's State Correctional system, beginning September 1973 through December 1979.

Walther, R.J. "Economics and the Older Population." In *Aging,* edited by Woodruff and Birren, p. 336.   *A*
"Warning: Home Repair Bunco Gang Operating again Fleecing Elderly." *Security Systems Digest* 12 (10 June 1981):10.   *A*
Washington, D.C., Rape Crisis Center. "Politics of Rape." Washington, D.C.: Rape Crisis Center, P.O. Box 21005.   *B, E*
———. *Testimony before the Public Safety Committee Task Force on Rape.* Washington, D.C., City Council: 18 September 1976.   *B, E*
Washington State Mental Health and Mental Retardation Committee. "Planning Comprehensive Community Mental Health Services." Task Force and County Planning Committee Reports, Mental Health and Mental Health Retardation Committee, 1965.   *E*

The Washington state plan for mental health services. Includes the task force and county planning committee reports.

Washnis, G.J. *Citizen Involvement in Crime Prevention.* Lexington, Mass.: D.C. Heath, 1976.   *E*
Wattis, J.P. "Alcohol Problems in the Elderly." *Journal of the American Geriatrics Society* 29 (1981):131–134.   *B*

Aspects of alcohol abuse in the elderly illustrated using seven case reports.

Weiss, K., and S.S. Bogges. "Victimology and Rape: The Case of the Legitimate Victim." *Issues in Criminology* 8 (1973):71–115.   *A, B*
———. "Victimology and Rape: The Case of the Legitimate Victim." In *Victims and Society,* edited by E. Viano: p.   . Washington, D.C.: Visage, 1976.   *A, B*
Weifhofen, H. *Psychiatry and the Law.* New York: W.W. Norton, 1952.   *C, F*
Weisberger, T.H. "The Elderly in the Roxbury–Dorchester Area: To Uproot or Not." *Journal of Geriatric Psychiatry* 5 (1973):174–184.   *E*

Identifies and examines some of the issues involved in the process of helping older people to uproot themselves from a familiar community and settle into a new neighborhood.

Welch, L. "New Role for PSROS: Abuse Reporting." *Hospitals* 52 (16 July 1978):34.   E

Wellman, B. "Networks, Neighborhoods, and Communities." *Urban Affairs Quarterly* 14 (March 1979).   E

Westermeyer, J., and J. Kroll. "Violence and Mental Illness in a Peasant Society: Characteristics of Violent Behaviours and Fold Use of Restraints." *British Journal of Psychiatry* 133 (December 1978): 529–541.   A, C

Thirty-five people labeled as BAA were studied in Laos, a country without psychiatrists or psychiatric institutions. Informant information was obtained for violence prior to becoming BAA, violence during the course of their BAA condition, and violence during the seven days prior to interview.

"What Works to Protect the Aged from Crime?" *Criminal Justice Newsletter* 8 (5 December 1977):2–3.   E

White, G. "Where Citizens Help Control Crime." *Dynamic Maturity* (July 1975).   E

White, R.W. "Motivation Reconsidered: The Concept of Competence." *Psychological Review* 66 (1959)297–333.   C, F

Whitehead, J.A., and M. Ahmed. "Chance, Mental Illness, and Crime." *Lancet* 1 (17 January 1970):135–317.   A, C

Whitehead, T. "The Gaslight Phenomenon." *Nursing Mirror* 145 (29 December 1977):31–32.   A

Wigdor, R.M., et al. "The Behavioral Comparison of a Real vs. Mock Nursing Home." *Gerontologist* 17 (1977):133.   A, E

Paper read at the 30th annual meeting of the Gerontological Society, San Francisco, November 1977. Describes behavioral comparison of a real versus mock nursing home.

Williams, J.D., et al. "Mental Aging and Organicity in an Alcoholic Population." *Journal of Consulting and Clinical Psychology* 4 (1973): 392–396.   B

Investigates validity of aging and organicity indexes for detecting deficits in mental functioning that may be associated with alcohol abuse.

Willis, R.L., and M. Miller. "Senior Citizen Crime Prevention Program." *Police Chief* 43 (February 1976):16–17.   E

Wilson, B. "The Impact of Social Isolation on Patient Satisfaction with Medical Care Services and Utilization: A Study among the Elderly on the Lower East Side." *Dissertation Abstracts International* 40 (1979): 213–B.   A, E

Discusses repsonses of elderly user of health-care facility on the lower east side of New York City to a self-administered questionnaire about subjects' satisfaction with the utilization of health-care services.

Wilson, J. Q. "The Urban Unease: Community versus the City." *Public Interest* 12 (1968).   *A, G*

Wilson, L. A. "Private and Collective Choice Behavior in the Provision of Personal Security from Criminal Victimization." Ph.D. dissertation, Department of Political Science, University of Oregon, 1976.
                                                                                    B, E

Wolf, R. "An Aid to Designing Prevention Programs." *Police Chief* (February 1977):27–29.   *E*

Wolff, K. "The Coordinated Approach to the Geriatric Problem." In *Geriatric Psychiatry,* edited by K. Wolff, p.   . Springfield, Ill.: Charles C. Thomas, 1963.   *A, G*

Discusses situation of the aged in terms of biological condition, psychological condition, and sociological status and needs.

Wolfgang, M.E. *Patterns in Criminal Homicide.* Philadelphia: University of Pennsylvania Press, 1958.   *A, B*

Wong, H.B., et al. "Sex Chromosome Abnormalities and Crime." *Modern Medicine in Asia* 14 (November 1978):11–15.   *A, B*

Women Against Rape. *Stop Rape.* Detroit: Women Against Rape, 2445 West 8 Mile Road, 1971.   *A, B*

Women Organized Against Rape. "Questions and Answers about Rape." Philadelphia: Women Organized Against Rape, 1220 Sansom Street, 1967.   *B, E*

Wortman, C.B. "Causal Attributions and Personal Control." In *New Directions in Attribution Research,* edited by J.W. Harvey, et al., Hinsdale: Lawrence Erlbaum Associates, 1976.   *A, C*

Wortman, C.B., and J.W. Brehm. "Response to Uncontrollable Outcomes: An Integration of Reactance Theory and the Learned Helplessness Model." *Advances in Experimental Social Psychology* 8 (1975): 86–93.   *E*

Yaden, D., et al. *The Impact of Crime in Selected Neighborhoods: A Study of Public Attitudes in Four Portland, Oregon, Census Tracts.* Portland, Ore.: Campaign Information Counselors, 1973.   *E*

Yin, P.P. "Fear of Crime among the Elderly: Some Issues and Suggestions." *Social Problems* 27 (1980):492–504.   *D*

A review of the literature on fear of crime among the elderly and its determinants. Provides a conceptual framework within which to locate the strengths and weaknesses of these works. Discusses variations in fear among elderly of similar backgrounds and residential settings and the fact that although the elderly comprise the most fearful age group, they are actually the least victimized age group.

Younger, E.J. "The California Experience: Prevention of Criminal Victimization of the Elderly." *Police Chief* 43 (1976):28–30, 32.   *A*

Discusses the special vulnerability of the elderly to certain crimes; examines ways that the California attorney-general's office is working with senior citizens to reduce the likelihood of victimization.

"Youth Victimized by Crime More Frequently Than Elderly, But Impact Varies Drastically." *Juvenile Justice Digest* 4 (23 April 1976):7.   *A*

Zaslow, J. "How Doctors Do Themselves in When Wrongly Accused of Medicare Fraud." *Legal Aspects of Medical Practice* 6 (July 1978): 55–57.   *A*

———. "A Lot More Than Honor May Be at Stake in a Medicare Contest." *Legal Aspects of Medical Practice* 6 (August 1978):60–62.   *A*

———. "Suspension from Medicare and Medicaid Dries Up Dollars For Doctors." *Legal Aspects of Medical Practice* 6 (September 1978): 55–57.   *A*

———. "What If the Government Thinks You're a Medicare Cheat?" *Legal Aspects of Medical Practice* 6 (May 1978):26–27.   *A*

———. "Why Innocent MDs Are Indicted for Medicare Fraud." *Legal Aspects of Medical Practice* 6 (June 1978):21–23.   *A*

Zinberg, N.C., and I. Kaufman. *Normal Psychology of the Aging Process.* New York: International Universities Press, 1963.   *C*

Zitrin, A., et al. "Crime and Violence among Mental Patients." *American Journal of Psychiatry* 133 (February 1976):142–149.   *A, C*

About the Contributors

Nancy R. King is currently deputy director of the Center for Women Policy Studies.

Frank Clemente, Professor, Ph.D. College of Liberal Arts, Pennsylvania State University, University Park, Pennsylvania.

Michael B. Kleiman, Asst. Professor, M.A. College of Liberal Arts, Pennsylvania State University, University Park, Pennsylvania.

Jaber F. Gubrium is assistant professor of sociology and anthropology at Marquette University.

Sheldon S. Tobin, Associate Professor, Ph.D. College of Human Development, University of Chicago, Chicago, Illinois.

About the Author

Joseph J. Costa is principal of the Shenandoah Valley Junior/Senior High School, Shenandoah, Pennsylvania (B.S., Bloomsburg State College; M.S.L.S., Villanova University; M.Ed., in reading, Kutztown State College; Ph.D., Columbia–Pacific University, San Rafael, Calif.; Principal & Superintendent Certification, Lehigh University). He has had practical experience in elementary, junior-high, and high schools as a teacher, coach, and librarian and has been librarian at the Schuylkill Campus of The Pennsylvania State University. His publications include *Child Abuse and Neglect: Legislation, Reporting, and Prevention* (Lexington Books, 1978) (with Gordon K. Nelson); *A Directory of Library Instruction Programs in Pennsylvania Academic Libraries* (sponsored by the Academic Library Instruction Committee, College and Research Libraries Division, Pennsylvania Library Association, 1980); and *Abuse of Women: Legislation, Reporting and Prevention* (Lexington Books, 1983).